RELIGION

RELIGION

BY

EDWARD SCRIBNER AMES

PROFESSOR OF PHILOSOPHY IN THE UNIVERSITY OF CHICAGO

NEW YORK

HENRY HOLT AND COMPANY

PREFACE

A striking feature of contemporary thought is the widespread awakening of interest in the deeper questions of religion. There has been a general clearing up of the controversies over the problems of historical criticism, evolution, and authority, and there are other signs of the passing of the warfare between science and religion. A calmer and more constructive spirit of inquiry has appeared which is providing the means for a more adequate assessment of the nature of religion, both in its practice and in its doctrines.

This book endeavors to present certain aspects of religion as they appear in the light of its history and of social psychology. Religion is here viewed as a natural, social, cultural process. The doctrines, which have often been regarded as the essence of religion, are seen to have intimate relation to the religious activities, being at once deposits or products and also instruments of such activities. Religion arises as a phase or quality of the complex life of the human spirit in its idealistic outreach, and is continually subject to restatement under the influence of the flowing stream of that life.

The conception of religion as a social process was clearly stated by John Stuart Mill, but the rapid and extensive development of the social sciences since his time has vastly enriched that conception. I have attempted to use the point of view and the method of these sciences throughout this work. After considering the origins and the values of religion, a comparison is made between religion and other interests such as science, philosophy, art, and morality, in the conviction that such comparisons are the most helpful means of defining and revealing the nature of religion.

The second main problem of this study is the nature of God. Here again the history of religion and social psychology have been employed as the best aids in discovering the meaning of God. From this approach, the question of the existence of God is no more and no less perplexing than the question of the existence of life, or the existence of the cosmos, but the nature of God and the processes with which God is involved become intelligible and meaningful in new and appealing ways. Whatever illuminates the idea of God also throws light upon all other phases of religion, upon prayer and worship, upon religious institutions, upon the quest of the good life and the salvation which it affords.

The chapters on "Religion and Philosophy" and on "Religion and Art" were recently published in the *Journal of Religion;* and the substance of the chapter on "Religion and Morality" appeared in the *International Journal of Ethics.*

I am indebted to Van Meter Ames, of the department of philosophy in the University of Cincinnati, for reading the manuscript and making valuable criticisms and suggestions.

E. S. A.

The University of Chicago

CONTENTS

RELIGION

CHAPTER I

THE SPRINGS OF RELIGION

It is not uncommon to find scientifically trained and otherwise emancipated persons who regard religion as outgrown. They think it but a matter of time and general education when religion will be relegated to the limbo of superstition and magic. It arose in primitive culture and that culture is rapidly disappearing. All manner of practices, now felt to be revolting, have been conducted in the name of religion—cannibalism, polygamy, infanticide, human sacrifice. Wars have sprung from it. The pioneers of science have been persecuted and put to death by it. Priests and prophets have opposed innovations and have slain those who championed new standards and experiments.

Even wise people do not often enough pause to reflect that these things are true also of politics, of trade and commerce, of family organization. Every phase of society and of human life suffers from the survival and inertia of old customs. It is not easy to introduce innovations in business, in industry, in education, in domestic service, in politics, or in religion. Human nature operates much the same in all interests of life. Ordinarily it is subject to habit and custom, and many customs are irrational but persistent. If those who reject religion because of attributing to it the evils mentioned were to judge the rest of life in the same manner

3

they would logically become thoroughly pessimistic concerning human nature and the world itself.

The immediate answer to the pessimistic critics of religion is to say that there are different kinds of religion as there are different kinds of government and systems of education. Religion, like other interests, undergoes change from age to age and from land to land. There are various forms of any one religion and each has its conservative and progressive parties. In Mohammedanism, Buddhism, Roman Catholicism, Protestantism, in every sect, it is the same. Innovation, modification of mores, modernism, come about in time, although in religion the resistance to change is more stubborn because the values involved are the most important and the most intimate. They do not submit themselves to analysis as easily as do other social values. When changes are made they are apt to be less conscious and direct. Religion may be said to be the last great human interest to feel the scrutiny of scientific method. It is only within a generation that the methods of scientific study have been applied to it and there are many enlightened people who still think that the subject is inaccessible and unamenable to scientific treatment. All social affairs were formally under this dominance of custom. They had no rational justification and they permitted no questioning.

The state promulgated its customs as laws which were given and received as if subject to no change or exception. The king ruled by divine right and the edicts of the throne were as the voice of God. To question them would have been treason; to disobey them was punishable by death. Anything like constitutional rights for the common man has been a late achievement and is yet only imperfectly accomplished. In the old world-view all the really significant experiences of life were thought of as emanating from a superhuman source. The inspirations of poets, the insights of thinkers, the achievements of leaders, were accredited to divine visitations. Likewise all established customs carried an authority and sanction which identified them with an order above and outside the ordinary experience of men. This is yet a strangely persistent and widespread attitude toward great men. They are called "geniuses," and the word carries the survival of the feeling that they are gifted with unique endowments indicating a nature different from that of their fellow mortals.

Religion is traditionally accounted for on this principle. The great religious geniuses, Buddha, Moses, Jesus, Mohammed, are regarded by their followers as supernaturally sent, if not themselves actual incarnations of deity. They have thus been able to bring revelations and to impose their teaching as authoritative and unconditional. Common men, by implicit faith in the prophets and by strict obedience to them, have been able to share in the salvation offered. With marvelous devotion masses of followers have adhered to these leaders and when the followers differed among themselves their differences were not ascribed to any limitations in the revelations, but to the misunderstandings and weaknesses of mortals. In the tragic conflicts and wars of religious sects, each party held unwaveringly to its own supposedly infallible standards and sought to impose them by logic and by force.

At last the civilized world has come upon the historical method of studying these faiths, and has been able to discover something of the genesis and social exfoliation of various systems. Knowledge of the sacred texts, of their discrepancies, of their successive stages, of their reflection of varying mores and ideals, has shown the fallacy of their claims to infallibility and complete perfection. They now appear to all critical, competent students as the products of the human spirit in the quest for satisfying principles of thought and conduct. They are the records of the spiritual aspirations of the cultures in which they appear, and carry the strength, as well as the limitations, of their respective settings. It is as great a mistake to reject them wholly as it was to accept them unquestioningly. Taken with discrimination they afford knowledge of the sources and the nature of religious faith.

The psychology of religion, working upon the nature of the individual in the total process of his experience, has furnished new clues to an empirical and scientific understanding of religion. The same genetic inquiry which has thrown light upon the origin of language, of social customs and institutions, has clarified many problems of religion. In particular it has shown that the most important single task is the discovery of the springs of human action, and the sources of those forms of human association through which fundamental needs have been mediated.

Psychology has greatly modified its answer to this question since that science adopted a genuinely empirical method. The discussion has centered largely about the subject of instinct. It is only within the last decade that the psychologists have definitely abandoned the term. Until that time, while differing widely in the specification of the number and character of the instincts, the concept was generally accepted. It has been discarded for several reasons. That no two scholars agreed concerning the number of instincts tended to create skepticism concerning their existence, but it was the tendency to formulate a more and more precise definition which led to abandoning the search. As instinct was described as a ready-made, inherited response or chain of responses of the organism, on occasion of appropriate stimuli, it became increasingly obvious that no such finished and effective responses could be discovered. Even in the lower biological forms it became evident, upon careful observation, that the nest-building of birds, for example, and the hunting and fighting reactions of animals, involved a learning process. These ends were achieved under the tutelage of parents, and were developed and elaborated in play activities. They did not arise in full strength and efficiency within the isolated organism, or in equal perfection in different individuals of a species. It was particularly apparent that no specific instinct could be found to account for complex phenomena like morality and religion. The more instinct was conceived as highly organized response to definite stimulus the less applicable the term became to the highly wrought, intricate process designated by religion. Its variability in individuals and races demanded a more free and flexible principle than instinct.

The outcome has been the substitution of impulses and reflexes to indicate original tendencies to action.

The propulsive, dynamic energy of all living forms is the first element. In the lower orders, simple reflexes, extending early into settled habits, prevail. Nature produces immense numbers of individuals in a species, as among fishes, and in that way accomplishes the continuity of its kind. In the higher types, a longer period of infancy, and greater flexibility in the learning process provide the possibility of better adaptation. John Fiske gave a permanent contribution to the "meaning of infancy" in the human species. He showed that the very helplessness of the infant and its years of dependence furnish opportunity for variation in habit and consequent adjustment to varying degrees of complexity in the environment. It is in the process of education, often carried on into scores of years and capable of extension to the whole span of life, that the human being achieves increasing power in meeting the demands of a changing physical and social world.

In general it is this adaptation, and consequent satisfaction of its needs, which the organism seeks. These needs, wants, wishes, ideal ends, as they are variously called, are the springs of action, the dynamos of behavior. They impel to self-preservation, to expansion and enrichment of life. Certain needs, like the satisfaction of hunger and sex, are basic and persistent through all grades of culture, but the manner of their satisfaction is modified by an indescribable wealth of associated interests, and by the emergence of new and complex ends. Men are so bound up with their fellows in this endeavor to fulfil their needs that the ends sought are common to groups of persons living together in family, tribe, and nation. A man strives for the welfare of his mate as identified with himself; parents seek the good of their offspring as part of their own ends; patriots sacrifice for their country as for their larger selves. There is no limit to this sense of participation and social solidarity. It may include the whole conceivable world of mankind and the illimitable ranges of imaginable sentient beings. The scope of this social sense varies according to the experience and sensitiveness of people, but it is difficult to conceive any one so dead to companionship and natural ties that he is completely "selfish" and without the broadening influences of social feeling. What men seek are the satisfactions of felt needs experienced in maintaining life which in all normal circumstances is an associated life with fellow human beings.

Religion is the quest for the largest and the fullest satisfaction of felt needs. These needs vary enormously at different levels of society but in fundamental, persisting patterns, interwoven with all manner of conventionalizations. As the human face is of a fundamental structure, though varying among races and groups in size, shape, color, slant of eyes, and lines of the nose and mouth, so the human organism craves food, the mind is curious for knowledge, and the heart longs for companionship through varying customs and institutions. Religion is this outreaching for the satisfaction of felt needs, and its expression in objects and ceremonials associated with these needs. It cannot be identified with any one set or system of needs nor with any particular objects or ceremonials. These are as various as the faces of the races and the tribes of mankind. It is doubtful whether there are any peoples entirely without religion. There may be some whose life is so easy, or so close to the edge of existence as in the far north, that they are without the incentives or the leisure which make for organization and the play of imagination. But certainly no people has attained a significant culture, marked by arts, social customs, and widespread intimate tradition, without some appreciable religion. In all the great civilizations it has been conspicuously and vitally a large and focal interest.

It is a common fallacy to regard social institutions as the sources rather than the products of great human concerns. Schools are easily thought of as the origin of knowledge, whereas they are the expressions of the desire for wisdom and are centers in which are gathered and made available for youth the deposits of information and intelligence. Schools feed and guide the learning activity but they cannot create it. If the existing institutions of learning were destroyed, others would arise in time; but if the desire for what they represent were to perish, the schools could not supply it. The same could be said of all forms and organizations in society, in family, state, industry, and religion. They are ultimately voluntary associations for the better realization of common wants. Such institutions quicken and vitalize for many individuals the interests which they represent, and they give continuity and power to the impulses from which they spring, but these institutions are secondary and not primary. They enhance and extend, elevate and objectify normal cravings and activities of the human spirit, but the foundations and the sustained meaning of social institutions are in this human spirit, and are without significance except as they express and satisfy it.

It is one of the main tasks of the psychology of religion and of the history of religion to discover and to show just how religion and religious institutions have sprung from the impulses and desires of men. For this purpose the study of early and simple forms of religion has been extremely fruitful. What is the nature of religious objects? How do they attain their sanctity and holiness? How do men come to have religious ceremonials and priesthoods and sacred places and temples? What and who are the gods; whence do they arise and what is their significance? The answers to these questions involve the whole mental and social life of man. The partial, special-interest statements made by scientists and travelers, missionaries and diplomatists, require interpretation in more adequate perspective. The total genius and concrete history of a people in relation to its complex environment would be needed for complete understanding of their religion. Materials and suggestions toward such understandings have been gathered in great abundance during the past fifty years. The natural history of religion has gained scientific standing, and a method is being developed which is applicable to all religions, to their different stages and forms. These religions have been reviewed in relation to their economic and social history, and the correspondence in every case is so organic and functional, so natural and illuminating, that it recasts entirely their meaning and value.

In the first place, the vital interests of a people are

the central concerns of their religion. Their "daily bread" is an insistent problem. The food objects and the activities involved in securing them are dominant in their rites. All this is interestingly written down in the records of the Hebrew people in the Old Testament. As nomads and hunters they celebrated the events of the shepherd's and the hunter's life; as migrating tribes in search of grass lands and living water, they told the stories and sang the songs of their roaming adventures; as husbandmen and tillers of the soil they introduced new rituals and new conceptions of God. All the time their family health and tribal integrity were cherished, and their wars and feuds were echoed in songs like those of Deborah and in exploits like those of David. They needed children for man power, and the occasions of birth, marriage, and death deeply marked their hopes and prayers.

The sacred places were those in which success was won, and the spots where the clans gathered for feasts and councils. The sacred objects were those upon which their life depended, the sheep, the bull, the well, the flowing spring, and the fertile earth. The moon, the stars, the mountains, and the rich valleys also focused their attention and elicited their awe and reverence. All these gained sanctity as they accumulated significance in the furtherance of life and well-being. Objects became sacred as they were felt to function in the fulfilment of primal needs. As social organization was seen to be important, the tribal chiefs and kings engaged attention and secured loyalty and affection. From these patterns of the daily, corporate life the whole world was modeled and the invisible beings of the imagination were the glorified figures of their eventful communal life. These sacred objects came to be regarded as the sources and the ends of existence. There was a natural and insistent tendency to transfer attention from ends to means, to lavish devotion upon the things which satisfy desire and to overlook the fact that the desires and their satisfaction are the determining factors in the selection and esteem of sacred objects. The psychology of the process of evaluation shows that ends which are attained with difficulty, through prolonged intense effort and associated endeavor, gain importance thereby. Because shepherd people had to exert themselves to care for their flocks, seeking grazing land for them, protecting them against wild animals, nursing them at yeaning time, watching over them by day and night in order to gain from them food, clothing, and shelter, they came to prize the sheep as sacred. It seemed to be the center of magical power. At the feast where its flesh was eaten, men who were faint with hunger and worn with labor gained new energy and spirit. In the communal meal where the sheep was shared by all, there was a sense of strengthened ties of kinship among the tribesmen, and between them and the sacred mysterious power resident in the sacrifice. During the feast, the stories of the tribal history were told, memories of heroic ancestors were revived, and the circle of the tribe extended in imagination to include all who were thus remembered. The same may be said of the Central Australians celebrating their totems, and of the American Indians gathered in ceremonial circles about the maize—the altar covered with it, their bodies sprinkled with it, and the ground marked in conventional figures with it. The whole ceremonial of "sacrifice" needs a reinterpretation to free it from the notion that the sacrificial object was offered to a deity, and to stress the fact that the sacred object was itself the center of power radiated to all who partook of it. That this is truer to the meaning of such ceremonials in developed and in early rituals may be emphasized by the observation that the highest point of Christian ceremonials is reached in the Mass or the Lord's Supper. What is the purpose and meaning of this rite in the minds of the strictest churchmen? It is that here men actually feast on the body and the blood of the Lamb of God. To Roman Catholics it is the literal appropriation of the living flesh and blood; through it the participants are infused with the life of deity. This is the great mystery and the supreme act of the communicants. By it they renew their life and overcome sin, weakness, and death. Their relation of intimate oneness with God is re-established, not by an offering to him, but by possessing themselves of his actual being through the literal assimilation of him into themselves. To Protestants the ceremony is observed with more or less rationalization. They have been taught doctrines of consubstantiation, of spiritual participation, of meditative union, but the idea is still that of renewing the bonds of power with the Sacred Being in which religious attention and affection focus.

Some of the imagery introduced into the Christian tradition has tended to exaggerate the conception of the Divine Being residing above the sky and outside the world. The writings of Plato and Aristotle represent the abode of the gods in that way. In the New

Testament, especially in the apocalyptic literature, God is pictured on a throne beyond the clouds. John Milton gave to this imagery the vividness of his poetic imagination. Religious ceremonials have been built around a high altar, remote and suggestive of a majestic divinity before whom incense and praise should be offered up. All this, and much more of the same, have contributed to the impression that religion is derived from a supernatural source and revealed to man; that man brings his gifts to exchange for blessings; that man does not grow his religion out of the depths of his life, but is endowed with it from the unknown and the invisible.

There is the further important trait of human nature, the tendency to substitute the symbol for the thing symbolized. The flag may easily be mistaken for something sacred in itself, but it is the heroism and devotion of the citizens which give sanctity to the flag. As the expression of those qualities, the flag does possess a certain derived sacredness, but it cannot generate or convey them. Likewise, sacred books, like the Bible, have their value from the life which produced them and which is portrayed in them. To a large extent, important individuals in great causes are great in so far as they embody the will and represent the achievement of numbers of men. It is the loyalty and support of the army which gives the general his greatness.

Men have also been blinded to the fact that religion arises from themselves by the tradition of their own inferiority. They have been so conscious of their errors and limitations that they have been unable to think of noble things as emanating from their life. In the religions of salvation the doctrine of sin has been stressed and magnified until it has been regarded as inherent, innate evil from which there could be no escape except through the ministrations of priests and ceremonials. It made the institution more powerful and more commanding if it were thought of as the only medium through which hopelessly sinful men could overcome their vicious nature and gain deliverance. It has therefore been one of the first steps of these religions in dealing with the individual to make him conscious of his lost condition, his shameful and wicked alienation from virtue and goodness. There are enough facts in the experience of every one, enough conflicts of impulses, enough remorse and self-abasement to give force to the doctrine of original sin and total hereditary depravity. The Apostle Paul gave vivid expression to the suffering a person may endure through the conflict of aspiration and established habits. He exclaims, "That which I do I allow not; for what I would, that do I not; but what I hate, that I do. O wretched man that I am, who shall deliver me from the body of this death?"

When such a dismal picture of human nature is presented, sharply contrasted with the perfection and beauty of the divine life, there is every justification for the assumption that the sources of the good life, even the desire for it, must lie outside of man himself. This traditional doctrine of the extreme sinfulness of man confronts every naturalistic account of the development of a refined religion. But the scientific study of human nature reveals a wealth of impulses and a wide range of stimuli within which a process of selection goes on. By the method of trial and error, by tests of happiness and welfare, by reflection and comparison, some ways are found to be good and others bad. Man is ever striving for a fuller and better life, yet often attributes the very desire for improvement to some other source than himself. A more adequate psychology and a freer assessment of his life show his nature to be mixed and uneven, but capable of self-criticism and of the pursuit of selected ends, even the ideal, spiritual ends which he sets up in his religious faiths.

CHAPTER II

RELIGION AS A SOCIAL PROCESS

Religion, like other great human interests such as marriage, industry, art, and government, had a long history before men began to think critically of its nature. Communal feasts were celebrated, temples were built, and ceremonials flourished for ages before inquiries were made concerning their efficacy and before the nature of the gods was questioned. Such thoughts as floated through the minds of devotees were of desires to be satisfied and of the prescribed ways by which they could be fulfilled. In reverie and flowing imagery men remembered their sufferings and their triumphs, and recounted them in stories and legends, in vivid traditions, in pictures and songs. Religion reflected the labors of the hunt, the battle, and the field, the ardors of love and the pains of death. From its symbols and myths, comfort and courage were obtained. Slowly it changed with the shifting life of the tribe, rose with the growth of cultures, and fell with their fall. The great historic faiths —Buddhism, Confucianism, Judaism, and Christianity —move through vast cycles of change with the fortunes of the peoples to whom they belong. Within the ranges of these religions sacred literatures sprang up reciting the deeds of gods and men and sometimes rationalizing their customs and aspirations.

Eventually, with the birth of philosophy, a more critical type of thinking developed which sought to test the truth of religious ideas by its own methods of analysis and proof. The Dialogues of Plato record the first significant efforts of western cultures to achieve an enlightened and systematic exposition of the central ideas of religion—God, the soul, evil, redemption, and the future life. From his time speculation has been busy with these problems, in explanation and argument, in criticism and defense. Often the relation of reason itself to the life of religion has been the crucial problem, and opinions have varied from the conviction that reason must be employed to determine what should be believed to the doctrine that faith alone can furnish the truth which reason expounds. Faith is sometimes thought to be above reason, and then the two may be held to be contrary or in harmony; again faith is subordinated to reason and all is held to be rational and open to understanding. The human mind still lies uneasy on this subject, unable to satisfy itself that an irrational religion can answer its needs but also doubtful whether a rational religion is possible.

Modern philosophy inherited these problems from the medieval thinkers and has largely been engaged with the questions of the nature, the extent, and the validity of human knowledge in all fields but with special reference, in nearly all systems, to the ultimate questions of religion. These inquiries still go on but there are signs now that they are coming into fruitage. The books on logic, psychology, and epistemology have become less controversial and more constructive and disclose more agreement.[1] The course of modern philosophy has been steadily away from the dogmatic rationalism which

[1] An excellent recent work of this kind is E. A. Burtt's *Principles and Problems of Right Thinking*.

undertook to establish the power of pure reason to supply conclusive knowledge of the objects of religious concern. Although Descartes, the founder of modern philosophy, remained largely within the shackles of the older rationalism, he made a significant gesture in the direction of a more empirical procedure. He deliberately cast aside the books of his Jesuit training and applied himself to the study of things, and of the "great book of the world." He sought a beginning in indubitable fact and admirably illustrated his intention by a searching examination of all his inherited beliefs and habits of thought.

Francis Bacon and John Locke display the same aversion to metaphysical speculation and fruitless syllogistic manipulation of words. They also turned to things, to matters of fact, and to objects perceived through the senses; they appealed to common sense and to practical activities. Bacon's motto, "Knowledge is power," expressed the spirit of the new time, meaning by it power to control natural objects and forces, and to promote the welfare and happiness of man. Bacon professed, and may well have sincerely believed in his time, that such inquiries do not in any way affect the truths of religion, which are matters of divine revelation and not subject to human reason. He said we must "believe in the Word of God though our reason is shocked at it." This doctrine of the separateness of the realms of religion and science or natural knowledge had had a long history before Bacon's time and has been reasserted by many scientists since. It has always implied impatience with the assumption of metaphysical speculation that it should dominate the whole field of knowledge.

John Locke, who began the great English enlightenment of the eighteenth century by his "new way of ideas," gave much attention to religion. He held that we must accept the truths of revelation, "only we must be sure that it be a divine revelation, and that we understand it right." [2] Thus he attempted to hold on to the authority and certainty of a revealed religion, while at the same time he followed the demands of an empirical philosophy. Without seeming to realize all the implications of his position he did assert the supremacy of common-sense reasoning, which later led to the development of Deism and the doctrine of natural religion. For him there are no innate ideas of any kind concerning God, the soul, equality, or justice. At birth the mind is a blank tablet which gradually has characters imprinted upon it by impressions from the senses. All knowledge comes from and through experience. Revelation came to men of old in the same way by their hearing the spoken words of God and by witnessing the miracles which attested the authenticity of his messengers. Locke did inconsistently accept from the old rationalism intuitive and demonstrative knowledge but held that these concern ideas alone. Knowledge of these kinds is certain but not "real," while knowledge from the senses is real but not certain. The latter may yield some notion of order and design in nature, it may enable man to satisfy his creature wants, but it cannot afford absolute certainty concerning the existence of

[2] *Essay on Human Understanding,* Bk. IV, Ch. XVI, p. 14.

God and other essential religious problems. So long as reason is occupied with the real world of things and events it must be content with probability, but this is sufficient for all man's practical needs, it being his duty to be content with the endowment which the Maker has given him. It is the duty of human beings to recognize their limitations and to accept contentedly the fact that their range of knowledge is limited by a short tether.

It was David Hume who made clear the implications of Locke's empiricism. With relentless consistency he carried through the doctrine of sensationalism to its logical issues. He saw that "the impressions of sense" taken by themselves are discrete entities and that as thus conceived there are no discoverable connections among them. Even the identity of objects as perceived in successive periods of time became for him an illusion, and the idea of any causal connection was resolved into a mere subjective work of the imagination owing to the force of habit built up by the influence on the mind of repeatedly noting the succession of events. The assumption that objects which follow one another are causally bound together seemed to him wholly unwarranted no matter how often such sequence might appear. So far as reason could show, the objects of perception and the impressions of sense had no real coherence or connection and there remained no actual relations between them which could be proved by any scientific or rational knowledge.

More desolating was Hume's application of his views to the inner world of the self, for this too disintegrated into passing states of feeling as piecemeal and chaotic

as impressions of the senses. The soul thereby lost
the unity and permanence which had been attributed
to it since the days of Plato. Even the ground of unity
within the imagination was thereby shattered and the
possibility of any kind of dependable knowledge was
entirely destroyed. But this dissolution of knowledge
is as complete for any negative assertions as for positive judgments, and therefore the claims of any dependable knowledge were destroyed by a complete and
irremediable skepticism. All religious ideas for Hume
were subject to this incurable skepticism. Miracles,
for instance, are beset by more difficulties than direct
observation of events because they rest upon the testi-
mony of men in the far past and run contrary to what
is observed in the present. The most persuasive argument for the existence of God is from design in nature, but the evidence is not conclusive. Nature is by
no means clearly a system of order. It shows many
imperfections, compromises the ideal of goodness by
pain and evil, and suggests several other possibilities
besides that of being the work of an all-powerful and
beneficent creator. The world might be the work of a
limited deity, of one who arrived at the present results
by many trials; or of one who was young and inexperi-
enced; or of one who had become superannuated and
left his work unfinished! Possibly the world is self-
generating by a vegetative or animal process. In any
case the observed facts do not warrant any rational and
demonstrable conclusion that the universe is the work
of an infallible deity. All this may not be sufficient
to dissuade human beings from a strong "belief" or
"faith" in the existence of God such as Deism held,

but it removes the foundation of any decisive proof of a God as the creator and sustainer of the world.

It was John Stuart Mill, in the nineteenth century, who, accepting these results of empiricism as applied to the claims of any establishment of *religion as a body of truth,* turned to an empirical view of religion as a *social process* and suggested a more fruitful interpretation of it in terms of experience. In his essay on "The Utility of Religion" he says, "We seem to have arrived at a time when, among the arguments for and against religion, those which relate to its usefulness assume an important place." He proposes to investigate "the belief in religion, considered as a mere persuasion, apart from the question of its truth." By its truth he obviously means the old conceptions of the truth concerning the existence of a perfect and infinite God. The specific questions he raises are: "What does religion do for society, and what for the individual? What amount of benefit to social interests, in the ordinary sense of the phrase, arises from religious belief? And what influence has it in improving and ennobling individual human nature?"

He suggests that religion may be viewed as a kind of poetry and still have very real value. "Religion and poetry address themselves, at least in one of their aspects, to the same part of the human constitution: they both supply the same want, that of ideal conceptions grander and more beautiful than we see realized in the prose of human life." "The value, therefore, of religion to the individual, both in the past and present, as a source of personal satisfaction and of elevated feelings, is not to be disputed. But it has still to be considered, whether in order to obtain this good, it is necessary to travel beyond the boundaries of the world which we inhabit; or whether the idealization of our earthly life, the cultivation of a high conception of what *it* may be made, is not capable of supplying a poetry, and, in the best sense of the word, a religion, equally fitted to exalt the feelings, and (with the aid of education) still better calculated to ennoble the conduct, than any belief respecting the unseen powers."

Mill cites patriotism, devotion to the welfare of humanity, loyalty to parents and friends, and the sense of the approval of the noblest souls of history as powerful incentives. "To call these sentiments by the name morality, exclusively of any other title, is claiming too little for them. They are a real religion; of which, as of other religions, outward good works (the utmost meaning usually suggested by the word morality) are only a part, and are indeed rather the fruits of the religion than the religion itself. The essence of religion is the strong and earnest direction of the emotions and desires toward an ideal object, recognized as of the highest excellence, and as rightfully paramount over all selfish objects of desire." There is still present here the influence of Mill's old association psychology according to which the emotions and desires are not spontaneously outreaching toward the ideal object, but need to have "strong and earnest direction." The same difficulty arose in his view of ethics that man is by nature egoistic, that it is only by education and long training that he may become altruistic enough to seek the greatest good of the greatest number. Although he was never able to justify by his psychology the social attitudes which he approved as essential to morals and religion, he did champion this social idealism, giving a new meaning to religion and preparing the way for it to find its place in the modern world of scientific knowledge and method of procedure.

In John Stuart Mill, philosophical empiricism reached its limit of negation concerning the traditional theological conception of God as a being whose existence could be logically and conclusively proved; but in Mill there was also the beginning of an entirely different conception of religion. He began to see religion as a social process arising from human desires and emotions directed toward ideal ends. That was a constructive and fruitful view which continues to make its way in the world with vital and fresh appeal. As the empiricist disclaims any absolute and demonstrative knowledge, but holds to useful knowledge; as he confesses his inability to find a final, demonstrable system of ethics, yet cherishes with intense appreciation the fallible standards of moral experience; as he estimates government, industry, and education on the basis of their value in human life; so while admitting the impossibility of justifying religion as a body of truth, perfect and complete, he does claim for it a place in the higher life of man, as an outreaching toward ideals and the promotion of a higher life for the individual and society. Mill turned his face away from the abstract, the metaphysical, the pure realms of absolutes and infinites, to the concrete, practical, mixed experience of actual human beings in their aspiration toward a more satisfying order of existence.

The nineteenth century developed certain tendencies

already suggested, though imperfectly grasped by Mill, which have given depth and clarity to this conception of religion. Among these are the logic of empiricism, the historical method, the study of the social nature of man, the conception of evolution, and the functional or behavioristic psychology. Since the beginning of the present century all of these tendencies have been interactive and together have combined under the method of the physical sciences to illumine and enlarge all of the social sciences. All inquiries in economics, political science, history, and sociology are sensitive to these tendencies. Studies of whole cultures, not only those of more primitive stages, but also those of advanced civilizations employ the evolutionary, social, voluntaristic conceptions of human nature. Specific application of these points of view to religion has been made by numerous scholars. It is now possible as never before to trace the genesis and development of the religions of various peoples and to generalize the processes of religious experience as we generalize the processes of science, government, marriage, art, and industry. All of these have been carried out of the earlier theological, metaphysical framework to be put upon an empirical basis. Each of them is now seen to spring from needs of human life, each is more or less responsive to the criticism and direction arising from the effort more adequately to meet those needs. It was formerly thought that no system of government or marriage could have value unless it made the claim of being the absolute and final system, but the experimental attitude has come to be widely accepted without surrendering the great values of society and family life. It is becoming apparent also that religion may not sustain the claim to any fixed and final form or authority, yet be cherished with all the intensity that continues to appear in patriotism and domestic fidelity. It is conceivable that a greater, more vital loyalty may support a religion conscious of limitations and struggling to employ the methods of science and practical experimentation to improve itself. If in every other sphere interest has grown with the recognition of the empirical nature of the enterprise, it would seem reasonable to expect that the same would be true in religion. Men did not discard government when they began to doubt the "divine right of kings," nor have they given up the quest for knowledge when they have turned from the rationalistic conception of it to the tentative and partial knowledge of modern political science.

Certainly the liberal leaders of modern Protestantism, under the influence of historical criticism, have abandoned the conception of an authoritative revelation in the Bible, and at the same time have found new values in the book considered as a record of the struggles and growth of the Hebrew and Christian faiths. They have surrendered the conception of an infallible church, yet are loyal to their churches. The divinity of Christ, in the old sense of conceiving him as a perfect deity, has disappeared, but the life and teaching of Jesus continue to wield their power. All the great doctrines of sin, salvation, and worship have been radically restated in the temper of the time and still persist in new forms.

Philosophical empiricism, after Mill, has its fullest

expression in the pragmatism of William James and John Dewey. The latter has been more concerned with logical theory, ethics, and education, thus far leaving almost entirely on one side the problems of religion. James gave much attention to the subject, not only in his *Varieties of Religious Experience,* but in numerous essays dealing directly with it. His criticisms of absolutism are from the direction of pluralism. He does not find that we possess Truth, capitalized and all-inclusive, but that we have particular truths in various fields of experience, subject to the atmospheric changes of interest and modes of life. Truths warm with vital interest often pass into the "cold storage" of outworn, outgrown concepts. The attempt to gather them all into a complete system of concepts eludes success, and is frustrated by the progressive discovery of new facts and theories.

His recognition of the part played by the will and by subconscious motivations involves the secondary character of intellectual systems and their reference to the controlling influence of practical needs and changing emotional attitudes. "The Will to Believe," though by no means the arbitrary and whimsical thing it is often mistakenly held to be, expresses in a striking phrase the dominance of the passional, volitional life in the operations of the intellect. The thought structures of man are not fashioned independently of his wishes and needs, but in the effort to fulfil them. Only in a realm of abstraction, undisturbed by the facts of concrete experience, is it possible to erect nice, consistent systems of reflection. Whenever a thinker comes to terms with his actual world of events and persons, of social change and outreaching purposes, he is compelled to regard his most careful constructions as partial, tentative, and provisional.

It is perhaps in his treatment of the soul or self that James applies most adequately his empirical interpretation of a problem central to religion. Refusing to accept the metaphysical, theological idea of the soul, he inquires what the self is in experience. He finds that instead of a stable, uniform substance the self is flexible, shifting, waxing and waning through good fortune and bad, becoming integral and unified at times, then divided by conflict to a diffused multiplicity of impulses and emotions. He bravely takes the experience of apparent unity in states of mind as actual unity. The continuity and identity of mind are not metaphysical elements underneath the changes, but are observed and describable connections among ideas and feelings. James says that states of consciousness have functional identity, that "this functional identity seems really the only sort of identity in the thinker which the facts require us to suppose." The evidence of this identity is in the "warmth and intimacy" which my own states have for me in contrast to those which I ascribe to other people. "Thus it is, that Peter, awakening in the same bed with Paul, and recalling what both had in mind before they went to sleep, reidentifies and appropriates the 'warm' ideas as his, and is never tempted to confuse them with those cold and pale-appearing ones which he ascribes to Paul. As well might he confound Paul's body, which he only sees, with his own body, which he sees but also feels. Each of us when he awakens says, Here's the same old Me again, just as he says, Here's the same old bed, the same old room, the same old world." [3]

It was this empirical test of continuity which James applied to the problem of life after death. He gave a surprising amount of time and energy to psychical research and to séances of various kinds, searching in his ardent way "these dingy little mediumistic facts." But he was never able to rest in any final conclusion. Like Sidgwick, who after twenty years of studying the phenomena confessed that he was in the same state of doubt and balance as that he started with, James confessed to indecision. These are his words: "For twenty-five years I have been in touch with the literature of psychical research, and have had acquaintance with numerous 'researchers.' I have also spent a good many hours (though far fewer than I ought to have spent) in witnessing (or trying to witness) phenomena. Yet I am theoretically no 'further' than I was at the beginning." [4]

It was this kind of detailed factual inquiry that he used in his effort to discover the nature of God. He searched the writings of those who claimed to have experience of God, gathering testimonies from many faiths and cults. He clung wistfully to the experiences of the mystics and analyzed their states of ecstasy, but never could experience them for himself. He was extravagant, as further research has shown, in his expectation of what the subconscious might mean in the search for God. From all these sources he ventured the suggestion that God might be an environing sea

[3] James, *Principles of Psychology*, Vol. I, p. 334.
[4] *Memories and Studies*, pp. 174 f.

of consciousness from which here and there contacts might invade some sensitive, receptive souls. It was the endeavor to deal with these actual, definite facts of experience, and to interpret them without prepossession or partiality which was the most significant feature of his search. He rejected the old rationalistic, dogmatic assumptions and arguments with their conclusions. For him all the reality of religion was sought within the realm of experienced fact, widely and patiently examined. He saw it as a complex, pluralistic, finite process, like government, too complex and too dynamic to submit to neat phrases of formal definition. He did not have the sociological and historical material now available through which to make an adequate interpretation of the social nature of religion. With the development of the sciences of anthropology and social psychology, Mill's suggestion that religion may best be understood as a social process has had fruitful confirmation. Studies of so-called primitive peoples, including "our contemporary ancestors" in the tribes of Australia, Africa, America, and the islands of the sea; researches in the cultures of Egypt, Greece, Rome, Israel, India, China, and Japan; and acquaintance with the multifarious sects of living faiths have shown religion to be a phase of the great stream of the life of mankind, revealing its nature in a wealth of institutions and literatures.

Religion, thus exhibited, is the cherishing of values felt to be most vital to man's life and blessedness, by means of ceremonial dramatization, expressive symbols, and doctrinal beliefs. These values and their representations change with the economic and cultural life.

In the more primitive levels they were embedded in routine custom and cult lore. In the metaphysical Middle Ages they were rationalized in impressive systems of thought and elaborate rituals. Today the most advanced societies are absorbed in the values of scientific knowledge, of universal human welfare, and in search for the means of control by which these may be made imaginatively dynamic and inspiring. The attainment of knowledge, development of personality, and the enjoyment of the fullest possible experience are the characteristic religious values. Religion is in a confused state because its conventional forms are still bound up with the values of the past, with submissive faith, otherworldliness, and the symbols which these have generated; while the newer interests of scientific knowledge, social welfare, and their appropriate symbolism have not yet sufficiently permeated the popular mind to make them generally religiously significant and commanding.

CHAPTER III

THE VALUES OF RELIGION

The attempts to define religion are so various and so unconvincing that the method of description has become the fashion. Although this does not escape all difficulties of interpretation, it provides a more modest and empirical means of dealing with the very complex and baffling phenomena. A living experience involving all the vital aspects of human culture, even more than a lofty mountain range, offers endless details for observation and numberless points of view and perspectives. The contemplation of the mountains may be at dawn or at sunset, in mist or moonlight, from the ground or the air, in reference to flora or fauna, gold or timber, time or space. No enumeration of the possibilities can be made, yet the results of any observation depend upon some definite position and interest of the observer. The recognition of this fact at the outset may at least caution both the writer and the reader against the assumption that any one treatise concerning religion can present the whole subject in every phase to the complete satisfaction of every need. It is important to reflect also that any view of such a vital human interest as religion has some justification and value. The values emphasized here are those which have emerged in the study of religion from the general standpoints of the social sciences. The values of religion are

34

practical. The word practical as applied to these values does not mean utilitarian in a narrow or vulgar sense, but is intended to suggest that they are ends, goals, ideals toward which religion strives. They may be growing ends, flying goals, and moving ideals. Religion seeks a city, another world, a heaven, nirvana, some state of blessedness. It comes that men may have life and have it more abundantly. It prays and labors for the coming of a kingdom. It pronounces beatitudes upon those who hunger and thirst after something which they believe to be better than that which they possess. Therefore human history is filled with quests, pilgrimages, purifications, asceticisms, sacrifices, penances, vigils, fastings, feasts, vows, and meditations, in the effort to realize the fulfilment of these powerful wishes. Religion is not always practical in the sense of being profitable or efficient as business corporations or labor unions might demand, but nevertheless it seeks ends and goals with intense devotion.

This aspect of religion is manifest pre-eminently in situations which are most religious, such as the great crises of life, when the surge and tide of existence offer the finest boons and the deepest tragedies. All religions celebrate birth and death, for then the world opens from the past and toward the future, and throbs with uncertainty, with fear and hope. The rites which are performed are felt to make the entrance or the departure of a human being safer, more auspicious, and to afford comfort and security to the family and the tribe. Everywhere religion mediates crises, helps men over rough places. Its ceremonials throughout the world are those of christening, initiation of the youth, confirmation, marriage, ministering to the sick, burying the dead. These are typical points of tension in the life-cycle of the individual. There is another group of ceremonials built around the emergencies of the food process—springtime, harvest, drouth, and pestilence. Other rites develop about the intercourse of peoples, as in war and hospitality. These three sets of ceremonials appear in practically all tribes and civilizations 'round the globe. They are the germinal centers of religion in all ages and they are the determining events in all stages of all faiths. Some cults may give special attention to interests which the accidents of the environment or of the life-history magnify. The ancient Egyptians specialized in rituals for the burial of the dead and in contemplation of the future. In their quest for health and happiness, Christian Scientists seek a technique for controlling the ills of life. All religion is thus concerned with salvation and is so far practical.

An investigation of the prayers of cultivated Christians at the present time shows how practical and even utilitarian their religion is. Does not the Lord's Prayer teach us to pray for our daily bread? Can any one who knows the world in which he lives doubt the tragic intensity of that phrase for millions of souls every day? Do not football players pray for success in their games? Probably there are still some college students sufficiently interested in their studies to pray for knowledge, or at least for passing grades. It is a deep conviction that righteousness is an asset in business and in the successful prosecution of affairs. Many people attend church to ward off evils, to set themselves right, to create a claim on the universe for security and prosperity. Thus the intention of religion is practical, by which is not meant that it is necessarily efficacious, but only that it is felt to be so. The religionist wants something, strives for something. His attitude is that of wishing, expecting, hoping, demanding. The objects of his desires may be little things or great, they may be of time or of eternity, they may be of the body or of the mind, they may be selfish or unselfish. He may seek not the fulfilment of desire but the annihilation of desire. Still, psychologically his attitude is a practical one. It is quite different from a purely reflective or appreciative attitude, and it is this difference that is meant by many writers who hold that religion moves in the realm of the will. They see that it is seeking salvation, overcoming the world, always active, striving, renouncing, enduring, aspiring, suffering in silence. Even the religions of renunciation exhort men to follow that way which few attain. They represent an active quest after a passive state! In so far their attitude is practical.

The ends which religion seeks are practical in the further sense of being regarded as good. However bad the world may seem, that which religion craves is felt by it as good. In some faiths, as in the ancient Hebrew, the blessings are those of basket and of store. In others, as in early Christianity, this present life and all its works are regarded as evil and unprofitable, but that which the believers fix their eyes upon is full of joy and delight. Man never strives for what he regards as finally a worse state. He may think of the future as evil, or of conceivable conditions as unavoidably bitter and profitless, but he does not labor to hasten them. The ends of religious faith and endeavor are felt to be relatively good and desirable.

In the highest religious culture this practical aspect becomes increasingly dominant. The good life, moral character, is set above all else. Virtues of honor, integrity, industry, courage, love, and reverence are made the real tests of religion. Creeds and rituals are but means to the development and maintenance of finer personalities and societies. As human nature is better understood and social forces are brought within the realm of constructive modification, religion begins to conceive its task more in terms of education, statesmanship, and promotion of social justice. It is a long way from early man dancing about his totems in mimetic, magic rites to civilized man imbued with scientific utopian dreams, but it is throughout a practical enterprise. The religious life is always bent upon the satisfaction of wants or is rejoicing in their fulfilment. It is hot with the sense of a cause, often cherishing hopes long deferred, attempting amazing tasks, and returning with new ardor after every defeat.

A second trait of religious values is their *social* character. Religion is cultivated in the associated life of groups of people. These groups may be of the natural kinship type or of the voluntary kind represented by churches, synagogues, and free assemblies. Man achieves all his significant ends in association. His language, moral ideals, science, and art are co-operative enterprises. All that belongs to his genuinely *human* nature is achieved in interdependence with his fellowmen. Even the creations of individuals in physical isolation and solitude bear the impress of the common

life. Thought is itself essentially conversation whether
in face-to-face exchange of ideas or in imaginative
discourse. Without this reference to other minds,
immediate or remote, mental activity loses its stimulus
and direction. Nowhere is this more evident than in
hermits, anchorites, and scientists who, while outwardly
alone, are inwardly in company with congenial souls.
Their problems are set by the traditions within which
they have lived and their solutions are tested by reference to the judgment and experience of their fellow
men.

It is a common fallacy to confuse physical solitude
with psychological isolation, as is illustrated by so great
a thinker as Professor Whitehead.[1] He declares that
religion belongs to a man's solitariness, but in order to
make the position plausible he is compelled to dismiss
early cults as foreign to religion, and to treat ritual
and ceremonial as negligible. Finally he is obliged
to admit that "there is no such thing as absolute solitariness," and that "man can not seclude himself from
society." It is clear that in the first statement he is
thinking of the metaphysics of religion and emphasizing the obvious fact that in creative reflection a man
must withdraw from the madding crowd and possess
his soul in quiet. But it is evident that when a man
"goes into the silence" and meditates in private he has
only gained a relative and not a complete detachment
from society. If he is a conventionally religious person he is likely to pray in his solitariness. But what is
prayer if not social intercourse with ideal beings? The
records of those who practice religion in the solitude of

[1] *Religion in the Making,* pp. 16, 137.

monastic cells make it clear that they live a vivid social life in imagination, conversing with numerous saints, angels, demons, and divinities. Indeed they seek such "solitude" for the express purpose of enjoying more adequately the society of the personages whom they prefer.

Religion is thus seen to be social in several senses. It is social in respect to institutional customs; it is social in terms of co-operation for the control and guidance of community action; it is social in the psychological meaning of a relationship between persons both actual and ideal; it is social in every sense that indicates participation in the shared life of other persons. It is not limited to a given, static order nor to the visible outer frame of action. It moves in the realms of memory and imagination, of the terrestrial and celestial, of the actual and the ideal. It is sometimes on the side of the old order, but it is often searching and striving for New Jerusalems. All the complexity and variation of the social process are found in religious groups. Some are fundamentalist and some are modernist. They do not fall far behind the general culture nor far surpass it. Religion is a social concern much in the same way as are education, business, and law. All are experiences in which associated individuals are interdependent and reciprocally determining. None of them can be carried on except by blending, interacting personalities.

Religious values are *inclusive*. Religious experience is always at the same time some other kind of experience. There are no ceremonials of a purely religious character. Their subject matter is from life. They are concerned with daily bread, with birth, death, love, and marriage. Religion is potentially responsive to every possible kind of event in human affairs and has something to say about it if stress centers upon it. The Prayer Book contains special prayers for all sorts of occasions as if nothing were foreign to its ministrations. It is well understood that in early society all functions of the group were included in one process of living. There were not even names for "law," "art," "education," "industry," or "religion," but these were all blended in a flowing experience, undifferentiated and whole. In more advanced stages, where specialization has distinguished many functions, religion still claims its unifying right. The welfare of the individual and of the group is its concern. Though different institutions have arisen in the service of particular interests, religion feels them all to be within its province. These in turn recognize the propriety of calling on religious organizations for moral and practical support. All community enterprises appeal to them. Patriotism, charity, education, moral reforms, naturally expect approval and aid from religious people and institutions. It is in religion more than anywhere else that men realize their common life, their brotherhood, their mutual dependence. More than any other agency religion teaches men these things. No other influence is so universal and so persistent in the affairs of the individual. From birth to death, in weakness and strength, in sorrow and joy, it speaks for him and to him. It is about him in infancy before the school opens to him, and continues after instruction has ceased; it makes a home for him when the family has been broken by time and death. For religion, he is never under age nor superannuated, never an alien nor an outcast, as he may be for every other relation. So long as he lives he is never utterly denied nor completely beyond redemption. After all evil and sin, the prodigal may return. As has been said, "every sinner has a future, just as every saint has a past."

This inclusiveness of religion implies another value of the greatest importance, namely, its *cosmic character*. The religious man regards the world and himself within an indefinitely vast set of relations. Every fact is for him fuzzy with mystery. It has its near and immediate aspect but it also has an immeasurable reach and indeterminate significance. Religion puts the individual and all his deeds in an infinite perspective. In the contemplation of the relations of the humblest event there may steal over the mind and heart an unutterable awe, for its consequences are interminable and unfathomable. Out of the past surge streams of life sweeping on into the remotest future. A footprint on the sand, or a pebble thrown into the abyss, contributes its influence to the momentum and the direction of the whole. This cosmic sense may be vague and inarticulate, but for some it is made clearer by a knowledge of electrons, of light-years, of the magnitudes of intricate mathematical formulas, and of the sensitivity of the millions of cells in human brains and bodies.

The religious man feels himself in the presence of the infinite. His conduct has import and meaning beyond all calculation and all definition. Therefore life gains for him in dignity and in moral worth. He is not only the child of time but of eternity. In the sheen of the sea and in the arch of the sky he beholds the beauty of

God. His soul stands face to face with the visible yet ever extending horizon, and there awaken in him reverence and deep humility.

All religious literature and ceremonial vibrate with this "cosmic emotion." Man feels himself in the presence of an order and reality which include him but which extend far below and above and 'round about him. Every strong wind which blows and every whisper of a friend remind him that he is but a small part of a vaster life and awaken the "feeling of dependence." This is one sure mark of the difference between the religious and the non-religious man. The former is sensitized to these larger aspects of his experience. He acknowledges them and he *feels* them. But the non-religious man is less responsive to such moods, either not feeling them at all or turning from them as meaningless or misleading. He keeps himself within the immediately factual level and declines to be a poet or an artist or a participant in sentiment. More often the non-religious man lives in this attitude not so much from choice as from habitual lack of response to the sublime. There are tone-deaf persons; there are prosy people; there are practical-minded and hard-fisted individuals to whom it seems childish and feminine to acknowledge the tender emotions. There are many scientifically trained men and women, specialized in analysis and in a limited kind of laboratory accounting, who refuse to acknowledge anything as valuable or significant which does not fall within their method and vision. Their work is important and they contribute much to knowledge and to mechanical manipulation, but they do not feel religious and they do not sense the importance and perhaps not even the reality of the religious man's experience. No more can a man who has not been in love appreciate the experience of one who has been set dreaming by soft eyes or by the lingering touch of a delicate hand. In the religious man there has arisen some realization of his relation to the whole creation which moves him with wonder and invites his soul into the heights and depths of profoundest emotions. These emotions are very mixed. Fear and love alternate as the tides threaten to overwhelm him or to bear him aloft. Life is precarious and serious to him in the dimensions of his wisest and loftiest imaginings. Therefore he knows in every event possibilities of both the love and the wrath of God.

But he carries also the conviction that God is on the side of man's deepest sense of the right and the good. Or at least he believes that the world, when taken in all its aspects, includes a moral order or is capable of supporting such an order. Here the tragic sense of life presses hard upon enlightened minds, for it is clear to them that man has conscientiously served the gods in ways and with offerings and sacrifices which now appear to be wicked abominations. What else to the modern moral sense are human sacrifices, ceremonial prostitution, holy wars, and the endless persecutions and inquisitions in the name of religion? But in spite of them all, religious men still believe that this very judgment and condemnation of customs of the past is the evidence that there is a moral quality in the nature of man's life. For who is it but man himself who turns upon the deeds of his past and rejects them with remorse and with hope for a possible better? His conviction that he should still seek and labor for a nobler world is itself proof to him that the universe, become articulate in himself, demands of him something greater than he has yet achieved. The imperfect laws which he enacts are his acknowledgment of the necessity of bringing to definition and working force some degree of righteousness. Much of the justice of the actual world is indeed rough, but its history and limited efficiency are nevertheless expressions of power to generate and to respond to moral ideals. Religious men therefore believe that they are fighting the battles of the Lord and that the enemy yields and falls back under attack. It is this tang of a real warfare which elates Mr. Chesterton in his novel, *The Ball and Cross*, where on both sides profoundly religious men engage to the death in defense of their faith. No other men fight with such spirit and devotion, for they believe they are laying down their lives in the conflict of the good against the evil, and that ultimately the good will be triumphant.

The religious attitude is therefore one of confidence toward reality and experience, with reference to the values which men at their best cherish most profoundly. This is a quality of disciplined optimism. Not infrequently religious people are blindly optimistic. They accept life with its varying fortunes as if all were decreed and sent for their good. It is surprising to what an extent devout souls, from Job to the Salvation Army lass singing on a street corner, can believe in the perfect goodness of God in spite of all the suffering and shame of human life which they keenly feel. All these hard things are but for the moment to them. Beneath all the confusion and perplexity they possess an undis-

turbed peace which truly passes all understanding.
Even when a religious person is discriminating enough
to doubt whether all things literally work together for
good to him, there is still the conviction that on the
whole life is rewarding and in the long run more satisfying than disappointing. It is usually very consciously
a matter of faith and admittedly without proof or experimental justification. This optimism displays a kind
of will to be content, a preference for looking on the
bright side and a refusal to be distrustful and unhappy
where so much is radiant and beautiful.

Religious persons may be intensely pessimistic about
some circumstances or elements of their experience, or
of the world at large, and yet be convinced that ultimately and finally happiness eventuates for the valiant
and faithful soul. Early Christianity despaired of the
existing order of society which it called "the world,"
but it had compensatory imagery of a future state of
bliss. Doubtless this thought of the final destiny has
been greatly modified in modern views, but the conviction of the possibility of improvement in this present
scene of action and through a long future still remains.

This sense of intimacy and security of the individual
in the midst of flux and immensity is another trait of the
higher forms of religion. It is the counterpart of the
emergence of the recognition and evaluation of personality from the solidarity of primitive group life. In
earlier stages the tribal unit is the absorbing concern as
is shown in such customs as that of blood revenge.
Only so late in Hebrew history as the prophets Isaiah
and Jeremiah is the conception of personal responsibility
made clear. Then it is decreed that "the soul that

sinneth, it shall die." Even in the time of Jesus the old idea that physical illness was the result of hereditary guilt still obscured and hindered appreciation of the importance of a man's own conduct, and the Pauline doctrine of the visitation of the sin of Adam upon the whole race reflected the ancient supremacy of the kinship group. It was in the teaching of Jesus that the worth of the individual soul was first emphatically declared. He carried further the "inwardizing" of moral values which had been suggested by some prophets, psalmists, and the dramatist Job. For Jesus the issues of life and death were from the heart and the imagination, from the motives and intentions of the will. The kingdom of heaven was within, and the inclinations to good and evil were sources and measures of moral worth more than the sayings of those of the olden times. The power of repentance, the ability to exercise forgiveness, the privilege of private prayer, the central place of faith and love, all illustrate the primacy of the inner life. Upon these qualities, rather than upon race, family, station or external ceremonials, depends the acceptability of men with God.

In such a religion the individual may feel himself in his own right securely allied with the divine. He is the child of a beneficent providence which guards and sustains him with infinite care. Outward fortunes are secondary and non-essential, often blinding and corrupting. It profits a man nothing to gain the whole world if he lose his own soul. Without goods or rank one may still possess the supreme treasures and belong to the eternal kingdom of light and love. The tendency of modern society has been toward the acceptance of such an ideal, as is evidenced by the rise of democratic states, universal suffrage and education, property rights, and the administration of justice. The goals of social reforms have been greater development and freedom for the individual. The claims of equality and natural rights for all men, regardless of accidents of birth and fortune, have been powerful factors in civil revolutions and in religious reformations.

All this has enlarged the individual's self-feeling and encouraged his sense of intimacy and oneness with God. In devotional literature this note has become dominant until it has created the illusion that the personal, subjective aspect of religion is the whole of it. It is an interesting result of the long and arduous efforts of associated life in providing the means for attaining freedom and inner worth that the individuals thus developed should claim independence of the very influences which have fashioned them. It would be absurd to assert that religion is experienced elsewhere than in particular persons, but it is of profound importance to realize that they are dependent upon association for their experience of it in their private lives. There is good ground for believing that the very God with whom they commune is really mediated through the Spirit of their associated life, and that without the nurture and direction of that communal power they never could have come to knowledge of God nor to the sense of participation in his beneficence and goodness.

Fortunately the sense of religious values is not altogether dependent upon an understanding of them. Seldom do religious persons wish to analyze religion or philosophize about it, and not infrequently any attempt

critically to investigate their faith hinders and weakens
its force and appeal. In the popular experience of religion this trait of personal intimacy and at-homeness
in the world is apparent in many forms. It is expressed
in the feeling of mutual relations such as those of
comrade and friend, lover and beloved, helper and co-
worker. Men tell God what they could not reveal to
any human being, so much do they trust his understanding love and forgiveness. Although they think of him
as one who knows everything they do, they are not kept
from him by their worst sins or their most devastating
weaknesses. They will not charge him with their fail-
ures nor with their suffering, but invent theories to ex-
onerate him from the evils they experience and make
the seeming evils appear as means to their good.
"Whom the Lord loves, he chastens," is an ancient and
still unworn word of comfort. Religion lives in the deep
and abiding conviction that the universe is friendly at
heart and that any appearances to the contrary are unreal and negligible. "The Lord is my shepherd, I shall
not want," is a universal sentiment of devout hearts;
"O Love that wilt not let me go," is a song from the
depths of the common faith; and the prayer, "Our
Father," is intelligible in every family on earth.

Freudianism interprets this sense of trust and intimacy as due to the child-father complex derived from
the conditioning of the infant toward its parents in
the early, susceptible years of unconscious life. Frequently this theory is regarded as discrediting man's
idea of the fatherhood of God simply because it is traced
to such an origin, but is such a conclusion warranted?
On the contrary, this doctrine may well be accepted as

illuminating the natural processes by which religious sentiments develop. Religion may become more concrete and appealing by the discovery of such intelligible explanations of its attitudes, and there may be found here serviceable means for the more certain development of desirable emotional responses to justifiable religious values. Many writers, so novel is the scientific treatment of religious experience, naïvely assume that to explain religious experience at all is to explain it away! Where else, if not in the most intimate and impressive relations of the family and kinship groups, may we look for the patterns of religious values and behavior? To treat these as fortuitous or vitiating would be to surrender the possibility of any valid interpretation of religion in terms of human experience.

In other chapters the tendency of religion to express its values through ceremonials and institutions is discussed. The ceremonials reflect all the values of religion, its practical spirit, its social nature, its inclusive and cosmic character, and its personal intimacy and aspiration. ᴸToo often these ceremonials become independent values on their own account, but when they do so it is a sign of waning vitality and of decadence.⟩

CHAPTER IV

RELIGION AND PHILOSOPHY

The nature of religion is revealed by comparison with other interests and activities which arise in the history of culture. For example, there is at all stages some ideational experience involved for human beings, but in religion it is kept subject to the fulfilment of practical interests. In primitive cults thinking goes on in a kind of reverie which gives rise to mythologies. This associative thinking is the oldest and the most natural kind of mental activity. It is subject to chance impressions and generates the most grotesque fancies. The folk-lore of all peoples abounds in stories of the strangest imaginings, mingled with the events of daily life. The world is peopled with spirits of undefined powers and caprice. Legendary beings throng through nature and take possession of man. There are no bounds between the real and the imagined. The strangest marvels happen. Inanimate things come alive. Animals speak with more than human wisdom. Men are transformed into lower forms and invisible shapes. The dead are alive and the living pass out of the body in their dreams. Words and signs have magic power. Omens are given in cloud and star, by the entrails of birds, and by the dew and hail. The sun is stayed by the word of a prophet. The serpent tempts a woman and the race bears the heavy burden of her sin, generation after generation. An axe head floats in water, a man lives in the body of a whale, a cruse of oil is miraculously replenished, city walls fall at the blast of trumpets, seas divide their waters for tribes to pass and then overwhelm pursuing armies, manna falls from heaven for the hungry, water bursts out of the rock for the famished. Such are the groping efforts of man's infant thought endeavoring to explain the events of life and the relation of the mysteries which surround him. Nor does he leave of a sudden that fanciful, mythical world for one more clearly defined and ordered. By the side of a more rational conception these old fancies still persist. Wise men, to this day, live next door to dark superstition, and in some corner of their being are likely to harbor some old irrationality of myth or magic. But this mythology was not the main stream of man's life in any age. All the time he was carrying on a life of action, loving and fighting, sowing and reaping, building and migrating, dancing and singing. He built cities and sailed the seas; he invented tools and developed the arts. Clumsily and haltingly but persistently he extended his power and increased the volume of his deeds. By restless energy and chance achievement he pushed on into new adventures and new mastery. His thinking was in terms of his experience and habits. It was "practical," just as at the present time people elaborate in their leisure and reverie dream pictures which review and extend the patterns of their daily tasks or build compensatory castles in the air. The world of ideas was molded by the things the hands worked in and by the processes of nature and man's interaction with them. The mythologies were often grotesque, the efflorescence of unchecked imagery, but they were in the character of the symbolism afforded by the habitat and by the enterprises of securing the means of existence.

Another tendency of thought in connection with religion is the rationalization of prevailing customs. Swine were taboo to the Hebrews. The reason usually given was that swine were not healthful food for them in their climate and circumstances. But an authority on such matters now says that the taboo may have been due to the fact that the swine were too sacred, the term "unclean" not having the meaning which we ordinarily attach to it. Likewise the observance of the Sabbath as a day of rest may have arisen from some superstition connected with the changing phases of the moon rather than from the recognition of the desirability of having a day's vacation each week. We rationalize the use of clothing as the expression of modesty, whereas it is now known that modesty springs from the use of clothing, and that clothing began to be worn as ornamentation. In our society marriage seems to be the basis of the family, but in the history of the race the family was the occasion of marriage, and remains so in some lands today.

Theology may be regarded as the systematic rationalization of customs and of the fragmentary, uncriticized ideas carried along in the practice of religion. Thus Christian theology has undertaken to organize and interpret the biblical system of religion. The doctrines discussed and formulated deal with creation, the fall of man, the nature of sin, the scheme of redemption, atonement, the trinity and each person of the trinity, revelation, rewards and punishment, immortality, and the destiny of the world. Some theologians have proceeded upon the theory that the Bible furnished answers to all such questions and that it was only necessary to make a systematic exposition of the Scriptures. The diversity of conclusions is obvious even to the casual reader of their works. Others have held that theology required enlightenment with reference to the original languages and institutions of the people whose records are given in the Bible. Still others, under the influence of modern critical methods, have concluded that no theology can be written simply as an exposition of Scriptures but that it always requires a process of interpretation. This process is of course subject to constant revision, not only from the side of discoveries with reference to biblical texts but on account of the growing knowledge of human nature and social institutions and other religions. To some extent each religious body has its characteristic theology. The Calvinistic, Lutheran, and Wesleyan theologies start with different presuppositions and arrive at different results. Or theologians who undertake to divest themselves of all partisan points of view are still influenced by the prevailing spirit of their times. Just now all advanced scholars work with the concepts of evolution, of genetic theories, of social justice, and of scientific methods. They incline to the moral theory of the atonement rather than to the judicial, the commercial, the legal, or any other of the older historic types. They are also more or less motivated by the attitude of the apologist, interested in the truth and value of the religion he expounds. Their thinking, usually with confessed awareness, is concerned with making religion more intelligible and useful.

In the philosophy of religion another stage is reached

in the function of thought. Philosophy endeavors to proceed in an objective and independent manner. It is more detached, more a spectator or observer than a participant or apologist. Here reflective thinking develops the attitude of searching for the Truth freed from the practical, emotional experience. Only a few philosophers have realized that their thought, however they strive for this objectivity, is yet influenced by motivations and evaluations which are deeper than their thought. Occasionally thinkers like William James appreciate the extent to which temperament, personal history, environment, occupation, and other phases of concrete living enter into the structure and color of the stream of thought. Fewer yet seem to see that thought may still have value and very useful functions within such limits.

The full realization of this fact has appeared only with the development of recent psychology which has discovered the realm of the unconscious and has given new importance to habit and impulse, and to custom within the group life. The school of Durkheim and Lévy-Bruhl in France, with Gilbert Murray and others in England, has shown to what extent the structures of society, religion, morals, and philosophy itself are elaborated under the practical pressures of life, and with far less objectivity than thinkers have usually supposed. The remark of Sumner that there are fashions in thought as well as in dress is a reminder that ideas bud on the branches of the tree of action and that a whole tree of knowledge is mythical. Whatever exaggeration there may be of this view in certain schools of thought it has carried conviction in varying degree to all types of thinkers. Very few, if any, at the present time escape this fashion of our thought. We are pretty generally convinced that our thinking is bound up with our habits of action and operates within the field of our "complexes" and our *milieu*.

It is interesting to note to what an extent the philosophers have dealt with the problems of religion. From Plato to Royce and James it has been a dominant interest. Descartes labored over the proofs for the being of God, Spinoza was finally dominated by "the intellectual love of God," Locke wrote more essays on religion and commentaries on the Scriptures than on any other one subject. Even Hume evinced a central interest in the history of religion and in miracles. Kant felt called upon "to remove knowledge [from undue claims to settle the metaphysical problems of religion] in order to make room for faith." Hegel put his philosophy of religion at the apex of his system. The English idealists—Green, Caird, Bradley—were philosophers of religion. Comte, Mill, and Spencer are known as much by their discussions of religion as by any other interests. Bertrand Russell with his *Free Man's Worship,* and Santayana with his *Winds of Doctrine,* and Whitehead with his *Religion in the Making* express in the titles of important works the inescapable subject of man's sincerest reflective thought. In writers like Bergson and Dewey, occasional references to the subject indicate that these questions are not foreign to their thinking though they may be, with effort, left on one side or deferred for later consideration. And even in those who do not use the terms of religious phraseology, only a slight change in their nomenclature is needed to make it fully apparent that they are not uninfluenced by the problems which arise in this field.)

It is not difficult to understand why philosophy moves so constantly within this sphere. Thinking centers upon the points of stress and strain in human experience. Religion deals with inclusive and pervasive ideals of life, with the tragedies of a fortuitous existence and the fact of death. The emotional tensions which pertain to these universal experiences center attention upon them with unavoidable pressure. Probably the great majority of professional thinkers have devoted their lives to philosophy because at some time or in some way these problems became vital and inevitable for them.

But when one enters upon the task of philosophizing about so live and urgent a matter as religion he finds himself involved in the opposition of two profoundly significant attitudes. On the one side is the living, practical interest in the ends or consequences to be obtained. He wants his faith justified, his hopes assured, his wishes fulfilled. But satisfactory reflective thinking requires detachment. It must be disinterested, cool, impersonal. How, then, is it possible for a warm, practical being such as the natural person is to go over to the attitude which thought requires? How can he be expected to absolve himself from all interest in the outcome of thought in order to be able to think impartially and truly? Or, if he succeeds in abstracting himself from his emotional life, how can he be certain that in his detachment he still is in possession of the "facts" of experience upon which he wishes to reflect? This is, of course, a kind of paradox which is involved in all scientific, disciplined thinking. For some thinkers

it has developed the conviction that we live in two
realms, one of appreciation and one of description.
Actual living experience is permeated with apprecia-
tions. Pure thought moves in the unemotional field of
description. Experience is on the plane of action toward ends which are colorful with desired satisfaction.
Thought lies on the plane of observation, analysis, and
logical relation. In the first, desires rule; in the second, truth is found. Thinking, in the form of associated
imagery or of practical solving of specific problems,
occurs in the former, but pure thought belongs only to
the latter. The one is known in the history of philosophy as "empiricism," and the other as "rationalism."
The effort to see things as they *are*, independent of all
feeling, leads to the Truth, capitalized and hypostatized.
The treatment of concrete, motivated experience allows
only of relative truth, spelled with small letters and
conscious of its modest function and power. It is an
instrument for action, for use under the demands of
the practical will.

From this predicament flow decisive influences, particularly in the study of religion, and therefore it de-
serves careful consideration. Those who hold to reality
as it is for pure thought cannot identify that reality
with the emotionalized world of religious experience.
They must, therefore, either take refuge in a paradox
such as "intellectual love," or relegate religion to the
world of symbols and metaphors as Kant did. They
may become mystics, holding on to religion in spite of
their philosophy, or they may discard religion as an
affair of the simple-minded and unenlightened. In all
such positions there is a cleavage between the sphere

of emotionalized action and conceptual thought and no adequate or legitimate interaction is recognized.

Another view of this difficulty is that thinking is only relatively detached, and for intervals of time. Thought does indeed for the time being ascend or withdraw to one side from the practical activity. But it remains in sight of the situation and is cognizant more or less closely of the fact that its problem arose from that field of living experience and that its answers must soon or late be referred back to it again for verification and use. The functions which thought performs are those of criticism and direction of activity. Both aspects are accomplished by affording a wider perspective for the survey of the situation in which conduct occurs. Just as an aviator may survey the field of battle more comprehensively than a soldier on the ground, and may also have more quiet and safety in which to make observations, so the thinker in his withdrawn position relates the narrower scene of the moment to the past and the future, and thus gets it in a perspective which brings out its purport and meaning. If the aviator loses all relation to the earth he has no bearings from which to make estimates of distance or danger or any other meaningful observations. It is impossible to imagine what kind of thoughts a disembodied spirit could have and yet the effort of some "pure scientists" seems to be to attain precisely this complete release from any meaningful problems of human interest or value.

Under the sway of scientific thought there is a strong disposition to regard the world as described by science as more objective and real than the world as seen through social interests. Science seems to give us Na-

ture as she is. In that view man and his human affairs
appear as transient and momentary and subject to the
processes and fate which the natural order imposes.
But it may be answered that these physical sciences
describe the world *from their point of view*. And there
are other points of view, probably indefinite in number.
There is the conception of the world as an object of
consciousness, or as a stage for the drama of conscious
life, or as a scene in which spiritual forces are gradually
transforming lower into higher orders of reality. Any
given object may be viewed from indefinitely numerous
and various points of observation. What I call my
pencil is also a piece of metal; it is of so much money
value; it is beyond price in its meaning to me because
it was presented by a friend one Christmas time; it
would be, on occasion, a weapon to stab with; it is a
reflector of light; it is a means of identification; it is an
ornament; it is the subject of discourse. In each relation it is just as real as in any other. The scientist
cannot say what it really is any more than a poet or a
salesman or a thief. The sciences have their points of
view which are just as much determined by interests
as are those of the religionist or the artist. If we con-
sent to let the scientific view play the rôle of the really
real, we may consistently do so. But to suppose that
it is really the real in any ultimate and objective sense,
other than this, is to ignore what all the sophisticated
people know and admit. Every judgment is weighted
and anchored by interests and specific situations. This,
indeed, gives limitation to the judgment, but it also
is the basis of any meaning or significance for judgment.
Limits have positive, as well as negative, functions.

The boundaries of a field reveal the area of the owner's freedom and may invite to certain kinds of friendly relations beyond. They show him the way out at the same time that they establish his place within.

An objection frequently made to such an interpretation of the function of knowledge is that it is subjective and solipsistic. The answer may be made that of course all thinking goes on in minds or persons and is unquestionably conditioned by their experience and character. But it is just this fact that they are in the world and part of it which makes their knowledge of it real. It is obviously quite impossible for the mind to deal with objects or entities entirely outside its experience. We get at past events through their relation to present events, and imagined future occurrences are projected upon the screen of the known. It is a favorite puzzle to assume the geological ages of the past and then ask whether they came into being with the birth of man or other sentient creatures. They are so obviously antecedent to mankind. But is not this antecedence a relation to the knower of the present? The very arrangement of before and after, of here and there, is undefinable except in relation to some posited point of reference. So much is this a feature of thought about the world that the attempt to think it independently is impossible. The attempt to assume objectivity of this kind is like trying to get an up without a down, or an in which has no out. But on this account to deny meaning to these relations is to dismiss all possibilities of description or thought. To assume that there is some particular kind of knowledge, such as that of geology or of mathematics, which escapes this condition, is to set

up certain relations of thinking as if they were independent of thought. Religious objects are not different in this respect from any others. These also appear
within the forms, and subject to the conditions, of
thought. Like all other conceptions of reality they are
related to the experiences within which they are conceived.

But this is quite a different matter from the assumption that the individual thinker imposes relations
and conditions which are his alone. Thought is not a
subjective process within the head of an individual
organism. Thought is bound up with language and language is a social fact. It is a shared experience. Minds,
so to speak, are more fluid than human bodies. They
interact and participate in ideas and emotions when
the physical organisms are at a distance. Meanings
are transmittable and simultaneous for the parties to a
conversation or a correspondence. It is of the very
nature of ideas to be communicable and to be group
possessions. They are events in time but they are not
isolated. Any idea is continuous with other ideas and
is a partial definition of a continuum of experience.
There are no individual life-histories sundered from all
other such histories. Each is an aspect of a flowing
stream and can be singled out and described only within
a social process.

This fact is the basis of a certain type of objectivity
which is of importance in dealing with the truth and
reality of the world. When an idea is true it is capable
of appropriation by other persons, and it is this possibility of appropriation which makes it more than subjective, individual fact. The truth of an idea is its

meaning for many persons in similar circumstances so that it is a cue for similar acts for them all. The true idea about a route of travel is one which represents the experience of persons in the past and of possible experience for others coming after them. The objectivity goes beyond the personal feeling of a single organism, is capable of being used by others, and guides action for all into overt deeds. In fact, the reality and validity of an idea become convincing and authoritative only when it is so recognized and used by others. In the field of social action the truth is finally established.

This is a form of objectivity very different from the entire detachment from human concerns which is sometimes demanded. This is the type of objectivity which Plato describes when he speaks of the state as the individual "writ large." The pattern is more intelligible and available when projected on the larger scale. But the pattern is still cast within the human, social experience, and yet it takes on universal and demonstrable reality. Such reality has concreteness and definition. It does not belong to the order of essences, pure being, and absolutes without attributes. It is not pure, nor infinite, nor absolute in the meaning of these terms as fixed by familiar doctrines of ideal Truth, Goodness, and Beauty.

As has often been pointed out, the difficulty springs from the attempt to establish knowledge by itself, in a vacuum, as it were. But every such attempt must end in a kind of mysticism where the very processes of demonstration and argument are carried out beyond the only sphere in which they are capable of having meaning. They can have meaning only in reference to action or within a system which finally rests upon the solid realm of practical action. Knowledge thus shows itself to be a means of dealing with action and the objects which are generated or brought to attention within action. In the simpler forms of life this action is of a sufficiently obvious kind and this continues to be the fundamental type for all men. Living organisms are inherently active. They are constantly in motion, seeking and appropriating food, mating, playing, fighting, in the endless struggle for existence and for the goods of life. The processes of perception, memory, anticipatory imagination, are ceaselessly operative. The function of percepts, memories, and imagination is to guide and select. They are the ever restless antennæ of the organism in relation to the environment, circling about, feeling for favorable experiences, withdrawing from objects which signify danger. On the higher levels of conduct the same process continues with varying degrees of refinement. The antennæ of human beings are vastly developed by the accumulation of traditions, of techniques, of capacities for assessing novel situations. But in principle it is the same process. The inventions of man are often characterized as the extensions of the organs of the body, and we now have man with telescopic and microscopic vision, with marvelous powers of locomotion, of discriminative ability to the millionth of an inch and the distances of light-years. With these refinements of the senses go enlargement of sympathy, deepening insight into social processes, and corresponding creativity in intelligence and art. This extension and refinement of goals, or ideals, is of the essence of the spiritualization of life. The assumption that the spiritual is of another order than the practical and the intelligible introduces into the conception of life a cleavage which obscures and confuses all important problems. It reduces everyday experience to the routine and commonplace, and removes spiritual values out of reach of the natural man. Whoever accepts that dualism thereby creates the impossibility of regarding religion as something to be understood and developed by reasonable methods, and leaves the simple and fundamental life-processes outside the pale. Then there appears the irreligious natural man, and the unnatural religious man. In such a view, no development of science could be of any help or enlightenment to religion, and religion would be incapable of suggesting any ends capable of enlisting or utilizing the services of science.

Wherever knowledge has been applied to concrete experience the result has been marked development. Many spheres of interest were once withheld from criticism and rational suggestion. It was so with custom, with law, with marriage, with what seemed the decrees of fate. "The king can do no wrong" meant that he was not within the province of criticism. Gradually various realms have been conceded to rational treatment. The one still most insistent on the claim of exemption is religion. But wherever it has been subjected to the light of knowledge significant consequences have followed. The Bible has been given a new place of importance for educated persons through its critical interpretations. The life of Christ as described by Renan and the long line of scholars since his time has generated a new appeal. A religion of social idealism has gained adherents in all creeds and is gradually remaking the conception and the symbols of the churches. Whenever religion turns to practical tasks such as healing the sick, educating the ignorant, organizing the broken and wavering units of the family and neighborhood, scientific knowledge is able to prove its serviceableness to spiritual ends.

Religion does not foreshorten the perspectives in which these practical tasks lie, but is interested (more than any other treatment of them) in the extension of their perspectives upon the largest possible scale. A cup of cold water may be given in the name of deity; an obscure soul is a brother of the most divine. But it is the brother whom we have seen who affords the starting-point. Any satisfactory idealization begins with the concrete and the empirical. It cannot end there. Religion performs one of its greatest services in the extension of the frame of thought and feeling from the immediate and the given to the most sublime proportions. This recognition of the far-reaching relations of the humblest events involves one of the most important functions of knowledge. Here all the sciences, including mathematical measurements and imaginative constructions, lend form and magnitude to religious conceptions. It follows that religious ideas, in their refinement and scope, reflect the level of the general culture. At every stage religion seeks the most inclusive and comprehensive frame of thought in which to set the lowliest experiences. But the attempts of knowledge to build conceptions of reality independent of such experienced realities lead it into mere fog and mist, while the efforts of religious feeling to assert other realities than those of actual experience end in the same unverifiable and indescribable nonentities. Religion needs, therefore, the factual elements and relations of scientific thought, and science needs the evaluations of religious attitudes. Neither one is complete or adequate in itself.

These attitudes, as we have indicated, are social attitudes, in the true sense of that term. It is from this common base of social life that all knowledge extends and to this it returns. The dining-table may be taken as a symbol of this center of social life and as a medium in which is generated the essentially human world of feeling and thought. Take, for example, the round table of a university faculty club. There may be seen gathered at luncheon several men, specialists in various fields, sciences, languages, law, religion, art, medicine, business. They order from the same menu, use the same kind of utensils, and employ the same speech. There is a limited range of conversation in which they are all equally at home—the weather, the news of the day, certain general features of the university life. But two men of the same department may engage in conversation concerning some problem in their special field of research and quickly absorb themselves in technical concepts and discussions which are quite outside the interest or understanding of their neighbors. In order to make their conversation intelligible to their friends they would have to go back to the beginnings of their problems in the field of common experience and gradually show the steps by which they were carried out to their special sphere of discourse. In similar manner each one about the table is at home in the simple, common processes of eating, drinking, and chatting about the items of the narrower circle of living. But from

that base of shared action and feeling radiate lines of
selected interests with their own technique, terms, and
values. The chemist, physiologist, historian, and lin-
guist are well enough served by the same menu and
understand one another sufficiently with reference to
hunger and satiety. Yet each one moves out from that
fundamental process and follows certain facts and relations into the great distances of academic expertness.
At the farthest points of their investigations they are
remote from the common experiences of the table group,
but are occupied all the time, it may be, with questions
connected with food. However diversified or technical
their knowledge, it is nevertheless engaged upon the
facts of that encompassing life-process and for its ultimate validation must justify itself with reference to that
process. Now and then some discovery occurs on the
frontier of a specialty which throws such light upon the
elementary activities as to be universally appreciated.
Such is the discovery of a new anæsthetic or the
excavation of an Egyptian tomb, or Lindbergh's non-
stop flight across the Atlantic Ocean. But the processes
and achievements of knowledge move out from and return to the world of common experience symbolized by
the table. The highest and the subtlest reaches of
knowledge have this setting and relation. There is no
material for knowledge outside this cycle nor any means
of proof or verification of alleged facts or truth apart
from a loop line ascending from this starting-point and
returning to it again. This does not mean that the basic
field of human action and emotion remains unchanged
by accumulating knowledge. It is constantly illuminated and modified by enlarging knowledge but it con-

tinues to be a life-process stimulated by the native springs of appetite, of curiosity, and of satisfaction. Knowledge does not come first. Action, impulse, sentiency, and habit in their diversity and conflict are the sources of reflection and the test of its value. Philosophy cannot go on without the social life of man, but the life of man generates philosophy and constantly summons philosophy to an accounting as to its results and value. Like all knowledge, philosophy is, in a sense, derived and secondary, instrumental and subservient.

Yet this very knowledge is the means to the greatest enrichment and development of the life of mankind. The attainment of the methods of accumulating knowledge, of making scientific discoveries, and of extending experimentation are the great agencies of progress and the enlargement of life. They have transformed the face of nature and the manner of man's life to an astonishing degree. Here lies his hope for further control in the future. But at the very height of this scientific era the wisest men are beginning to see that no amount of knowledge is adequate to the demands of human life in its deepest needs. Bertrand Russell and other observers of our civilization see that the development of scientific technique affords no guaranty of any significant use of that technique. The great question of their later thought is as to where and how there are to be found means for relating knowledge to the great values and ends of life. These values are the qualities which belong to the natural social bonds of the fundamental social units, the face to face groups of mutually sympathetic and helpful individuals. These values are the concomitants of social attitudes and these attitudes at their highest are the religious verities.

CHAPTER V

RELIGION AND SCIENCE

One of the acutest problems in current thought is the relation of science and religion. The solution would be greatly simplified and clarified if the discussion were prefaced by more adequate definition of terms. We have emphasized the fact that religion is a practical concern in the sense that it projects ends and ideals and works for their realization. It seeks a kingdom, undertakes to build a better social order, and its contemplative aspects are occupied with meditation upon those ends and the joyful thoughts of their fulfilment. In this contemplation is implied reflection upon the nature of man and the world, and of the forces operative in attaining some adjustment between them.

Science is the detailed examination of these factors and of their relations. Each of the sciences deals with a small sector of reality, investigating with the utmost care its facts, describing them and discovering whatever laws may be operative in them. Particular sciences are concerned with specific, practical matters, as in medicine, which seeks knowledge of a disease like cancer by all the objective methods of analysis and observation known to the laboratory procedure of physiological chemistry, bacteriology, and pathology. The scientist studies the facts in their setting and relation as objective phenomena and without the emotional stress of being himself a subject of the disease or near of kin to any

one suffering from it.   For him it may be just a scientific
problem whose implications for human weal or woe are
relatively remote.   That they are not entirely indifferent to him as a human being is evident from the most
casual knowledge of such a disease as cancer which must
come to the attention of any reader of the papers or to
any one who has ordinary contacts with his fellows.
The fact that the inquiry has entered his laboratory
shows that it involves human interests, and this sense of
a social basis of the problem contributes to his interest
in dealing with it. Scientists do not spend their energies
upon matters in which no one is in any way interested.
If the questions with which they deal are taken in
their history and larger human setting, they reveal, in
their past and future reference, relations with situations
which men desire to understand and perhaps to control.

Science, like philosophy, belongs to the reflective attitude.   Unlike philosophy it limits itself to specific
problems. Its work is more piecemeal, more limited,
while philosophy undertakes to construct a view of the
whole upon the basis of the discoveries obtained in the
different partial fields.   Science does indeed require certain attitudes toward reality and may betray curiosity
about anything relative to the world of facts.   There is
also the conviction of the right to investigate, to probe
into any phase or type of experience; and success has
developed confidence in the fruitfulness and value of
such inquiry.   Out of the practice of the scientific
method and its results has arisen the assurance that
when any problem is presented, science possesses, or
may develop, the appropriate method of dealing with
it.

Naturally if religion is identified with a dogmatic attitude toward any facts or practical ends, the spirit of modern science is in conflict with it. Or, if religion is thought of in terms of the scientific concepts now outgrown, it will be in conflict with the newer conceptions. But this is essentially due to a difference between varying scientific views of the world and should not be attributed to religion and science as such. Both science and religion are constantly subject to revision and one may not properly be regarded as static while the other is subject to change. Frequently the charge is made by religionists that science is always changing while religion remains the same, but the history of religion shows that it also undergoes enlargement and refinement.

Or it is held that religion belongs to the sphere of belief while science claims knowledge. But as a matter of fact science frankly admits that its most fundamental concepts are hypotheses, although as well verified as is at present possible. It looks to the future for further discoveries and builds upon the belief that these are possible. The assumption that religion deals only with what is undemonstrable and therefore requires to be taken on faith simply puts the stress upon the unsolved aspects of life, while ascribing to science the field of the known. In reality, if the inquiring function of science is emphasized, science may be thought of as dealing with the unknown. There is thus a tendency to put the two interests in contrast by selecting extreme phases of each and making them stand for the entire procedure. There is a settled and assured area of both science and religion, and there are areas in each which are incomplete and conjectural. Neither one has reached complete finality, and it only begets confusion to compare the developing side of one with the achieved results of the other.

Even the most elusive problems of religion, such as the doctrine of the future life, may be approached by the method of science. Science may investigate the history of the idea, may show when, where, and under what circumstances this belief came into prominence. It may point out the kind of evidence which is needed to deal fruitfully with the subject and devise suggestions for gathering such evidence. Perhaps this kind of question is not fundamentally different from that of conjecture concerning the possibility of life on other planets, a question concerning which science has so far no definite answer. Yet studies are made with reference to atmospheric and temperature conditions thought to have some bearing upon the problem. In every field some things are known clearly or in part, while others remain dark and unfathomed. This is as true in scientific matters as in religious and in religion as in science. To generalize in science upon those things which are well determined, and contrast those generalizations with the less known things in religion is as fallacious as it would be to compare all the tentative guesses of science with the settled and sure aspects of religion. In both subjects knowledge is partial and progressive. In both there are phenomena well understood and verified, and in both there are things partially determined, and other things quite unknown and full of mystery. Inquiry goes on in each realm and reliable results are obtained.

However, this comparison of science and religion, as

if they were separate fields of experience, is itself likely
to be misleading. It would be truer to regard science
as the method of all possible knowledge, and religion
as one of the subjects to which it may be applied. Then
the correct observation would be that knowledge of
religion is comparable to knowledge of other social interests, such as politics or economics. In these subjects,
too, much has been learned and much is still obscure.
Politics is not science but may be dealt with scientifically. Not all political questions can now be answered
by scientific knowledge but progress is under way concerning many of them. In all the social problems
science is in its infancy but already has established confidence in its value. Religion is one of the last subjects to be approached by scientific inquiry, and it is not
strange that as yet the possibilities in this realm are not
appreciated.

There are peculiar difficulties in every type of subject matter where thorough knowledge is sought. One
of the commonest barriers in opening new sciences is the
force of tradition and habit, of sentiment and apprehension. The subject of eugenics affords abundant illustration of this. Just because custom and uncritical attitudes have prevailed, it is difficult to make a beginning.
Scientific investigation of the questions involved seems
at first like an impertinence. Emotional opposition is
encountered, and an irrational fear is awakened that
such studies may undermine cherished institutions and
have only negative and destructive results. It is indeed impossible to allay such fears for it is never possible to foresee what the results of knowledge will be,
but the achievements in other interests give reason to

hope for significant results in the study of religion. Because of the depth and intimacy of religious experience, and because of the intense emotional life which accompanies it, religion has withheld itself from scientific treatment more insistently than any other human interest. Inquiry into these religious states may easily appear sacrilegious to religious persons, and when put into objective analysis and description the facts may appear entirely incommensurate with the feeling of the events themselves. But the same is true of any lively emotional phenomena. The descriptions of romantic love seem weak and colorless as compared with the pulsations of passionate affection. Our verbalizations manifest their limitations and shortcomings when used to express such experiences.

Moreover, religionists have so long been accustomed to associate their ecstasies with marvelous supernatural causes and influences that the matter-of-fact reference of these high moments to natural conditions such as bodily impulses of hunger, thirst, and sex is incredible and revolting. Nowhere has this correlation been more thoroughly established than in the phenomena of conversion and in mystical exaltation, and nowhere have the facts been more vehemently denied than by the subjects of these states. Devout souls often refuse to recognize the reality of these correlations, but their emotional protest in itself is no invalidation of the facts which scientific studies disclose. It may easily seem unbelievable to the lover of roses that the delicate coloring and perfume are in any way related to the black earth and fertilizer which the gardener put about the roots of the shrub, but few could now doubt the efficacy of his methods in producing the bloom and beauty which result. It is indeed incomprehensible why the sight of the sun setting in a sea of gold, banked by masses of cloud, should stir so deeply the thought and emotion of man, but the frequency of the experience leaves no doubt that such is the case. To discover and verify the humble conditions in the human organism and its environment in which moods of adoration and reverence arise is scientifically possible, and yields a certain acquaintance with the moods themselves. It may even afford a measure of control of those moods.

Science is sometimes said to deal only with material facts and with phenomena which can be quantitatively measured, and that therefore it is incompetent to deal with the central experiences of religion having to do with the soul, spiritual reality, and God. It has just been shown that religion touches upon the factual and measurable side in the correlation which exists between the highest states and known psychological factors. What is more important, science is extending its sphere into various social fields, and is applying its methods of observation and description far beyond the realms of mere physical events. The social psychologists are beginning to investigate the nature of personality and its attitudes. Whatever else it may be, religion is certainly a matter of attitudes. It is bound up with awe, reverence, and faith. It is expressed in emotion. All these are being brought within the range of the methods now employed by scientific psychology. It is possible to know the conditions under which they occur, the varying degrees in which they appear, and the results to which they lead. Further prosecution of this type of inquiry waits upon more adequate refinement of method, and the co-operation of more trained and skilful workers, but beginnings have been made which already prove that the phenomena are not beyond the reach of patient treatment. As the social sciences become more adequate to their tasks in dealing with the institutions and attitudes which human nature achieves, it will become clearer that science is able to understand and illuminate many more features of religious experience. It has been natural that science should be identified with the physical realm because it was here that its first triumphs were made, but its success as a method of definite knowledge has given it courage to go farther and to deal with more and more complex phenomena. In the early stages also, scientists themselves thought of their work as concerned only with the objective, physical world and sought to avoid conflict with religious prejudice by asserting that they had nothing to do with the fields of religion.

A review of the fruits of the application of science to religion will show that it has already proved itself a useful aid and handmaid to religion. First, it has been exceedingly productive in the practical good works of religion. Science has afforded the means of great alleviation of human suffering and want. It is unquestionable that the more advanced forms of religion have regarded this ministration to human life as of central importance. Healing the sick, opening blind eyes, unstopping deaf ears, and straightening bent limbs are among the objectives of the Christian spirit. No one can doubt in these days that science has achieved marvels in these things. It is not the business of science itself to do such deeds, but it is a prime duty of religion to do them, and to use science as a means for their accomplishment. The founding of hospitals, employing the best instruments and methods which science can devise, has been one of the most conspicuous contributions of Christian philanthropy. Probably the majority of the great hospitals of the world bear the names of the churches which have built and manned them. There is nothing in the nature of science itself to determine that its knowledge and skill shall have such uses. It lends itself just as readily to processes of destruction, as all the world knows to its sorrow from the recent great war. (But it is also equally apparent that religion, without the aid of modern science, would be as helpless still as it was in the days when it had no other means than magic and incantation for its humane ends. This principle might be illustrated in many directions. It is part of the aim of religion to bind the race together in bonds of neighborliness and human understanding. To this end all means of communication and transportation contribute. The highways, cables, steamships, and railways, built by the aid of the various sciences, furnish the framework for the more adequate practice of brotherhood and good will. The value of these things depends upon the spirit in which they are used, but the will to use them for these spiritual ends belongs to religion at its best. The world could not be as effectively religious as it is, in a practical way, without the instruments furnished by science. The realization of further degrees of practical kindliness and neighborly love are promised by researches and experiments now in progress. In this field certainly, science makes no reservations in regard to religion. It offers all its resources for the uses of devout and earnest workers for the kingdom of heaven on earth. The fact that these same resources are also available for evil-minded persons does not destroy the value of science for religion, but only requires greater alertness and enthusiasm among religious people in recognizing and utilizing this possible ally.

A second definite contribution of science to religion lies in the field of contemplation. This seems more intimately religious to many than the practical good deeds just mentioned. Those who find the essence of religion in meditation, or worship, may well ponder the help which science yields here. The psalmist said, "When I behold the heavens, the work of thy hands, what is man, that thou art mindful of him and the son of man that thou visitest him?" If the observer of the heavens with the unaided eye could be brought to such ecstasy by what he saw, how much more meaningful is the exclamation of the modern man who looks out through telescopes and spectroscopes upon the millions of suns and stars in the vast spaces through which light is now known to travel? Or if the seas and rocks known to ancient men could awaken reverence, to what depths may those be moved who know so much better the story written in the rocks and in the tides of the sea? Every field which science has surveyed has opened out into amazing wonders and beauties beyond all powers of perception or imagination. The human body, so wonderfully and fearfully made; the atom with its swirling protons and electrons; electrical forces, playing about all the world and carrying messages into the walled retreats of man; tremendous energies within the smallest grain of sand or drop of water—all these as disclosed to boys in school set the frame and action of a universe so vast and so full of order and beauty that a new type of contemplation and reverence arises. When these things are more commonly known and appreciated, who can doubt that they will inspire new poetry, art, and piety?

To some minds this gigantic world is a fearsome and overwhelming immensity, within which they see man moving as a fragile, helpless fleck of dust. But that is only one interpretation of the picture, and even that is not entirely lacking in its significance for religion. It is one indispensable attitude of religion in all its stages and forms to recognize the greatness and power of the forces within which man lives and moves and has his being. There is ground here for a genuine awe and respect for the order of nature; there is the possibility of recognizing that amidst all this ocean of being man has his place, and that he is able to rise to some comprehension of its vastness and complexity. He has reason to know that not only may the world overwhelm him, but that it carries him within it, and yields him power and happiness in the midst of its force and change. It is through just such a world of hazard and precariousness that man has grown to be what he is. His emotional life is attuned to risk and possible achievement, and as the world widens through better knowledge, the scale of his experience is extended into new dimensions of adventure and hope, as well as of fear and tragedy. This larger, wider universe may therefore afford new intensities of religious emotion as far beyond those of the older days as the new order of reality is greater than the old.

A third specific indication of the contribution which science makes to religion may be illustrated from the special branch of science which is concerned with the most intimate phenomena of religion, namely, the psychology of religion. This study has taken its place among the organized sciences only since the beginning of the present century, yet it has already achieved results which furnish a more adequate understanding of religion and of the possibilities of its development. Applying the methods and concepts of general psychology and especially of social psychology, it has rapidly grown to an important body of knowledge. The first studies were devoted to the problems of conversion. The work of Starbuck, Coe, and Hall establish the fact that religious interest awakens in early adolescence, with the maturing of the whole organism, and the emergence of love between the sexes. This awakening is occasioned by the suggestions of the group in which the individual lives, and is a response to the larger social attitudes of the group. The form and content of the experience is conditioned by the habits and customs of the family and community life. These awakenings are of two types, which James called the once-born and the twice-born types. Coe showed that persons subject to automatisms, under normal suggestion or under hypnotism, have corresponding conversion experiences. The peaks in the curves of the statistics show that the ages of twelve, sixteen, and nineteen are the high points in the number of those who become religious during adolescence, and each of these periods is characterized by differences in their reactions. The earliest is more directly a response to suggestion, the second evinces more emotion, and the third is more definitely reflective. Three-fourths of the persons who become members of churches do so before the end of adolescence. Variations were traced in the correlations between conversion and age, temperament and sex.

Much study has been given to mysticism, particularly by Professor Leuba. He had made it clear that the mystical states are emotional states which stand in close relation to bodily and social changes. Many prominent mystics, like St. Theresa and Madame Guyon, were disappointed in their married life, and in the early twenties sought the ministrations of religion in what may be regarded as compensatory experiences. Their love life, however, still dominated them, their visions and ecstasies being concerned with celestial companions. The more they endeavored to suppress the flesh the more it asserted itself though in sublimated forms which prevented the subjects from recognizing the true source of their experiences. Further, the patterns of the mystic's visions and ideas of religious matters reflect clearly the patterns of the beliefs and doctrines prevalent in his social environment. All religions, Jewish, Mohammedan, Christian, Buddhist, have their mystics who employ the vocabulary, conceptions, and attitudes which are characteristics of those faiths. These studies already make it possible to read in psychological terms the genesis and development of the phenomena which have heretofore been described only in the unscientific and conventional terms of devotional literature.

Other fruitful investigations have been made in the psychology of faith, inspiration, genius, prayer, prophetism, and the phenomena of religious groups or sects. Beginnings have been made in the study of the prevalence of specific beliefs, such as belief in immortality and in God. These studies, illustrated by the work of Professor Leuba, have undertaken to find out the relations between these beliefs and the education and social status of respondents.

Significant studies have also been made concerning the development of religious customs and values in the light of the tendency of psychologists to discard the older ideas of instincts. If there is no religious instinct, how do the religious attitudes arise? Various answers have been made, but there is sufficient agreement among the scholars to indicate that the answer is to be found in the conditions of the genesis of social values, and in the differentia which characterize those values which we call religious. By the same approach, new light is being thrown upon the central ideas and symbols of religion, such as the idea of God and the ceremonials of sacrifice, purification, and initiation. Here, as in all scientific fields, it is a question of finding the facts, and estimating their evaluation.

Professor Coe has suggested another point of view from which science may be appreciated in directly religious terms, and this is in reference to the spirit in which the scientist pursues his tasks. Science requires those qualities of character which religion has long extolled—patience, courage, humility, and disinterestedness in the presence of facts; superiority to material rewards and to the fears and hopes which dominate ignorant men; and not infrequently the heroism of those who forego comfort and social life to attain unselfish ends. Many scientists, especially in the biological field and more still in the growing social sciences, believe themselves to be devoted to the cause of humanity in the highest sense. Not only do they discover immediately useful facts, but they furnish knowledge which yields mental release, stimulation, and possibilities of æsthetic contemplation.

There are certain general features of the scientific spirit which are also imbued with genuine religious quality. Science is a work of the imagination at its best. It has furnished H. G. Wells many topics for his novels, not the least important of which are his utopian dreams of the future of man's life on this planet. Alfred Noyes has caught the inspiration from the history of science for putting into poetry the epic of its great adventures and achievements. Many of the problems long prominent in religion may find their answers through the discoveries of science. One of these is the problem of creation. By finding out how nature works at the present time in the great cosmic laboratories there may come knowledge of the nature of life itself. Already the astronomers tell of the beginnings and deaths of heavenly bodies and they have formulated theoretical explanations of these phenomena upon the basis of the facts they observe. The rough outline of man's life on the earth has become clear to anthropologists, and sociologists are searching out the secrets of his growth and culture. All interests have been enhanced by better knowledge—language, art, government and religion; and the fruitful study of these things is only begun.

CHAPTER VI

RELIGION AND MORALITY

In the older view the contrast between religion and morality was sharp and clear. Religion had its source in revelation, while morality was man-made. The former was absolute and perfect; the latter, uncertain and fallible. Religion came to the individual with the transforming and illuminating power of divine grace through conversion, but the morality of the natural man was the imperfect work of human reason and experience. Morality might easily become a hindrance to the work of grace by leading men to trust to it instead of seeking the true righteousness of a converted life. Not infrequently the pulpit has inveighed against the merely moral man as the worst enemy of pure religion, since he might claim that the goodness obtained by natural insight was equal or even superior to that of pious churchmen. Men in the community who were good neighbors, honest and upright without the help of religion, seemed to disprove the contention of churchmen that the offices of religion were essential to the good life. The virtues of such moral men must be spurious and, at most, poor imitations. Whatever value such goodness might have in this world, it could afford no assurance of salvation in the world to come.

The great ethical systems of modern philosophy did not soften this contrast between natural morality and revealed religion. Immanuel Kant held morality to be obedience to the rational will, to the sense of duty inherent in human beings. It is true that he distrusted the desires and the inclinations of man's sensuous nature, but he regarded the rational will as a universal possession of mankind which gave categorical commands to all alike. The good man for Kant is the one who lives in all good conscience in conformity to the dictates of the moral law within. This law is known intuitively and directly, with the same clearness and impressiveness as attends the vision of the stars in the heavens. No special revelation is needed to teach a man right conduct, for the moral law is written in the nature of his own reason. The will to obey this law is the mark of the highest good and it allows no admixture of counsels of prudence or pleasure.

Religious institutions and observances, for Kant, are only means of moving and directing the will in the fulfilment of the moral law. Religious history is the story of man's endeavor to realize the moral life. That history is figurative and symbolical, not factual. Its claims of divine origin and peculiar authority are in effect concessions to human nature, and they have their significance as aids in leading men to follow the commands of pure reason. Theological doctrines, such as the incarnation and atonement, have real value only in so far as they illustrate and elicit moral conduct. The importance of religious personages, like Moses or Christ, lies not in their unique metaphysical nature, but solely in their exemplification of obedience to conscience and duty. Religion, at least in its popular forms, is accordingly superfluous for those wise, understanding souls who are able to discern the moral law intuitively and to follow it consistently. Ritual, ceremonial, public observances, are merely aids and supports for weaker, less rational people. They are temporary devices in the childhood of the race, and tend to disappear as men attain true moral insight.

Only as means of realizing the natural moral law does Kant think it possible to justify the central ideas of religion. The traditional proofs for the being of God are all fallacious and inconclusive to scientific thought; so also those for the existence of the soul, and for its freedom and immortality. Knowledge can deal only with the world of phenomena which it sees woven in a complete mesh of laws, determining all events in the rigid framework of cause and effect. Therefore the three great ideas, God, freedom, and immortality, which religion employs, cannot scientifically be established. Nor are they rationally justified as matters of revelation. They are merely demands which human nature makes, and such confirmation as they have is involved in the moral law. The Kantian philosophy in this way separates morality and religion, leaving revealed religion on one side, minimized and outgrown.

John Stuart Mill, who may be taken as the exponent of the other great school, ethical empiricism, also separated morality from dependence upon religion as traditionally conceived. He accepted the general doctrine of hedonism and recast it into the theory of utilitarianism, holding that the moral ideal is "the greatest good of the greatest number." For him the good is the satisfaction of wants and the avoidance of pain. Human happiness involves the fulfilment of the higher nature of man as well as the securing of creature comforts. A noble character like Socrates cannot be content with the pleasures of the fool. The moral goal is to realize the satisfactions which are sought by "the best people." Only cultivated persons are worthy to be considered in determining the kind of happiness which should be cultivated. Mill was an apostle of popular education, and of social reforms looking to the amelioration of the conditions under which the masses live. He believed that morality would be greatly advanced if the general welfare were improved. Health, temperance, freedom of women, improved legislation, and other social enterprises engaged his labors. Although Mill set out with an individualistic, egoistic conception of human beings, he believed it possible to develop an altruistic sense of duty toward one's fellow men. These social interests are appealing when once awakened and generate their own sanctions and moral obligations. Mill was critical of the prevailing religion for not concerning itself more with the practical and immediate problems of social amelioration and progress. Religion seemed to him to divert attention from these things to a fruitless worship of the supernatural, and to a wasteful absorption in doctrines and forms which produced small returns in present happiness and welfare. Utilitarianism, under various names, has continued to emphasize the difference between morality and religion, often holding religion to be an enemy rather than a benefactor. Naturally both the doctrine and the attitude of such moralists have aroused the opposition of religionists and widened the chasm between religion and morality in popular thought.

The systems of Kant and Mill were formulated while

religion was still conceived in terms of revelation and authority, and more as a body of truth and beliefs than as a social process. Kant died in 1804, and Mill in 1873. Since that time a new world has opened to man's view of himself and the universe. The physical sciences have made marvelous conquests and the social sciences have entered upon a new era of achievement. The world of thought has been revolutionized and the traditional schools of philosophy and ethics have been displaced by new methods and inquiries. (All cultures and institutions are now seen to have had evolutionary histories and to have passed through many stages.) The religions of the world have been subjected to searching inquiry and have been related to the concrete life of the times and peoples among which they flourished. Morals have been shown to have undergone evolution from the levels of unreflective custom and folkways to very diverse, prolific forms of social life. The Christian Scriptures have been minutely studied by the methods of literary and textual criticism, and important discoveries have resulted with reference to their meaning and the doctrines drawn from them. In general these studies have made for a naturalistic, in place of a supernaturalistic, interpretation of this religion, and with new evaluations of its teachings.

Psychology, so fundamental in all social sciences, has only lately escaped from the trammels and dogmatism of metaphysics. Laboratory and statistical methods have been employed in these subjects only within recent decades. Genetic conceptions of human life and thought have come into general acceptance since Kant and Mill passed from the scene. They, especially Kant, belonged to a static order. Neither was able to conceive an evolutionary account of morality, although Mill made some attempt to do so. The latter's idea of the possibility of disciplining naturally egoistic, selfish, hedonistic beings into sympathetic, altruistic patriots and philanthropists, however inconsistent with his premises, indicated the new trend. For both of these philosophers, psychology was still under the departmental faculty theory, and morality was just beginning to be naturalized in the world, by means of man's "intelligible" nature for Kant, and by his "acquired" nature for Mill. Scarcely any one thought of religion in other than supernatural terms, for to do so was practically equivalent to rejecting its claim to any significant value.

The newer conceptions of morality begin with this more adequate psychology and keep close to the facts and the analyses which it provides. Professor John Dewey may be cited as a contemporary representative of this more scientific view of morals to which the designation self-realization has been applied. In this system human beings start below the threshold of moral responsibility. They are impulsive, unco-ordinated organisms with only a few elemental reflexes and emotional reactions. Habits develop rapidly and in great variety, including the very complex and important ones of walking and talking and manipulating objects. Attitudes toward people, animals, and things appear along with this process of locomotion and communication. After some years these habits and attitudes become more or less conscious, especially as conflicts arise among them and the interests which accompany them.

At this point, where selection between different ends and means has to be made, there begins the truly human nature, the self-conscious, reflective, individual personality. That which he desires and which satisfies when obtained he considers "good"; the bitter, disappointing, unrewarding things are "bad." What the people around him permit is "right"; and what they forbid is "wrong." On through the world he goes under the influence of these trial-and-error methods of finding his way. Always he lives in a world of many people who also have interests and rights which he must consider. At times these coincide with his own, and again they are in sharp conflict. He learns the rules of many games, and engages in many enterprises. Everywhere he hears and sees that certain qualities are approved and are efficient, while others are decried and are rejected. These are the virtues and the vices as judged by the world of men and women: industry, integrity, courage, justice, wisdom, sympathy, candor, humility, patience, temperance, and their opposites. That which makes the virtues good and right is the fact that they contribute to the expansion, the harmony, and the joy of life. They are characteristics which imply a life shared with others and a life interacting with others so intimately and spontaneously that there is no hard-and-fast line between the self and others. Selfishness means a small self in a small group; unselfishness means a generous self participating in a larger world.

Morality in this view is the criticized life, developing continually broader and finer ideals and finding means to their fuller realization. It is primarily the work of individuals in reflection upon their own problems of conduct in relation to their place in the social institutions to which they belong. Morality, as such, builds no institutions of its own. It is a way of thoughtfully evaluating and modifying personal conduct, and consequently effecting changes within the social order itself.

The older systems of morality are subject to the criticism that they locate the ends of conduct outside the process of experience itself. They posit a moral law standing over against the impulses and inclinations of the natural man to which the latter must be brought into subjection, or they assert pleasure to be the end whose attainment measures the moral value of conduct. There is thus created a chasm between the processes of habit and reflection and the goals of endeavor which robs the former of any vital part in the determination of the good. So long as the standards of morality lie outside the deliberations of the agent, they remain given and imposed, and the only work left for intelligence is that of conformity to fixed goals. The regulation of action by set rules is the only type of behavior left and the essential condition of genuine responsibility is precluded. The best of rules, for example, the Golden Rule, furnishes no specific guidance for particular situations. They may indicate desirable attitudes and dispositions, yet they fail to afford specific indication of the proper course to be followed. Rules are only general formulas, while the demands of every moral situation are concrete and variable. The injunction to love my neighbor as myself does not yield the desired information as to whether the amount of money he wishes to borrow should be lent to him, or whether he should be assisted in securing work from which to earn what he needs. Each case implies a very complex network of factors, and one instance which justifies immediate and direct assistance may be followed by another where such treatment would be disastrous. Even the question as to what love of self involves from a moral standpoint is not always clear. A thoughtful person is not certain at all times just what he wants for himself, or what his own highest good requires. People are constantly seeking for themselves many things which turn out to be to their disadvantage. Their own wishes, as well as those of others, have to be criticized and estimated in the light of their whole complex nature and station.

The same observations apply to the pursuit of pleasure as an end. Pleasure is attainable only in concrete forms, such as eating when hungry, playing a game when in need of recreation, or prosecuting an unfolding, cumulative enterprise through successive stages. What is pleasurable at one time may be boring at another, and what is morally satisfying under some circumstances may be repellent under others. The statement of the good is always qualified in so many ways and by so many relations that the positing of ideals is conditioned and relative in every instance. These facts are not cited to deny the possibility of moral conduct but to emphasize the fact that it cannot relate to prescribed or preconceived ends. Morality consists in the fashioning of plans and purposes as much as in their realization, and unless both ends and means function in the same process of experience they lose their full moral quality. Much of the strain and discontent of the present social order springs from the divorce between routine labor and its remote, unshared objectives. This is the bane of formal education and of all forms of drill which lack the vitalizing stimulus of chosen and appealing ends. Such militaristic discipline, which trains men in the technique of battle, without enabling them to share in the planning of the campaign, may produce excellent machines but it does not develop responsible moral agents. Such a procedure doubtless vitiates much of the so-called character training which sets up the virtues—courage, courtesy, obedience, patience—in abstraction from the situations where these qualities are naturally called forth and where they bring their unforced fruits.

It is from this view of the need for more unified and organic conceptions of conduct that the advocates of self-realization find so much to criticize in the prevalent types of religion. The religions of authority represent the ends of conduct as prescribed by divine wisdom which it is the duty of man to accept and follow by faith. It is contended that this logically results in making men automata within a fixed system of behavior. Rules and commands are given, with a system of rewards and penalties for their conformity or disobedience. Divine examples, models, and regulations are provided for man's "good," which he disregards at his peril, but the effect of such religions is to produce timid, slavish, weak, and sentimental personalities. Doubt of the rightness or the efficacy of the system is treasonable; initiative and experiment are bold effrontery. In some systems of theology, certain areas of conduct are regarded as prescribed by revelation while others are left to the domain of opinion and common sense. In the more progressive sects the realm of the established doctrines and ordinances is narrowed to a few "essentials," while great liberty is allowed to private judgment and decision in all other things. Many influences of scholarship and of practical life have operated to reduce and weaken the essentials and to multiply and enhance the non-essentials, until in their actual working functions, religious groups have in many cases achieved emancipation from the old ideas. But in the most advanced of these there yet lingers much theoretical dualism between the given ideals and the free methods for their fulfilment. True freedom in religion, as in morals, requires that the confusion and inconsistencies in practice and in theory be overcome by a thorough restatement of the place and function of reflection in all human conduct, and of the value of criticism and insight in the pursuit of all forms of the higher life.

Religion has gradually taken over into its standards the growing moral insight, but it has often done this by force of public opinion rather than by clear choice and conviction. Illustrations of this are abundant in modern times. The undiscriminating acceptance of the Bible as final authority in the morals of society has led to the sense of having its support for new convictions even though a little time before it was quoted in behalf of the old customs. The Bible covers the long ranges of human development from the days of savagery to a high degree of civilization; therefore it records divine approval of widely diverse practices. When the old institution of slavery in the last century came to be questioned by Christian communities, the Bible and the New Testament, too, it should be remembered, were quoted in favor of it. But now that the Christian consciousness disapproves slavery, it is commonly held that this institution is denounced in the sacred literature. More recent instances of this significant process might be cited, as in the questions of woman's suffrage, prohibition, and political democracy. With developing appreciation of the right and duty of all members of society to share in responsibility for its institutions, women have been drawn into political activities in spite of the Pauline teaching that they should be silent in public assemblies and receive instruction from their husbands at home. Scarcely any minister in American churches would now advocate such a practice, but interprets religion as favoring for women the same participation as men exercise. The religious consciousness has summoned to its aid a new set of texts to support its convictions. Again, biblical sayings formerly were used to defend the moderate use of wine, but now these are neglected or explained away in showing that the "spirit" of Christian teaching is on the side of complete abstinence. In matters of government, many passages exhort Christians to obey their rulers and accept the prevailing order, but now it is felt to be the duty of religious people to take initiative in creating better laws and selecting administrators who will carry out their wishes. The old passive acceptance of kings and monarchs has been superseded by the vigorous prosecution of democratic policies and popular government. Similar changes might be cited with reference to "bodily exercise," birth control, divorce, material possessions, and the use of the fine arts. In all such interests practical religion tends to be guided by the claims of a freer and richer life for the individual, although its historic forms do not lend the sanction of the letter to the innovating ideal. Only when religion candidly recognizes the method which it employs and frankly discards the assumption of having a ready-made system of morals for all situations can it gain full approval from the creative spirit of modern society and render the most adequate service to constructive living.

The very intensity of religious conviction sometimes prevents its exemplification of the flexibility which morality demands. Not infrequently singleness of purpose is emphasized to the point of narrowing the outlook of the religious man to a fanaticism which cramps his response to wider opportunities and interests. Some one concern, such as a special social reform, or the cultivation of the devotional life itself, withdraws him from the fuller stream of experience and hardens his character into insensitivity to other vital issues. He has little difficulty in seeing the sin of overspecialization on the part of men bent upon business or sport, but is blind to the fact that his own devotion to a special religious object may lead to the same vices of exclusiveness. The fact that an interest is pursued in the name of religion does not guarantee that it is morally wholesome. The conscientiousness of the pious man has falsely led to the belief that he is beyond criticism, and that his zeal justifies his neglect of wider horizons.

When both morals and religion are conceived in naturalistic ways the line of demarcation is not so clear as when morality is assigned to human reason and religion to the divine, but there are still two appreciable differences. One of these is that religion emphasizes the wider perspectives in which all conduct lies. It takes account in conscious and significant ways of the vast implications of every deed and of the long consequences of present deeds. While a man who acts morally acts within the situation in which he stands and does his utmost to take into consideration the full import of his deed, he realizes that the issues may run far beyond his calculations. In spite of all reflection the ranges of his influence go farther than his vision, and touch upon other lives and events in the mysterious interrelations of an immeasurably complex and delicate existence. The recognition of this phase of conduct gives tang and adventure to the homeliest acts and deepens incalculably their meaning and scope. It is the source of much joy and elation, as well as of the sense of seriousness and awe, in living. A single conversation with a friend, the gift of a book to a child, a journey to a neighboring city or foreign land, a view of a landscape or a waterfall, or a chance acquaintance, may change the course of a life and involve the conduct and happiness of countless persons. A common topic of conversation is the strangeness of the coincidences and consequences of just such experiences. Attention to these implications is involved in the religious way of living. This forward thrust of every deed into an unknown and inexhaustible future calls for faith, and for a certain commitment to the nature of the world, to what may be meant by the providence of God. While religion teaches duties to the neighbor who is near, it sees those duties as related to the infinite, the divine.

The religious man thinks of what he does for a human being as done also for God, and of what is done in a moment of time as continuing into the future. Seemingly little things may be surprisingly big, and obscure deeds may flower out into portentous and conspicuous events. Morality therefore has religious implications, as religion has moral character. To attempt to separate them falsifies and vitiates both. It is of less importance to magnify the differences than it is at the present time to recognize such identity as they have.

There is another contrast between morality and religion as they are found in practice, and this concerns the use of ceremonial observances. Religion employs ritual and symbols to dramatize and illuminate the meaning of life and the various aspects of conduct. Stories and parables, narratives and biographies, poetry and music, are woven into the interpretation and elaboration of the central values of life at its best. This symbolization gives more forceful expression to the attitudes and emotions which center in these values. Such ceremonials are didactic in their effect but they are more than this. They aid in revealing the implications of ordinary activities and they furnish means for the enjoyment of contemplating more adequately the issues of conduct. Morality does not found social institutions in its own right. It consists in the reflection of the individual upon his own problems of behavior, which may indeed be social, but are primarily particular and specific. Religion, through its institutions and public assemblies, as well as through its private meditation and self-examination, gives the individual the experience of sharing in the recognition and approval of a group con-

sciousness directed toward the highest and fullest life.
This institutional dramatization of religion furnishes a
kind of objective expression and stable representation
for the high moments which the individual now and
then achieves. The energy and vision of a person are
not always at their best. Through the conflicts and
toil and cares of the common tasks the sense of the
ideal values may be obscured and weakened, and need
to be refreshed. These values are implicit in daily life
and in the most effective symbolization they are shown
to spring from it, so that every one may see them as
related to his own life and capable of recovery in it.
Too often the ceremonials of religion embody only ancient forms of the ideal, presenting them in archaic
speech and dress. It is one of the great assets of the
Christian religion that its founder spoke in the vernacu-
lar, both as to the words and the subjects he employed.
The common people saw that he dealt with their world
of human interests, and showed them its spiritual qualities and possibilities. For this reason they marveled at
his teaching, it was so full of their daily concerns, and
yet set those concerns in a new and wondrous light.
Effective religious ceremonials do that today. They
do not merely revive the past, but they speak in parables based upon the occupations and the incidents of
the present flowing life of living men.

Religion is not adequate to its opportunity when it
is austere and merely solemn. When it succeeds in
seizing upon the nobler and the more valuable aspects
of experience, projecting them enlarged and enhanced
upon the scale of its magnitudes, it becomes the source
of the finest joy and blessedness. Then the dullest

mind is enabled to catch some realization of what life would be if men lived up to their best. There the careless and preoccupied man may find again the portrayal of the patterns he has forgotten, and live in them once more as the true realities of his inner world. Through such experiences of expanded imagination, awakened conscience, and ideal beauty there springs up a spiritual fellowship whose inspiration to better living and to fullest satisfaction has diviner possibilities than any other experience of life. There man finds himself one with the divine and in possession of priceless happiness. The frequent sense of the failure of religious services to yield this effect is an evidence that this is what they really seek.

CHAPTER VII

RELIGION AND ART

Studies of early life have made it clear that preliterate man did not divide and specialize his activities as do modern men. Nor did he have words to express the various interests which are now characterized as religion, business, and art. It is a striking fact that in the Bible and other sacred texts the term religion scarcely appears, although it is the dominant interest. Ceremonials of celebration of great events in the history of a people and of their recurrent experience with the procession of the seasons are the conspicuous facts of religion. In these ceremonials many forms of activity are blended which under later and more highly individualized functions develop into artistic expression. All of the arts are potentially within the ceremonial. The ceremonial ground, located in some secluded spot secure from observation by forbidden eyes, is the forerunner of the inclosed, protected space of architecture. The dress and ornamentation of the participants, worked out in a wealth of symbolism, are prophetic of the garb and insignia of priests and clergymen. The cult-lore, recited or chanted, becomes the sacred literature refined into poetry and the forms of elevated speech. Flaming torches change into chaste and delicate candles and the sweet incense of the altar. The rhythmic beat of drums and tom-toms grows into the strains of organ music. Mimetic dances evolve into sol-

102

emn processionals and into postures of reverence and petition. Encompassing clouds of witnesses are symbolized by ancestral tablets, statues and pictures of saints and deities. The whole intricate scene, originally acted out in great detail, is sublimated into a wealth of symbolism and imaginative dramatization.

The central themes of the ceremonials vary from one people to another under the influence of their habitat and history. The Egyptians developed a great cult of the dead. Successive dynasties reveal by their monuments and tombs the increasing attention and skill lavished upon their mausoleums, the figures of the dead, the statues of servants employed in their occupations for the deceased, the articles of personal adornment, and enormous treasures of household furnishings, royal dress, and magical emblems. This refinement of technique and care of detail indicate the emergence of the various arts. Inlaid work in precious woods and stones and illuminated texts within the series of sarcophagi were also done with infinite care. The temples of Assyria, Babylonia, Persia, and Greece bear witness to the same process working in the materials and interests peculiar to these peoples. When Solomon built his temple in Jerusalem he brought skilled workmen from neighboring cities to adorn it with handiwork to express the genius and faith of the Israelite shepherds now become a nation and a more self-conscious body of worshipers of Jehovah.

The same process goes on in the great religious bodies within Christian history. All of them carry in the heart of their rituals the symbolism of the life and death of their highest deity. They re-enact, as the most sacred feature of their faith, the drama of man's participation in the power and saving grace of Christ. The celebration of the Mass, or the Lord's Supper, is the expression of the historic conception and central office of the Christian religion. It puts into action the meaning of the atonement and the recovery of man from the depths of sin to an eternal life of blessedness and peace. Around that focal point are built the cathedrals, the processionals, the music, the altars, and the ministries of priests and prophets. Christian art, as the shrines and galleries of Christian lands testify, creates its pictures, its statues, its vestments, its carvings, its candelabra and crucifixes, with the utmost thought, affection, and skill to embody as effectively as possible the meaning and power of the redemptive work of Christ. Even Protestant churches of the puritan tradition do their utmost with their resources of wealth and culture to enhance those few forms which they cherish. For them the emphasis falls most upon the arts which appeal to the ear and to the imagination: music, oratory, and poetry.

In this process is revealed the nature of religion from the side of its relation to art. When dealt with separately and stated in terms of its characteristic functions, art may be said to be a means of self-expression. It furnishes the means and methods for the fullest and richest expression of man's experience. It employs forms and symbols for putting the immediate and concrete events into settings and perspectives which are idealistic and imaginative. It combines the real and the ideal, the immediate and the remote, the casual and the meaningful. It illuminates the present with the inheritance of the past and with the outreaches of the future. By it the instant and the given are generalized upon the scale of the wished for and the possible. Perceptual experience is magnified by the conceptual. Events are represented with their implications and irradiating consequences. Particular deeds are displayed with their meanings. The thread of a human life which may appear small and tenuous in its prosaic routine and hard sequence of events is revealed as imbedded in a great texture of fabrics and patterns, colored and toned in a wealth of relations. The "Song of the Lark," by Breton, takes a simple peasant girl in the field at sunrise and portrays in her posture and uplifted face her rapt response to this voice of nature. It suggests realms to which her spirit answers with eagerness and wonder. She is then not merely a drudge of the soil, but upon her face glows the evidence that she responds to an ideal life of joy and beauty. She typifies unnumbered peasants regal with a life rich in dreams and shapes which hallow and transform the workaday life of toil and care. And thus not only is she a type of peasant life, but of all human beings. Therefore every one finds something akin to himself in her listening, wistful face. The picture is also the expression of the artist. By it he has released his own spirit and conveyed the meaning of a common scene in terms of the idealization of an ordinary, familiar situation whose beauty and significance would too easily escape the eye.

Art is just this interpretation of the artist, his enlargement of the meaning and potency of life. He makes natural events vibrant with his own imaginative conception of their ideal portent. But this is not the work of professional artists alone. It is the characteristic achievement of all significant human living. In the degree to which any man puts into his life imaginative construction of thought and feeling he is an artist. This he may do to some extent in any kind of work, in building houses, operating a business, directing organizations, playing games, making scientific experiments, as well as in writing poetry or composing music. Wherever he contributes thought and enrichment of inventive skill to his activity in the pursuit of ends he adds the refinement of art. In this sense all creative, orderly, effective effort has an artistic quality. The subject matter may be found in the humblest enterprises or in the most comprehensive and refined endeavors. Viewed in this way the common distinction between the industrial and the fine arts is resolved into a difference of materials and technique. In both there is the same constructive, idealizing process of reflection and skilful execution. Religion as a practical enterprise, the quest for salvation, exemplifies this kind of activity. It conceives the simplest acts as moving within a larger perspective, and encourages devotion to them in their ideal bearings and significance. It gives a cup of cold water in the name of divinity and cares for the wounded man by the wayside as if he were a cherished neighbor. The plainest and most alien human being is for religion never a means only, but a final and supreme end in himself.

Art is therefore unifying: it orders and harmonizes the diverse and disparate elements of experience into forms and patterns which make them contributory to significant ends. It brings the brute facts of impulse

and physical existence within a frame of ideas and projected plans. Because of this, every fragment of a
work of art becomes a symbol of the whole and calls for
reinstatement within the total structure to which it
proclaims itself to belong. Like the arm or torso of a
broken statue, it defines and proclaims the lines and
proportions of the entire body from which it has been
severed. No matter how great the complexity of detail or how numerous the parts, every feature carries
the character and quality of the whole. The greatest
art is that which reflects in every part the richest and
most far-reaching life. Works of art are therefore identified with the whole life of the peoples which produce
them and with the entire culture which they achieve.
A Greek vase or a Roman lamp carries the marks of
the Greek spirit or of the Roman genius. Each expresses the soul of the race from which it sprang. Even
within the great diversity of theme and motif which
different arts and artists employ there still pervade
them all the strange likeness and distinguishing character of specific race and time. The unity which the
artist consciously labored to achieve is thus attained
within a deeper and encompassing unity of unconscious
attitude and trend of life. The satisfaction which a
work of art evokes is partly due to its making explicit
in more adequate expression this underlying unity.
Partly also it is due to the further projection of the
mind or spirit of a culture into new forms which add
enrichment without destroying the continuity of spirit.
    Art is therefore creative as well as reproductive.
When it becomes merely repetitious and only multiplies
copies of masterpieces it is decadent and stricken with

age. Living art continues to extend its themes and to display novel forms. The so-called classic types of art content themselves with adherence to traditional forms and make their stand upon correctness of form. Romantic art, at the other extreme, minimizes the form and stresses fresh impulse and intensity of feeling. Each becomes one-sided and inadequate, and the opposition between them calls for the resolution of the conflict in modes which keep the form flexible under the requirements of fresh insight, but also strengthen the new impulses by shaping them in favorable and sustaining forms. Art, like religion, moves with the general life of society. In an age of settled and stable conditions it emphasizes and elaborates the established and traditional, while in a time of change and aspiring outlook it takes on new rôles and projects prophetic, adventurous ideals. Whether it glorifies the past or turns confidently to the future depends upon the temper of the age or upon the social group or school of thought with which it is allied. The humanistic painting and sculpture of the Renaissance illustrate the embodiment of the novel and forward-looking tendencies as over against the settled and reminiscent products of the medieval period.

Another function of art may be described as the objectification and stabilization of the ideal values reached in the great experiences of individuals and communities. The master-artists are the understanding and articulate souls who portray the insight and emotions of a people in symbols which perpetuate in enduring stone and canvas and drama the great hours of the spirit. In such symbols these values become

available for less discerning men and for the renewal
of noble sentiment for all who need to be reminded and
inspired anew. It is in the works of art that the transient vision and luminous moments of the profoundest
minds are caught up and fixed in shapes and tones
which endure and continue to radiate inspiring ideals.
Through them men find their better selves again and
are lifted to the heights of their fairest dreams. In
such symbols there is always more than has been made
explicit, for it is their very nature to suggest more than
they express. The mind dwells upon them with the
sense of inexhaustible wealth, of fruitful and fructify-
ing contemplation. Such symbols are alive with stimulating power. The lines and arches of Gothic architecture continue to greet the eye with new invitations to
aspiration and assurances of grace and strength. The
stone tracery never rests, but continues to evolve new
mysteries. Lights and shadows play through it in endless variety. The cathedral itself is the embodiment
of the drama which it shelters. Along its floor runs
the pattern of the cross. Over the altar glows the light
of faith. The arches leap toward heaven, and in the
niches stand the guardian, protecting spirits. Even the
fantastic gargoyles escaping from the roof signify the
evil sprites which have been driven forth and made
powerless by a mightier hand. No wonder that a cathedral is a congenial place for man to meditate upon the
meaning of his life and upon the riches of his spiritual
possessions.

It is no accident that religion has supplied to art so
much material and so much inspiration. The casual
traveler through the scenes of the ancient civilizations

of Egypt, Greece, and Rome cannot fail to note after
the lapse of so many centuries that the most enduring
monuments in every place are the temples and the
shrines of man's faith.   They were built with enormous
labor and at fabulous cost.   The gigantic columns, as
at Baalbek, still stand like sentinels about the immense
temple areas, witnessing to the mighty effort their builders made to represent in permanent form their religious
piety and devotion.   The most frequent figures of stone
and bronze, in temples, homes, and tombs, are the figures of the gods and of worshipers in processions and
at the sacred altars.   It is still true that in the galleries
of Europe and America religious subjects dominate
to a striking extent.   If contemporary artists occupy
themselves more with nature and other "secular" subjects, it may be said also that their art lacks something
of the significance and strength of religious art.   Our
art, like our idealisms generally, is short-breathed in a
transition period where the old systems have lost their
appeal and the new have not yet found adequate interpretation either in ideas or in imaginative symbolism.
When the larger problems of life and death are undergoing criticism and skeptical uncertainty they do not
furnish the same opportunity for artistic representation
as when the whole society is bound together in common
conceptions and practices.   And in America we are yet
occupied predominantly with the exploitation of natural resources, with business and engineering, with the
immediately practical problems of industry, and with
the sciences and politics bound up with this industrial
revolution.   Our art is therefore highly self-conscious,
hesitant, and piecemeal.   It does not venture upon the

greater themes which are necessary to great epics and dramas, paintings, and sculptures. In the great ages of art it was a more natural, and in a sense a less independent, development. The artist worked within the religious atmosphere, and his interest was absorbed in the expression of the ideas and the forms set by the spiritual life. He did not think so much of art for art's sake, but was occupied with the more adequate representation of the experiences which the imaginative life of the people sought and enjoyed.

From these various points of view religion and art may be seen to have much in common, religion furnishing themes and the projection of ideals, while art refines and makes vivid, stabilizes and enhances them. Religion seeks for its ceremonials the highest and purest forms available—offerings without blemish—and art is occupied with just this purification and idealization of all the subjects with which it deals. But there are conceptions of both art and religion which put them in sharp contrast. In general such conceptions arise where either one becomes separated from the living stream of experience and takes on the character of an isolated or overdeveloped tendency.

One such contrast springs from the conception of art in terms of its technique, where it is concerned to an extreme degree with its means and forms. This is sometimes what is meant by "art for art's sake." In that conception there is scarcely a place for ideals or ends. It is not interested in "ideals," but only with lines or colors or rhythm or tones. The artist has no "story" or purpose in mind beyond the representation of an impression or a fancy, and the observer is told that he should regard himself as free to make of it what he will or can. Of course religion, being set for the realization of ends, for salvation of some kind, feels that such art is alien and remote. But this tendency of religion to be practical and to achieve results may lead also to an overemphasis on immediate ends, and such emphasis only widens the breach between the two fields. Art then appears to religion like a student of music absorbed in the practice of exercises who never produces a melody or weaves the elements of tone and cadence into a whole.

Opposition between these interests often arises from making one historic and the other contemporaneous. Art for some people is only what they see in museums and identify with the life of the Greeks or ancient Japan. Then its subjects are far removed from religion as they know it. There is an inheritance in the traditions of Christianity from the Hebrew taboos against pictorial and plastic art which heightens this antagonism, for the Hebrews observed with strict devotion the injunction not to make to themselves any graven image of god or man. It was to them a safeguard against idolatry, but it became also an inhibition with reference to the production and the use of most of the arts. There was present, too, no doubt, a natural antipathy to the cultivation of anything so characteristic of the gentile world as the arts of sculpture and drama. Christianity has felt the force of this tradition, especially in its puritanic sects. Only a limited development of literature and of music and of architecture has been accepted by this Hebraic-Puritan attitude. And any Christian, belonging to any of the traditional forms of that faith, may feel himself in a merely "worldly" atmosphere the moment he steps into any but the ecclesiastical sections of modern galleries.

On the other hand, thoroughly modern artists may share the widespread impression of many who are trained in the current culture, that religion is at home only in the past and represents a lingering survival of a system which is no longer vital, while to them art seeks its subjects in the life of the present day. Or, if they appreciate the artistic quality of certain religious subjects, they do so, not for the theme or the idealism, but only for the perfection of the artistry. To them such works are just "quaint," a more or less unconsciously patronizing judgment which human beings are apt to pass upon whatever lies outside their own times and customs.

To the religious mind there is something lacking in artistic activity which devotes itself to small, superficial, or limited subjects. Much current poetry is of this character, dealing as it does in a few lines with a single sensuous impression such as the color of a passing cloud. In the effort to avoid all interpretation by remaining within the terms of pure description the artist forfeits the scope and fulness of experience which are necessary to the proper exercise of his gift. At least for religion the refusal to go beyond the given sensations and the passing moment of time deprives experience of all that makes it worthy to be registered or remembered. Religion, at its best, does not ignore the immediately real nor the infinitesimally small, but it sees them in their relations and follows the natural tendency of the mind and imagination to fill out the scene and include the movement of expanding interests.

Art also becomes foreign and antithetic to religion when it calls attention to itself by overemphasis upon its technique or by its effort to produce effects. It is repelling to have a performer betray an undue amount of satisfaction with himself in his rôle. The actor who struts or shouts or moves mincingly in his manner obscures the character he plays unless it is his part to exhibit burlesque or buffoonery. Even then the act becomes more effective under restraint or by the submergence of the technique within the movement of the plot. At times the stage effects overwhelm the theme and draw attention to themselves. This principle is nowhere more important than in the use of art in religious ceremonials. The requirement here is called "sincerity." If a minister gives the impression of acting his part, or of striving for fine phrases, or of introducing devices of elocution, he is that moment shorn of power. At once he stands over against the task he has undertaken and obscures what it is his function to clarify and enhance. The qualities required are naturalness, simplicity, and unalloyed devotion. Consciousness of the arts employed is likely to be as disastrous as those forms of self-consciousness which call attention to the person through awkwardness or confusion. The highest art loses itself in the action for which it is employed, and is so much a part of the whole that it is discerned only with difficulty.

The quality required in genuine art is that quality which is lost when it is commercialized. It is difficult to describe, but it is easy to recognize, for the feeling for his vocation must be such that the artist cannot allow himself to be influenced by the thought of financial reward. When that happens something inimical to real achievement appears, something which threatens the spirit of true workmanship. In this sense true art is thoroughly disinterested. It is absorbed in its representation of experience and in the expression of what the artist beholds. Any other interest than the setting forth of what is seen and felt is a prostitution of power and talent. Just because the artist has had to learn by self-criticism and by much conscious effort to master his materials and his technique, he may have difficulty in forgetting them and merging them in the execution of his task. Unless the artist is first of all and continually an actively experiencing human being he is in danger of becoming artificial and inadequate to employ his gifts in the spirit of genuine art. It is important that the consciousness of art be absorbed and made oblivious of itself in the representation of adequate subjects.

In other words, æsthetic appreciation is at last, not the contemplation of the technique of the artist, but the enjoyment of the subject delineated with such understanding and skill as to make it appealing as a whole. Otherwise, æsthetic demands could be as well satisfied with a poor subject as with a good one. There would be no moral quality necessary for great art. But in reality the contemplation of a noble subject done with insight and feeling renders more satisfaction than an inferior subject treated with the same ability. Undoubtedly shoes may be polished artistically, but that process could scarcely elicit art of the quality and significance which could be wrought into a temple or into the portrait of a hero. In other words, works of art differ as much in terms of their subjects as in the manner of their execution.

Perhaps the best way to indicate the function of art is to state it in terms of the enhancement and ease which it lends to whatever it touches. Whatever gives to the beholder the sense of release and enlargement has for him the æsthetic quality. Whenever a person performs his task with skill and mastery, with energy and pleasure, he is an artist, whether driving a motor car or painting pictures. Any object which conveys to the spectator the impression of grace and ease in its construction and of free adaptation to its use is a beautiful object. Or anything which awakens pleasing associations and symbolizes the charm of delightful companionships or stirs the imagination toward ideal tasks is so far beautiful. A graceful, fleet runner, a swift-moving, circling plane, a ship under full speed, a scientist delicately testing solutions in his laboratory are æsthetic because they express with free co-ordination the skill of the performers and awaken admiration and appreciation in the onlooker.

Undoubtedly much passes for art which is felt to be such because of quite extraneous elements. Antique objects tend to elicit appreciation beyond their importance in the society in which they were produced. It is interesting to see things judged beautiful simply on the ground of being rare or old. Correspondingly, things are often rejected from the sphere of art on the ground of their novelty. Those who are most satisfied with Gothic architecture hesitate to admit that the modern steel sky-scraper is beautiful. Generally, people do not think of any machine as a beautiful object: steam shovel, motor car, linotype, or locomotive engine. But the man who handles any of these is likely to have a very real affection for them and to see in them that release of power and mastery of circumstance which belong to art.

Art is significant to religion in the balance and proportion which it requires. In the pursuit of great causes, such as are involved in religion, there is a tendency to strain and to fanatical narrowness and intensity. The cultivation of these interests with the artist's soul encourages wider perspectives and better-balanced proportions.

CHAPTER VIII

THE GODS OF RELIGION

Students of the history of religion have made us familiar with gods of many forms and kinds, of many degrees of divinity and varying importance. They have shown that the gods are the greater spirits, and that the spirits are of indefinite number and variety. The enumeration and description of the spirits of any culture present a task which cannot be completed for new spirits are constantly appearing and old ones change their form. Only a few have constancy and continuous significance. These facts have led to the psychological question concerning the nature of spirits. Why are they so numerous and why do they change in such astonishing and confusing ways? To the psychologist it becomes clear, upon acquaintance with a number of cultures in different stages, that spirits are not fixed objective realities, but reveal interesting and enlightening relations to human interests and habits.

I have shown elsewhere [1] that, in the early experience of man, whatever catches attention may be regarded as a spirit. It is well known that unusual objects, gnarled trees, queer-shaped rocks, dwarfs, giants, albinos, white elephants, maniacal men, are commonly regarded as possessed by spirits, or as being spirits of peculiar power. Earthquakes, eclipses, volcanoes, the sighing wind, the

[1] *Psychology of Religious Experience,* Ch. VI.

raging river, and other strange events within the recurring scenes of daily life, are regarded as spirits or the work of spirits. Such spirits appear when the phenomena occur, and disappear when the disturbances cease or become commonplace. Primitive man sees no clear boundary between what are now called the real and the dream worlds, or between the world of sense perception and the world of imagination. "Nature," as an ordered and law-abiding system of objects and forces does not exist. Anything may become anything else, animals change into men and back again, inanimate objects come alive, and marvels riot around and through the life of man. All these weird things become quiet and non-existent when man does not encounter them, or when his attention runs in settled and familiar grooves. It is when his nerves are taut and his senses or imagination assailed by unusual phenomena that he sees these things as spirits. Consequently spirits are inconstant and indefinitely various. Observers are baffled in endeavoring to name or enumerate all the deities and little divinities. Their lists are never complete and never could be, for these beings are generated out of passing experience, and their life-cycle is for the moment, or the day, or the age, according to the substance which they embody.

This substance of spirits is a combination of the processes in the environment and the reaction of the human mind. Some of these experiences recur with regularity and with felt importance to human life. Such are the sun, the rain, the birth of animals, and the growth of vegetation. Because of the intimate relation of such things to the deep and urgent interests of man, they live in his attention and tend to become familiar and important spirits. The world within which they appear is so precarious and so changeful that even these recurrent things are accompanied by concern and nervous tension. Even with farmers of the present time the successful planting and reaping of crops is attended with sufficient uncertainty and expectancy to make it clear that in earlier society the most stable things might easily become the focus of anxious attention. It is for this reason that birth of the young of flocks, ripening of fruit, hunting of animals, and gathering the harvest, are all centers of emotional stress, or at any moment may become such. Attention rises and falls, varies in amazing curves, and attaches to irrelevant, minute, and remote features in such baffling complexity that the interpreter of these things is constantly surprised at what surprises or does not surprise preliterate people. The principle proposed for explanation of the phenomena takes account of this fact. This principle is that whatever catches the attention sharply or in recurring situations of felt importance tends to take on the character of a spirit.

There is little hope of answering the question whether people make a distinction between the object and the spirit which inhabits it. This is a problem which exercises the wisest of scientists in our own day. It is particularly noticeable in the discussions of the nature of the self or mind. Is the mind different from the body, or is what we call a mind just an organism, the body, functioning in certain ways? In current psychology, mind is said to be present when certain types of behavior appear, namely, behavior which is adaptive in

varying situations, which solves problems, or which occurs in delayed responses to remote or complex stimuli.
In this view one organism may be said to be more highly
mental than another, or it develops mentality in the
sense of acquiring ability to deal with novel and difficult
circumstances. It would then be misleading to speak of
the mind as a separate entity residing for a time in the
body. Even the hyphenated expression, "mind-body,"
is not free from the suggestion of two things somehow
related. "Organism-displaying-mental-ability" might
be more adequate to the facts and less suggestive of
the old dualism.

If scientific men have not been able to agree upon
statements to indicate the nature and place of mental
activity, it should not seem strange that pre-scientific
people do not make clear, consistent statements regarding the nature of spirits and their relation to objects.
The assumption that spirits are substantial things but
more ethereal, like the breath as contrasted with the
body, only puts the puzzle into other terms; it solves
nothing. The conclusion would seem to be that spirit
is identified with object, or is conceived as a smaller or
more volatile object capable of dwelling in, or passing
in and out of, a more perceptible object. In one way
or another, spirits are substantial objects, though their
substance may be subtle and elusive.

Specially sacred objects such as totem animals, or
rice and maize, have this strangeness all the time. They
might be called primary centers of *mana* or *maya*, while
other things derive this quality in a secondary way, by
contact or some other relation. The things which possess this *mana* in greatest degree are the most impor-

tant spirits; and the converse of this is true, that those objects which are felt to be most important are those that possess this *mana* in the greatest degree.

Objects central in the ceremonies are of this nature, and performance of the ceremonies tends to enhance the sense of their possession of it. The chief objects in the ceremonies are centers of the actual life-process, subjects of constant attention, and they persist in this relation to the social group through long stretches of time and in the life of many generations. Familiarity and use tend to enhance their value, but they are never quite certain in their behavior. Drought and failure of crops, disease and disappearance of herds and flocks, pestilence, and death of children keep alive the uncertain and precarious nature of all the important objects of man's dearest interests. Precariousness is a great factor in keeping alert, or in reviving under stress, the sense of the significance of sacred objects or spirits.

Greater spirits come to be designated as gods, although this word carries something of the vagueness and changeability of the word spirits. Gods are the greater, more powerful, more persistent, more generally recognized spirits. But the gods undergo change with the fortunes of their social groups. When a people flourishes and attains dominion over more territory and more subjects, the gods of that people wax greater and more awe-inspiring. When battles are lost, territory forfeited and people subjugated, the gods are defeated, made vassals, or eclipsed by conquering gods. Gods reflect the fortunes and the cultures of their people. God is the Spirit of the Tribe. The various gods of a group designate different interests and functions of the group.

Each divinity presides over his appropriate segment of the common life, while a grand divinity, like Zeus, reigns over all.

Two changes are of special importance, the humanizing and the universalizing of the God. In Greece and in Israel, where religion reached a high development, these processes are clear and impressive. Not even the rewriting of the history and the tendency to obliterate the cruder forms of their religion succeed in destroying the evidence. Such authorities as William Robertson Smith for the Hebrews, and Gilbert Murray for the Greeks, show that the earlier divinities were species of animals. The sheep and the bull were conspicuous. The life of the group was felt to depend upon them. So-called sacrifice was the process of killing and eating the sacred animal to renew the wholeness and vigor of the group. When the welfare of the tribes came to depend more upon human leadership through the function of judges, warriors, and kings, attention centered more and more upon men, and the pattern was set for anthropomorphic deities. The transition was gradual, and the animal gods survived in the temples long after Yahweh and Zeus were officially conceived in kingly form. It required urgent and persistent activity of generations of prophets to purify the popular religion, and to lift it to the level of great gods of human form and character.

The struggle was not merely against the influence of the animal and other nature gods of alien peoples of the environment. It was a process of transformation and of substitution within their own mores. Tending of flocks and use of the date palms was closer to the everyday life of the people than processes of government and battles of kings. Only after centuries of conflict did affairs of state reach such organization and importance as could make people feel dependence upon kings and overlords to a degree that set the human pattern in the center of experience and imagination. Only with the attainment of that stage was God conceived as a king and judge, enthroned over the affairs of his people. The development of human traits of justice, mercy, and wisdom slowly emerged with the increasing realization of the importance of these qualities in the rulers of the nation.

Universalization of the gods was still slower and more difficult. Yahweh remained a local, provincial deity until the Exile. The exiles felt it necessary to carry with them soil from his land of Palestine upon which they might stand to be acceptable to him. When this became impossible on account of numbers and the slackening of the force of custom for the second and the third generation, the conviction began to arise that Yahweh could also be at home outside his ancient abode. It was by means of travel, commerce, foreign residence, colonial settlements, and diplomatic relations with neighboring nations that the idea emerged that Yahweh was the God of other lands also and finally the God of the whole earth. The conception of Yahweh as the God who ruled over great Babylon, Syria, and Egypt was a magnificently audacious idea of the prophets of Israel, born of the necessity either of universalizing their God to the dimensions of the world in which his people lived and struggled, or of regarding him as reduced and humbled to the proportions of the little, subjugated, buffeted land of Palestine. The strategic location of their country and the rivalry of neighboring kings for alliances with them, furnished a basis for this extension of their imagination and their sense of importance. The audacity of such a claim was an expression of the vitality and persistence of the intense national consciousness of the Hebrews. In this, as much as in anything else in their history, was displayed their peculiar genius. It is true that their idea of the relation of Yahweh to other peoples was as yet external. He managed them by strategy, by confusing the minds of their rulers, or by planting his will in their secret thoughts. These other peoples were not thought of as his own people or as those for whom he was responsible as he was for Israel. But the extension of his dominion by any means, on such a scale, was a new achievement, and it gave the prophets and other leaders new hope with reference to their destiny, and new faith in the greatness of their God. The conviction that he exerted such power upon the mind and heart of kings and peoples introduced a further principle of control besides that of armies and brute force, and afforded a kind of rationalization concerning the impossibility of measuring the potency of God by the numbers or wealth of his subjects. This seems to have been the view of Isaiah, who held that the safety of Israel depended more upon her faith in the power of God than in her military strength.

Among the Greeks the humanization of God reached its climax in the doctrine that Reason is the supreme attribute. It is wisdom that dignifies and ennobles man. Through wisdom the individual achieves proficiency in his tasks and understanding of the world; wisdom is the source of order and justice in the state. (Wisdom is the practical application of knowledge or reason) The Greeks not only thought of the best king as a philosopher, according to Plato, but also conceived God as the perfect philosopher, the entirely rational being. The Stoics made this humanization and rationalization of God a vital religion. Because the supreme principle of reason is in all men in some degree, and because of its importance for the right conduct of life, it is to be regarded as the bond of kinship and brotherhood for all mankind. It is not the mark of any one race or society. The Stoics felt themselves at home among all peoples; they thought of themselves not as citizens of Greece but as citizens of the world, and their God was not local or provincial but universal. It was the collapse of their own national life that gave deep practical significance to this view, but it had a vital historic basis in the experience of the Greek people. They had been colonists and travelers, scientists and philosophers. Athens, in her heyday, had been a more cosmopolitan city, where wise men of every race mingled their culture and their quest for truth concerning man and God. Thus there was prepared through a long and brilliant history, in the abstract thought of mathematicians and philosophers, the framework for the idea of one God which crowned the centuries of political and reflective endeavor. The Stoics carried this conception throughout the world with the ardor and zest of a reasoned, buoyant religious faith.

Modern metaphysics, beginning with Descartes, has undertaken to deal with this idea of God as an independent object. Taking it over from the concrete religious thought of the past, philosophy has sought to establish the idea of God by means of abstract logical processes. (But the result has been the conclusion reached by Kant that human knowledge is incapable of finding final proof for the existence of God.) His problem and the strength of his contention rest upon a procedure so characteristic of the method introduced by Descartes and employed by his successors for three centuries that it is necessary to examine that method in order to understand its inability satisfactorily to justify or prove the existence of God.

Descartes set the mold of the problem of knowledge that has engaged the minds of thinkers in the western world since his time. He was bent upon establishing the scientific method in philosophy. In order to do this, his first step was to sweep away all questionable assumptions and to make a starting point with solid matters of fact. After a rigorous effort to dispossess himself of all his inheritance of traditional ideas, he seemed to find the one indubitable fact of experience in consciousness of the self. But this self was assumed to be the old entity of familiar thought, a kind of kernel of solid substance, lodged in the pineal gland of the brain. With that assumption the whole world of experience split in two. On the one side was this self or soul, with its thinking; on the other, all the world of objects, other persons and God. The efforts of wise men for centuries have been to find a way to span the chasm between the self and other things. But with ideas as events in the head, and things existing outside, there was no sure bridge upon which to make the passage that alone could guarantee that the representations in the head were true to the objects in the outer realm. Upon the two sides of this gulf have been arrayed the armies of philosophers: the idealists upon the side of the self, vainly trying to stretch themselves to reach the reality they had posited as separated from their grasp; and on the opposite side the materialists, striving to ignore the self or to regard it as a phantom, an epiphenomenon, a breath or mist, exuding from the physical world itself. Some, called dualists, assumed the reality of both the psychical and the physical, but allowed each its place and never succeeded in an adequate answer to the question as to how the mind goes out of itself to so different an object, or how the object could be itself and yet be known.

For the materialist, the problem of God could be dismissed as more fatuous than that of the self, but for the idealist it remained the most perplexing of questions. Kant summarized the experience of all the idealists by insisting that it was a quest which reason could never forego, yet a quest which in the nature of the case could never be successful. He reviewed all the great, historical arguments: the teleological, the cosmological, and the ontological, with the searching, ardent criticism of one who is desperate to know. His conclusion was that these arguments will continue to be employed but will always end in disappointment. Reason impels to the task but never can settle the dispute. There is at last as much to be said, by strict reasoning, against the idea of God's existence as in its favor. Thus did the strenuous labor of philosophy, through centuries of toil, issue in the futility of a drawn battle.

The only possible answer was in terms of despair of the power of reason to answer its own questions, and in the endeavor to find some other means than knowledge by which God could be found and verified. All efforts of this type are represented by mysticism, asserting the impotency of reason and of sensuous knowledge, and then, unfettered by any concern for scientific procedure, making its claim for access to God through feeling and suprarational means. The contention of the mystics was the natural outcome of the confessed failure of the old metaphysics. Many men claim a real and satisfying experience of God, without the means of bringing this experience within the rules of evidence or of logic. Since they cannot explain it and yet do have it, they feel driven to the conviction that it lies beyond or outside knowledge and comes by ways which are inexplicable. God is of more importance to them than rationality, and between the two they choose God. This issue is pressing upon reflective religious minds of the present time with the greatest intensity. Many who have been influenced by modern scientific method and have followed the way of empiricism through other problems, such as those concerned with the soul and with moral judgments, turn aside from the implications of that method when they reach the problem of God. But it is incumbent upon those who essay empiricism to make a serious endeavor to carry it through the whole realm of religious experience.

In taking up this task it is important to recall that radical empiricism has demonstrated its fruitfulness, as well as its novelty, in dealing with the problem of knowledge by showing that the problem itself is unreal and artificial. No answer is needed to the question concerning the relation of the knower and the known when the process of experience is itself adequately analyzed. The naïve or common-sense person has no such question concerning his relation to the world in which he lives. He possesses the real world through his sensuous commerce with it. The objects about him are not elusive or particularly mysterious. He weighs and measures them, carves, burns, or decorates them, in keeping with his purposes. He knows objects in so far as he is familiar with the uses that they serve, and in so far as he has skill to manipulate and control them. This knowledge is expert, minute, and detailed; and it is real, intelligible, practical, and verifiable. The questions which the modern scientist asks concerning the world are questions that arise in connection with experienced situations, not abstract or general questions concerning the essences and hidden attributes of objects. He inquires about weight and measure, analysis and synthesis, motion and density, employing the instruments and processes of the laboratory to answer his questions.

This method of empiricism is not limited to a study of the physical world. There are facts in the life of human beings, in their impulses, reactions, imaginations, and associations; and these are open to investigation and understanding, although with difficulty and with slow returns. It may be true, as has been asserted, that the social sciences are a thousand years behind the physical sciences, and it is evident that the phenomena of man's experience are complex and baffling to the inquirer, but the empiricist is not defeated

by the discovery of these things. Great advance has
been made in the last half century in the development
of the social sciences, in gathering data with reference
to the cultures of preliterate people, in recovering the
records of early civilizations with their arts, social organization, and religion. With this has gone the discovery of man himself through study of the evolution
of mind, of morality, and of social institutions. Especially important in the inquiry concerning religion are
the processes that show it in the making, in its birth
and growth, and in its relation to other interests.

It is important to pursue this factual method, with
careful interpretations, to the last and greatest problems of religion. For example, what does the idea of
God signify when taken in the light of its history and
in terms of social psychology? It has already been
shown that this idea moved with the life of peoples,
and was most intimately bound up with their history.
The application of the empirical method of knowledge
would take these facts into account. It would no longer
attempt to proceed in terms of abstract reason to determine the nature and the meaning of God, but rather
would review the experience of men in the actual use
of God. When the latter is done, it is found that men
have proceeded with God much as they have with other
realities of their experience. He is something vital and
important in their life, as real to them as their fellows
and as the earth they tread. When questions were
raised concerning his existence by philosophers and
others in our modern period, the answers were made
under the limitations of a certain theory of knowledge.
Caught in the long-standing dualism of the mind and

its object, thought could only conceive of God as an object over against itself. It could get no farther in this than in other phases of the epistemological enigma. God seemed to become either a mere idea of the mind, or an inaccessible entity beyond the reach of knowledge. The latter horn of the dilemma had the advantage of leaving the religiously disposed person free to posit an unknown or an unknowable God. So long as there was confessed inability of the mind really to know any object, although many objects made certain claims to existence, it might be conceivable that God existed outside the range of definite knowledge. Such was the answer of Kant and it has been the view of the prevailing schools of theology since his time.

The empirical approach to the question goes back of the problem of existence and inquires first concerning the *nature* of God. To answer this demand for an understanding of the nature of God, the history of religion and of racial cultures is reviewed. From such a survey, the lesser gods, and the great gods of all religions, are seen to be the life-process itself, idealized and personified. Every god bears the marks of the habits and moral character of his worshippers, and he undergoes the changes and transformations that profoundly affect his people. When they are militant, so is he; when they are peaceful, so is he; when they have a monarchy, he is a monarch; when they become democratic, he becomes friendly, renounces external authority and rules by reason and justice. God is thus shown to be the Spirit of a people, and in so far as there is a world of humanity, God is the Spirit of the world. When men are divided and separated into various groups, there are many gods. If there is little conflict between the groups each may recognize other gods as well as its own. But when cultures come into conflict so that political and moral tensions arise, the tendency is for each group to regard its own deity as true and real, and the others as false. As the world of mankind attains more and more unity, especially in the fields of letters, science, and moral ideals, God becomes more really the God of the whole earth and of the spiritual universe. God is conceived as the soul of social values, the embodiment of ideals, the reality of the good and the beautiful, the meaning of the world.

Such a conception of the nature of God involves no longer the old difficulty concerning his existence. His reality is as demonstrable as the world itself, indeed it is given in the living experience of all socially minded people. And who is not socially minded? If there is any reality to the life of a city, or of a nation, or of humanity, then there is that kind and degree of reality to God. No doubt the reality of God is greater but it is of this kind. It is a natural tendency of human reason to conceive all rationality as consistent and corresponding. Men cling to the conviction that what they call good is really good, on any planet or in any heaven where the conditions are similar enough to make the statement of the case applicable. This may be seen in such realities as Alma Mater and Uncle Sam. Alma Mater is not a myth or mere idea. It is the reality of an organization of things and people. Any school boy can appreciate the fact that his college is an entity, objective to himself and yet closely identified with himself and others. Buildings and grounds, endowment money, alumni, donors, faculty, and students belong to it. These are welded together in a life-process, definite and describable. Alma Mater exists in certain forms of activity, in a character which involves specific requirements, offering appreciable rewards for stated conduct and achievement. Toward her, attitudes of devotion and loyalty are awakened. Songs are sung to her, gifts are made in her honor and for her use. Her life flows on through the years, often from father to son, generation after generation. Her influence remains with her children through their life, and the molding power of her spirit continues a living source of strength and control. It is the same with any group constituted by the common life of numbers of people. It has a being over and above any individual belonging to it.

God is the Spirit of the world of living beings, taken in their associated and ideal experience. God includes the so-called material world which is the stage of their action and the condition of their existence, and God signifies also the order of their intelligence and conduct. He is the grand total, living process, in which they live and move and have their being. Men cherish this corporate life. They celebrate it in their hymns, in their ceremonials, in their reverence, and in their sense of ideal companionship. God is their world, idealized and personified in accordance with their deepest, most spiritual insight and endeavor. He is as real as their own nature and as vast as the unmeasured and inexhaustible implications of their aspiration and imagination. With every discovery of science and every increment of knowledge God is better known, more profoundly revered, more definitely and vitally experienced.

CHAPTER IX

GOD AND THE SELF

Social psychology is working out a genetic account of the nature of the self which begins to afford light on the nature and function of God in human life. It shows that the self arises under definite conditions and through specific processes. The infant organism does not possess consciousness of itself or of the world in which it lives. Through the maturing of the organism and through its functioning in relation to other organisms and the world about, the child gradually attains some realization of itself and of others. Language is the great instrument for this achievement for it is in developing the ability to use speech that the self and its knowledge of other selves mature. Speech begins with impulsive cries and gestures, reflex activities of the organism. To indicate its continuity with related forms of expression, speech is often designated as "vocal-gesture." Because of its flexibility and possibility of development, it affords the great medium for the growth of consciousness and of communication. Language is the great means or instrument for the unfolding, or creation, of the self. Mere babbling of sounds or repetition of words is not true language, nor does it indicate the presence of a true self. This is but a preliminary stage. Real language does not appear until words are definitely employed to designate specific meanings, intended objects and acts.

The steps by which the infant comes to consciousness of self, and at the same time of other selves and objects, is now well stated by the psychologists. The process is vividly revealed in the speech of children, who pass beyond the parrot stage when they are able to recognize objects by their names, and to indicate by words objects which they desire or to which they point. The words of the infant when he first begins to use them are mere sounds, as they are for the parrot. Neither one can handle his vocabulary freely, with flexible adjustment of his speech to the complex environment about him. His use of words is routine and mechanical, repetitious and unenlightened. Gradually the child draws away from the parrot stage, and accumulates a larger assortment of words which he uses with increasing accuracy to indicate things, himself, other persons, and actions. By more and more numerous words he can be directed and controlled in his behavior. A dramatic illustration of this emergence of the real use of speech is seen in the case of the deafmute, Helen Keller. Her teacher had tried faithfully to give her the cue for the use of words to indicate familiar objects, but without success until one day when the child was seven years of age. They were pumping water from the well and as the water flowed over one hand of the child her teacher spelled the word "w-a-t-e-r" into the other hand. Of a sudden the child grasped the relation between the word and the object. At once she realized that various things about her could be referred to in the same way, and she ran about in great excitement asking the names of all objects she encountered. Thus, at a stroke, she really entered the human world of language and rose to the plane of intelligent communication with her family and friends.

Bound up with this experience of communication is the emergence of consciousness of the self and of others. This consciousness need not be regarded as anything metaphysical or transcendental. In its simplest aspect, it is the recognition of the child's own organism by its name, and of other persons by their names. Much more, however, is involved; for these organism-objects, in their complex behavior, motions, interactions, affections, and conflicts, develop numerous, varied habits and attitudes. Through contact with other individuals, the child not only learns to distinguish them and call them by name, but learns to do the same for himself. It is at the point where he begins to designate himself by his own name, and to note the difference in behavior of himself and of other particular people, that his sense of himself comes to birth. The play of children is one of the great means in the accomplishment of this end. By taking the rôles of other people, children refine their awareness of themselves and of others. To play father, mother, sister, brother, teacher, preacher, store-keeper, conductor, and policeman is to "go out of themselves" and yet to keep a very definite sense of their own proper character. Perhaps the whole enrichment of personality through life is just the attainment of sympathetic understanding of other persons to the point of being able in imagination, if not in actual performance, to take their part in the living drama of real social relations.

This social process is essential to the realization of the self, as well as of others. Consciousness of the self apparently comes about in this way, so that contact with other people is just as essential to the knowledge of one's self as of them. Many fallacies have appeared in the history of psychology and philosophy because this fact has been overlooked. It has too often been assumed that a person knows himself directly in some other way than that by which he knows others, but the accumulating evidence shows that a man becomes acquainted with himself precisely as he learns to know others, namely, by observation and by experimentation. The self-feeling of the organism comes to be associated with the organism or with a particular part, only by experience. The infant's pain is not in his toe any more, as has been said, than the toe is in the pain. It is some achievement to learn that he has toes and fingers and a body, that is, to know himself as an organism in distinction from his clothing or his crib. This differentiation does not take place on one side alone. It carries with it the correlative world of objects and persons. To learn to know himself as a son it is necessary that he learn to know his father. He cannot understand what it is to be the first baseman on a ball team without understanding the other positions on the team, and recognizing the fact of the team. All knowledge of self is correlated with knowledge of something else at the same time. The self is not isolated, nor separate, but is in a network of relations.

Throughout the play experience of the child, and in all his habits, there is a more or less defined sense of the rules of the game, of the forms of procedure. Any casual observer of children must have noticed that they are meticulous about carrying on their performance

with scrupulous regard for the customs of the activity
in which they are engaged. If they are playing at
housekeeping, they insist that things shall be done
according to the pattern they have seen in operation.
There is constantly the tendency to follow the manners
and habits of the organized social process they are re-
producing, whether it be the home, the store, the school,
the workshop, or the playground. In order to have the
play satisfying, it must conform to the regulations belonging to these institutions. The participants defer to
the system involved in each activity.

All the individuals are held within a frame of discourse and action, which all more or less consciously
recognize and accept. They submit to the ways prescribed by the group in its interaction. There is thus
developed the feeling of guidance by a common standard. Every one feels himself answerable to this law,
to the way things should be done. Offenses against this
general procedure are punished by the disapproval of
the leaders, and many times by the expulsion of unruly
members from the game. The self is not only in relation to the other individuals, but to the order and co-
operation which serve as controls. There is something
over and above the participants, and this is the group
pattern within which they move. They arrange themselves within a structure of custom which is designated
as "playing Indians," or "playing school." As Indians
they talk and act in character, and as pupils they deport
themselves according to the practices of the school. As
Indians they belong to a tribe, having a chief, a method
of hunting and of fighting. This group consciousness
varies with the play they agree to enter, but it is always

present, for there is always the assumption of a scheme of behavior without which the game can have no meaning, progress, or end.

The same principle operates in the activities of adults. They are workers in organized fields of interest, in families, in professions, in labor unions, in business associations. Such functions presuppose and imply definite forms of procedure; there is a kind of overhead system to which all must be respectful; otherwise there can be no understanding, no bargaining, no satisfactory eventuation of activity. Every self is in reciprocal relations to this structure of action or habit. It is symbolized by the laws of a vocation, by the leaders of an industry or profession. Each individual is a member, a participant in a body. That body or social unit is constituted by all the individuals, *in certain relations to one another*. The unity is not external to the members, and yet it is something more than the mere presence of the persons. It is defined by the function they wish to perform. Often a professional or business group, after the conference for which they primarily met is ended, adjourn to enjoy social pleasures—conversation, games, or a tea party; but they are still participants in groups, for these interests also have their proprieties. The groups in which a person finds himself in the course of a day are very diverse—the home, office, dinner party, recreation, study-class, political meeting, religious service—all these having their character, ways of behavior, and standards of conduct.

The self lives and grows in the midst of such social structures. Everywhere it is in reciprocal relation to organizations that determine the direction and nature of action, and that are modified in turn by the personalities of the participants. Not only is each member conscious of his relations to other members, but he is aware to some extent of the specific situation in which all stand within a club, or class, or school, or church. There is an entity designated by each of these terms which is definite and unique, toward which the self takes attitudes, and from which it derives stimulus and direction. Loyalty to this group-entity is a very real part of the self which feels itself expanded or shrunken with the development or losses of this larger situation. The older psychology conceived the self as a separate thing, as distinct as the body from other bodies, but the self is now seen to be constituted of meanings, purposes, and imaginative ideas that are sharable and capable of simultaneous possession by any number of persons. By such means it is possible to have common experience and to identify ourselves with others. So much is this the case that association with other persons is essential to the existence and happiness of the self. The approval and disapproval of a man's friends are the most powerful influences that touch his life. The loss of an intimate companion through death is the death also of a part of the survivor, but the loss of a friend through alienation of affection is just as real a loss. In a sense the latter is a deeper loss, for one who has passed away in death remains in our thought and is cherished in memory, and thus continues to be a part of us.

There is here afforded an approach to the importance and significance of another fact of social psychology. This is the fact that the self develops a feeling for the group, for the social *alter*. Through intimate associa-

tion with the members of the family, clan, and tribe
there emerges the notion of a common life to which all
belong.   This inclusive being is symbolized by the
coat of arms, the totem object, the flag, the representative individuals such as noted ancestors, powerful
leaders, chiefs, or kings.   Some peoples, like the Kaffirs,
definitely use the concept of a group-soul and have a
name for it.   All groups, wrought together through vivid
and prolonged experiences, manifest a sense of this inclusive entity.   There has been much discussion of the
nature of this fact.   Doubtless the group-soul has often
been conceived as something apart and external, as if it
had an independent reality over and above the individuals who constitute it.   It is so constant and so impressive that an illusion easily arises of an ontological
reality, self-subsistent and transcendent.   But this may
be taken as evidence of the importance of the phenomenon, without regarding it as literally apart and meta-
physically existent.

What is the reality answering to the group-soul?   It
is the order and structure of the associated life of the
individuals constituting the class.   It is a work of the
mutual interdependence and interaction of many persons woven together in a common tradition of customs
and ideals.   The individual is born into an inheritance
of language, forms of government, arts, and occupations.   He participates in institutions that are on hand
when he arrives, and through which he is molded in
thought and feeling.   This group life stretches into a
dim past, and survives its transient members; it imposes the authority of its standards, inspires loyalty and
reverence, and offers rewards of approval and judgments

of disapproval; its sanctions come to be the supreme measure of right and wrong, of honor and disgrace. By the relatively feeble and dependent individual it is felt to be the enduring and supreme reality. The patriot, giving his life in its service, evinces the highest possible devotion to it. It becomes the subject of song and story, the theme of ceremonials, and the object of religious worship.

When this spirit of the group is subjected to historical and reflective inquiry it seems to some minds to dissolve and vanish, because they cannot locate any specific object or external reality corresponding to it. But there are different kinds of reality, and that which is involved in the group or class is constituted by the order and framework wrought out in the experience of its members. An ordinary college class furnishes an illustration. The class is more than the enumerated persons in it. As a class they stand in definite relations to one another, to the teacher, and to the school to which they belong. They have a realization of its peculiar characteristics distinct from other classes. Certain attitudes are induced in them by it; specific requirements arise from it. The class stimulates its members, and responds to their efforts and achievements; it remains a localizable, describable thing through the lifetime of those who belong to it; it is easily a point of reference in the records of the college, and it continues to exist with force and meaning. Here, of course, the life-activities of the group are limited and highly specialized as compared with those of a family, where the interests are varied and intimate. But the family has the same kind of reality, though deeper and more vital. Each member

comes to have a sense of "the family," of its mind and
heart. This mind of the group is not merely the thought
of any one person in it, however dominant. The youngest child contributes something, if nothing else than the
problem it presents, and the need for care and direction.
An invalid member may condition all the rest as to their
sympathy, co-operation, and planning. Even a guest
in the house easily perceives the structure and conduct
of the whole. In addition to all overt acts and expressed
ideas, there is an atmosphere—a taste, a form, and spirit
—which determines the very furnishings as well as the
intellectual temper and social congeniality or antagonism. The individual member moves in the situation
with an adjustment of sentiment and manner, revealing
the depth of the unconscious control exerted by the
common life.

In larger social units this process is so operative
that it begets a quality and character, known as the
genius of peoples. The elements and forces which enter
into this result are too numerous and subtle for specification. The contour of the land, the fertility of the soil,
the occupations followed, the wars fought, the leaders
developed, the literature produced, the arts achieved,
the religion cherished, these and many other factors are
merged in the racial and national character. It has
become an interesting and fruitful enterprise to portray
and interpret this "soul" of America, of England, of the
Jew, or of the Slav. Outward signs, such as physiog-
nomy, dress, and speech, may furnish clues to this
inner life, but it is more adequately expressed in literature, music, architecture, and ceremonials. This genius
of peoples has been fashioned unconsciously, in the

cumulative life and exigencies of long and complex history. This enveloping life makes its impress upon the individual, and through it he finds self-expression and support for the operation of his will.

Through the power of generalization and imagination the self constantly moves with more or less clearness in relation to these larger wholes. They live in a man's thought as working realities to which he defers and by which he is inspired. Religion carries this process to its highest form. In religion the self stands in relation to the largest whole, to the universe, to God. This relation appears in those situations where the self meets the supreme crises of life, as when facing death, or the ultimate demands of honor. The whole meaning and urge of life then enters into the Other. This Other is of the same nature as all the lesser "others," constituted of social groups of varying scope and function. It is not a figment or an illusion any more than the state or the family is an illusion. It has the substance of the actual world of things and people, of history and projected action. Philosophy calls it the Universal or the Absolute; science designates it as Nature or Life; religion names it God. Psychologically it belongs to the inescapable experience of the relation of the self and the other. The "other" may be another human being, or a set of human beings held together as a family or a city or a nation, or it may be Humanity or the Universe. In every case this other is reality functioning vitally and impressively in the behavior and emotions of the self. We love God as surely and as intelligently as we love our country or our Alma Mater, but with deeper and more consummate affection.

There are certain limitations in all these relations which appear to reflective thought but are disregarded in the practical and emotional attitudes of action and appreciation. Few patriots conceive their country as absolutely perfect. They idealize it, they love it, and they labor for the ideals which are identified with its institutions and enterprises. Reflectively, they know there are imperfections in leaders and laws and methods of government but they work to overcome and eliminate these. The intentions, plans, hopes, and purposes of founders and of great statesmen furnish the true measure of their nation, and it is for these they sacrifice and struggle. Similarly, the religious man knows there are evils in the world, that justice is not complete, that tragedy and suffering exist, but he knows too that there are good and happiness and some fulfilment of righteousness. These qualities he identifies with the divine. God is not taken as the equivalent of all that is, but as the ideal being who seeks the realization of the good. Frequently the evil is held to be unreal and transient, a stage in the process or an incident in the unfolding of the ideal. God is "the Power which makes for righteousness."

This is the answer to pantheism which holds to an absolute, static reality, mechanistic and complete in itself. Religious faith contemplates a living process incompletely manifest in the will and purpose of individuals. That faith, in many forms at least, views men as allies, as instruments and aids in the realization of the divine will. By this faith men share responsibility for the coming of the kingdom of heaven; their devotion and labor count in the vast scheme of things; they hinder or accelerate the fulfilment of God's victories. The self participates in the life of the universal; of the great Other, it feels its part small but actual, just as the citizen of a republic knows that his deeds are slight events in the determination of national destiny, but still important. Without his co-operation and conscientious effort the course of events may be different, and through his loyalty the good may be augmented and enriched. Otherwise the self becomes unreal and its effort appears futile and illusory. There are religions which so emphasize the supremacy and self-sufficiency of God that the only objective of the self is to become merged and lost in the infinite. In such religions the self does not really count; the divine has no real need for its support or fidelity. But the empirical estimate of life grounds itself upon the conviction that the whole of things is modified by the activity of each factor.

The nature of the self and the quality of self-feeling depend very much upon the general social order within which it lives. In a society where an aristocracy prevails the forms and customs set limits to the interaction of persons, and tend to induce in each the sense of a fixed and predestined place and character. The very symbols of the organized life deepen this attitude. Where a king rules, he stands over against the humble subject at such distance and with such prerogatives that the latter accepts his own subjection and insignificance. The pattern of his thought concerning the cosmos is set by the pattern of his social experience. He may be the passive recipient of favors, but, if so, they are by the grace of his sovereign. The relation between the self

and the ruler is external. Humility, awe, obedience,
and unquestioning loyalty are the virtues natural to
that relation.

But in a society where the will of the citizens is
the final authority, a different pattern prevails. Here
the individual feels himself responsible, and tends to
develop interest and knowledge with reference to the life
of the whole. The rulers, in some true sense, represent
him, and are in need of his support. They appeal to him
for co-operation and are sensitive to his claims. The
individual is called upon to exert himself, to radiate
conviction, and to create good will on behalf of measures which affect the entire community. No limit is
fixed, outside his interest and disposition, to the extent
of his participation. Here and there he has opportunity
to see the results of his endeavors and is stimulated by
the conviction that the results of political and social
enterprises bear some relation to the work done by himself and his associates. The self expands with this
kind of sharing in corporate undertakings, and the world
in which he lives is felt to be somewhat open and im-
pressionable to his hand. The ruling power is no longer
symbolized by an individual set high above the common man, but by a citizen, like himself, who has proved
his worth, and has attracted to his side the combined
strength of like-minded persons.

CHAPTER X

GOD AS IDEALIZED REALITY

The scientific method starts with the facts of experience and forms its generalizations and hypotheses in terms of those facts. The first efforts of this kind undertook, naturally enough, to discover God as a single fact or object in the universe of facts. Their failure is well illustrated by the remark ascribed to Laplace, who said, "I have swept the heavens with my telescope and find no God there." That was a severe shock to the traditional, uncritical notion which thought of God as a great manlike being sitting above the world. The discovery of the rotation of the earth and of its movement in space about the sun demolished the old naïve cosmology. The words "above" and "below" became purely relative terms and the direction of heaven from any given point shifted at every moment and reached opposite positions every twelve hours. Neither in the heights or depths of space was it possible to find the throne of the universe. Probably more than anything else it was observations of this kind which discredited the old ideas of the doctrine of transcendence and led to various theories of immanence. But the search for God as one definite object or observable fact somewhere within the known world of phenomena has also been fruitless. Therefore the question, Where is God? has given way for the deeper question, What is the nature of God?

There is an analogy in the search for the human soul. The soul was long sought as an element or object within the body of man. Its seat was located in various organs, in the stomach, in the liver, and, by Descartes, in the pineal gland of the brain. But no anatomist or psychologist now holds to such a view. Some still use "mind" in much the same way, and a few are content to think of it as an existent fact belonging to a different order from the physical. The prevailing tendency is more and more to raise the deeper question as to the nature of mind or soul. Professor Otto, in his book, *Things and Ideals*, explains the concept of soul in terms of character or personality. If a man is considerate and sympathetic with his fellows, we say he has a soul; if his nature is refined and idealistic, we credit him with a soul. If he is hard and unimaginative toward others, we say he has no soul.

In similar fashion the endeavor to locate the mind as a specific entity is relinquished. Mind is increasingly regarded as a term descriptive of the behavior of some organisms, particularly those called human beings. When they behave in certain ways they are said to exhibit mentality. The selective character of their actions, their apparent deliberation before action, their ability to deal with novel situations effectively on the basis of past experience and imagination, are evidences of mentality. Mind is not therefore something separable, so far as science knows, from the organism, but mind is none the less a fact recognizable in the nature and behavior of men. The inclusive term is persons. A person is an organism which functions in complex and characteristic ways. He is not merely a physical thing, nor purely a psychical reality. He is a manifold, plastic, adaptable being for whose experience neither the material nor the spiritual terms are adequate designations. Few scientific psychologists deny the reality of mind, but they now seek its nature in the concrete, describable experience of man's life.

An analogous procedure is taking place with reference to the conception of God. Instead of trying to locate God as an object in space the search is made in the nature of the life of the world including man and the human cultures which the world sustains. Here again the conventional habit is to envisage the world as a physical substance and to seek God as an object outside or inside of this material universe, just as men have taken the bodily organism as a physical or material thing and the mind as an object alongside or inside of it. But it is possible that a more fruitful course is to inquire whether God may not be more truly and more fully understood as the reality of the world in certain aspects and functions—in what is here characterized as reality idealized.

One of these aspects is a degree of orderliness. The structure of inorganic and of organic forms illustrates this, as do the procession of the seasons and the social institutions of mankind. The formation of snow crystals, the ascertainable and dependable behavior of gases and liquids and solids, the reactions of chemical agents, the reproduction of living beings after their kind, the laws of habit and of custom in animal and human life, have impressed all who have had most intimate and thorough knowledge of them. The marvelous development of control over the forces of nature which man has achieved, especially in this age of science, has been due to the discovery of these structures and their interactions. The work of Louis Pasteur in the field of bacteriology was the discovery of microscopic organisms which cause fermentation, disease, and immunity. In the past such phenomena were comprehended under the conception of design in nature and made the basis of inference from order and design to a supreme designer. This method transferred attention from the inherent order of the world and overshadowed its importance by emphasis upon the source and first cause of order. The thoroughly empirical interpretation, on the other hand, rests with the fact of this order as an evident and significant characteristic of the world and of life itself. If the reality which we immediately experience and live by discloses to competent observers so much order, power, and beauty, why not accept these phenomena as belonging to the reality as known and felt? So much orderliness as we find is valid and it is good. It is not invalidated by man's wish for complete perfection, for that wish has often led to the forfeiting of the actual good at hand in the quest for some imaginary or whimsically desired good beyond. Philosophical man may have to learn, as naïve man has to learn, that his wishes may be better satisfied by the actual though limited realities which he possesses than by dismissing them for something which he cannot reach. The known order may be more truly something to be enjoyed and used as it is found, than as sign or promise of the existence of another kind of reality designated as Creator or First Cause. It is an interesting fact that the positing of such a First Cause does not of itself satisfy the questionings of the mind which thinks in that way, for it is possible still, as the child often does, to ask, Who made God? If the mind once sets out upon such a serial journey from one event to another, it is not likely to be content when it is told to stop at some particular object no matter what claims may be made for its perfection, absoluteness, and infinity.

If the understanding of a thing is sought in the concrete relations which it bears, it has within itself and in these relations all the values and all the reality which it signifies. The order and beauty found in the world and life are themselves inherent and actual, and give reality meaning and significance. Reality is in so far good, beautiful, and divine. Doubtless the reality we experience is in these respects limited and finite, and we are, on these grounds, required to be content with a finite God. We have constantly to face the fact that we have either a limited and finite world or no world at all. It may not be so difficult as it seems to recognize also that we have either a finite God or no God at all. It is usually easy enough for the student of other religions than his own to see how finite the Gods of these religions are, nor is it impossible for Buddhists and Mohammedans to see limitations in the Christian God. Successive generations of Christians readily sense the limitations of earlier conceptions of God in their own tradition. It is a mistake to suppose that religious loyalty, any more than other kinds of loyalty, such as patriotism and romantic love, depend upon demonstrated perfection in the object loved. We admire and love life as we know it, and if we identify

God with the degree of order and loveliness which we find, we may also love and reverence him. The development of this general conception in reference to other features of the life we live may help to make clearer and more forceful this line of reflection.

Reality is characterized by love; that is, love is present in the world and in life. It is the matrix of life in all orders of being, in mating, in friendship, in the good will which creates and binds together the higher forms of living beings. There is also hatred and envy and malice in reality, but love is pre-eminently identified with God. Here, as in other respects, God is not equivalent to all reality but to certain phases of it. Only where love is, God is. But wherever love is, in the higher and in the lower living forms, there God is manifest. Those who experience love, parental, filial, conjugal, communal, or cosmic, experience God. God, as love, is not far from any one of us. In love we live and move and have our being. This love exists as personal, intelligent, and active in the living world of actual reality. Hence we say God is reality idealized. This idealization does not mean fabricated or imagined. It means selection. God is the world or life taken in certain of its aspects, in those aspects which are consonant with order, beauty, and expansion. That these features are present in reality as experienced, as known, is obvious. To assert that love is not present in rocks and tides and winds may be true but these do not exhaust reality, nor do they state the elements of reality which are of most dominant and pervasive importance. Love is present in animals and men and these belong to reality. It is manifest in lovers and families, in states and in world-societies, and these belong to the world and to the cosmos. Therefore reality, taken in its most inclusive and far-reaching significance, manifests love, and this empirical fact is the ground for the religious interpretations of reality as God. Any conception of the world without love is an inadequate and so far an empirically untrue representation of it. Even if love is regarded as merely the flickering flame of the candle, still it is there and its light and warmth may be more significant than any other factors. A candle is not a candle without its light and it is not a world without love.

In a similar way it may be shown that other attributes of reality are included in God. Intelligence and rationality are in life, not perfectly nor universally, but in degree. Modern psychology has greatly extended the recognition of intelligence in creation, finding it in the orderly and effective behavior of birds in their migrations, in their nest building, in their care and guidance of the young, in their communications by cries and calls and various "gestures," and in many complex adjustments to their environment. Notably among animals, the horse, the dog, and the ape profit by experience. They learn by their trial and error, and often arrive at amazing skill. In man, thanks to a larger brain and nervous system, to a higher sensitivity and a longer, plastic infancy, intelligence appears to have unlimited possibilities. By the devices of written language which make available longer and wider ranges of experience, and by deliberately developed records for the preservation of the hard-won treasures of discovery, man increases his grasp of the world and himself, thus

freeing himself from many limitations and evils. Intelligence is thus evident in the world and life. It is
not the whole of life. There is much brute force, sheer
impulse, blind activity, but a degree of rationality is
present. To the rational beings who appreciate it, it is
regarded as valuable beyond any quantitative relation
in which it seems to stand to other measurable aspects
of life. Religion thinks of this wisdom as a quality
of reality conceived as God. God is reality manifesting
the functions of intelligence. The world thinks, reasons,
understands, in and through the rational beings which
appear in it. For the argument now under consideration it is not necessary to show more than this. The very
fact that there is an order of beings in the world and
of it which manifest some degree of rationality is sufficient to justify the claim that reality includes this characteristic. The idealization of reality is illustrated by
the tendency to select and magnify the significance of
intelligence, and by including it in the nature of reality to identify it with God.

So conceived, God is found present in the daily and
commonplace experience of living. Order, intelligence,
and love are the qualities of his nature. Such a statement does not exhaust the divine nature of the world.
No statement does. The theologians and the philosophers have never satisfied themselves that their descriptions and arguments have entirely compassed the
whole of reality. But this statement, proceeding in
purely empirical terms, does move within the sphere of
the actual and verifiable. It presents reality as loving
and lovable, as known and knowing, as orderly and
ordering. Life, in such a view, may make a genuine

appeal and may afford guidance, comfort, and rewarding tasks. Reality is understanding and responsive, dependable and friendly.

There is here no compulsion to take a religious view of the world. The old challenge still rings through the world, "Choose ye this day whom ye will serve." Fools may continue to say there is no God, and pessimists may still arraign the facts of their experience in such ways as seem to them to support the conclusion that all is mere vanity and vexation of spirit. There is hatred and stupidity and confusion in life, and if one looks at these only or chiefly, he may generalize from them to the conclusion that life is cruel and chaotic, may posit evil spirits, and picture the Devil as the true nature of things.

There are two arguments for the validity of the identification of reality with order, intelligence, and love. One is the fact that only by them is sanity and achievement possible. Unless there is some degree of order it is impossible to set up ends and to work for them; even the building of houses and the direction of the state would become illusory and self-defeating. But we do build houses and railroads and radio stations and empires and democracies. They are not perfect, let it be admitted, but they are remarkably successful and every advance points to yet further possibilities. The other argument is that along with this degree of orderliness and rationality goes a positive and pleasurable emotional tone. In a world where effort was always finally blocked and defeated, the result would be mere pain and nostalgia. Religions have been pessimistic about some aspects of life—the present world of un-

regenerate human nature—but they somewhere find
escape into a more optimistic mood, as in the doctrines
of heaven and nirvana, which afford salvation, positive
or negative. The religions of Western culture, at least
in modern times, have been more optimistic, especially
about the value and possibilities of life here and now.
As scientific knowledge of nature and of man develops
and is applied in the control of disease, and in other
ways which make for human welfare, the sense of the
friendliness of the world is increased for the masses of
men, though pessimism is not without its prophets.

As has been pointed out in an earlier chapter, the
positive, optimistic religions are characterized by the
will to live, by the practical attitude of transforming
both nature and human nature in the interest of fuller
and better living. All religions cherish in some form the
ideal of salvation. Even the so-called pessimistic religions, such as Buddhism, emphasize some ideal of
escape from the ills of life, if only by way of suppress-
ing desire and attaining the negation of pain and suffering. The Hebrew and the Christian faiths vigorously
project ideals of kingdoms of righteousness and peace
among men here on the earth. They employ educational, economic, and social methods of alleviation to
achieve these ends. They teach that the world is at
heart a moral order, and that the fulfilment of moral
ideals depends upon the co-operation of mankind in
the service of spiritual ends. Their God is not the whole
of reality as it appears in the tragic course of history,
but he is identified with the will to attain the good
through the dominance of order, intelligence, and love.
The impulses and desires of the hearts of men on behalf

of moral ideals are evidences of the presence of God and the will of God. Because men are constantly striving for greater harmony, knowledge, and good will, they are by this very fact giving proof of the increasing realization of the divine in nature.

There is another type of idealization with reference to God which arises in connection with the conduct of life. This might be called the emergence of absolute attitudes and judgments in practical situations. The necessity of action brings to an end the tentative and reflective attitude of deliberation. This principle appears in both the smaller and the larger aspects of life. When a person goes to the shop to buy a suit of clothes, many possibilities are presented as to material, style, and cost. There is really seldom any fixed standard. It is a matter of taste and of the willingness of the purchaser to do without other things. He may be very conscientious about the use of money and sensitive about his appearance, and he would like to know what it is "best" to do. But there is no view of the situation which does not suggest other alternatives. It is an open question. If nothing else forces a decision, loss of time and the worry of indecision, as well as the need for the suit, demand action. At length the choice is made. One out of several suits is selected. The transaction is finally completed as decisively and conclusively as if the buyer had really had at hand some absolute criterion. This is what I have called "the practical absolute." [1]

In more important problems of life the force of this

[1] "Religious Values and the Practical Absolute," *International Journal of Ethics,* July, 1922.

practical absolute is poignantly felt. It is impossible to determine the absolute correctness of a vote in an election, or the choice of a companion in matrimony, or the decision of a jury deliberating over the death sentence where only circumstantial evidence has been presented. Yet the decision is completed in action as finally and irretrievably as would be the case if the agents possessed infallible wisdom. In all truly moral situations the deliberation is empirical and tentative, but the action is final and absolute. The action is absolute because only one course can be realized and fulfilled. The agent is often in doubt until the last moment, but finally he acts as definitely and completely as if he had been guided by supreme wisdom.

It is in these practical situations throughout the history of religion that the need for God and the sense of his presence are most powerfully felt. It is in crises where one faces momentous decisions that one feels unable by himself to shoulder the responsibility. He seeks the aid of God by the methods at hand in the mores—by casting lots, by looking for some sign, by petitioning God through prayer. Whether the answer is an outward sign, or an inner conviction, the religious mind feels that the decision is the will of God. Often the course of events, of seemingly inescapable acts, moves on with so little conscious control or awareness of the implications that there seems to be a power operative beyond the will and the decision of the agent. So impressive does this aspect of experience become with some that they regard the divine as the one real actor in the drama. Their attention is so fixed upon the point of action that the whole field appears to be inevitably determined. Carefully laid plans do not eventuate; unexpected implications arise and unforeseen consequences spring forth; vast movements flow from mere incidents of simple circumstances. From the compulsion to end deliberation and to precipitate action with its incalculable results, is developed the feeling that events have their own necessary form, and that these are the work of God who overrules and directs the affairs of men in his own ordained way. The tentative and hypothetical situations of deliberation are reduced through action to definite, fixed forms. Social enterprises are so conspicuously of this nature that they are often attributed to a Power not ourselves.

The sense of the "practical absolute" is expressed and enhanced by the use of honorific terms. This is especially notable where personal affection and intimacy are involved. A mother sees her child in superlative characters; lovers are proverbially blind to defects; political partisans glorify their leaders; and religious devotees ignore the evils of life lest the recognition of them should qualify the perfect goodness and wisdom of God. This assertion of perfection in honorific titles of social usage and address evinces an æsthetic and compensatory tendency of practical life which is more easily discerned and assessed in ordinary affairs than in religion. The values and the loyalties of religion are so engrossing that they allow little opportunity or tolerance for analytical and critical estimates. The religious view of the world, in its emotional intensity and affectionate appraisal, naturally employs vivid and intimate personal symbols of the most perfect and absolute kind. In religious appreciation, God is Reality idealized and glorified with the attributes of complete and flawless personality.

In lesser matters the human mind employs the honorific terms of perfection without confusion. A homely and humorous instance of this fact I have captured from our modern world of industry and trade. It is a trademark, stamped in metal, which I removed from an old oilstove still doing service in my summer cottage. The trade-mark reads: "New Perfection No. 62." Presumably the inventor of this stove, elated by the creation of such a convenient domestic device, was moved to call it "Perfection." When some improvement was developed, with no apology to the philosophical absolutists, he advertised his, "New Perfection"; and with the successive inventions he boldly continued to number his growing perfections through the long series up to sixty-two!

Since God was first conceived in personal terms, he has been to religious souls the perfect Person. With the development of wisdom, mercy, justice, and love in the world, he has been the infinitely wise, merciful, just, and loving God. In spite of all evil in the world, regardless of the injustice, hatred, and falsehood which exist, God is to the hearts who love him, omniscient, omnipotent, complete and absolute perfection.

CHAPTER XI

GOD AND PERSONALITY

Personality is a difficult word, especially when applied beyond its ordinary use in designating specific persons. Even there it is not easily defined, for to state just what constitutes a person is more complicated than the free and constant reference to persons would suggest. Psychologists are still investigating the facts; they speak more of organisms and behavior; they are in doubt about the fact and the meaning of consciousness; they question whether animals have personality. Perhaps it is safe to assume agreement on the point that a person is a human organism displaying mentality and engaging in the usual social relations with his fellows. It is, so considered, a functional term and indicates characteristic forms of action which men and women display. On the side of values, those of personality are of supreme importance, and the various systems of ethics, in some form, turn upon the primacy and the worth of persons. The great ends of all cultural processes, such as education, government, and religion, are the enlargement and enrichment of personality. The worst crimes are those against persons. All social idealisms have for their objective the release and freeing of persons for fuller and happier life. Any man is a physical object, an economic unit, an animal, a thinking being; but he is also a person and it is as a person that he feels himself most significant. That term gathers up more meaning and value than any of the others. It is in persons that Nature reaches her highest expression and presents her noblest creation.

In the same way and with the same cogency we may say that reality is personal, as we have said reality is orderly and intelligent and possessed of good will or love. Not all of reality is personal, any more than it is orderly, but there is personality in it. Since man is a part of nature, nature is to this extent personal. There seems, consequently, the same ground for asserting that God is personal as we have had for saying that God is order, intelligence, and love. Everything depends on the empirical fact as to whether man is a part of nature. Our position is that he is, and not merely in his physical being, but also in mind and personality. The evolutionary view leaves nothing out of this process. It provides no ingress from another order, of any factors of man's being. For some, this implies that man is all body, a merely physical being, but that is an *a priori* manner of judging the matter. The scientific method of dealing with the case is to take man as he is, and to note the unfolding of his powers in the process of nature. If his mental and personal traits can be accounted for as well by natural processes as are his physical and social life, then it is unnecessary to go outside the sphere of nature to account for them. But that modifies the conception of "nature." It is essential to recognize all that appears in his experience. If he develops mind, consciousness, and intelligence, these belong to the process in which they appear. Few scientists question this view. Whatever man possesses they regard as arising in the due course of nature. Sometimes they are inclined to minimize the reality and significance of the intellectual and cultural life which have developed. It would seem that here lies the whole problem of an empirical estimate of human nature. If it is granted that all that man develops and achieves belongs to the nature within which he exists, then nature has the qualities which man has. Either the characteristics must be denied to him or they must be held to be a part of that nature to which he belongs. It is the acceptance of the implications of this conception which is the basis for the position taken in this chapter. In other words, it is maintained that since man is possessed of personality, the reality which we call nature, or the world, is to that extent personal. Therefore, God conceived as reality is so far personal.

One objection to regarding God as personal is that personality, as we know it, is limited and relative; but we have definitely accepted the idea that God is finite on the ground that empirical reflection leads to that conclusion. There is a tendency to infer that all limitation means insignificance or worthlessness, and it should be remembered that finite and limited things may be very great and significant. Space and time, electricity and thought, appear under limits, but they are vast and inexhaustible. Superlatives—perfection, infinite, absolute—have been so written into the conceptions of God that to many minds it sounds like a contradiction in terms to speak of a finite God. But when it is realized that grandeur and sublimity are compatible with finiteness, the admission of some kinds of limits and relations does not contradict the recognition of real and profound values. The conception of God as personal is the same in principle as the conception of a group as personal, for example, a corporation or a state. A railroad is a person before the law, and in many relations. It owns property, employs men, constructs great engineering works, buys and sells commodities, erects hospitals, is accessible to pleas, and is sensitive to the opinion of its public. These functions are carried on through specific individuals *in their official capacity*, never as private citizens. The particular agent in any transaction acts not in his own name but in the name of the corporation. The railroad is a certain organization of material things and human beings, and it acts with the definiteness and power of a great person. The same is true of God. He is the world of nature, including human beings, operating for certain ends through individuals and institutions. He never speaks except in concrete terms, through the voice of man, or through the significant facts of nature. A railroad puts up signs of warning at grade crossings, and God sets up directions, through human agency, at many important junctions of life. The lowly section hand is a representative of the railroad and at the same time is an agent for carrying out the will of society, and is no less a functionary of God. The individual may not see himself in these wider relations, but it is one of the ideals of religion to get him to do so, to see that he is very truly doing God's work, as well as the railroad's. A good deed may be done without the feeling of its greater significance, but it is always the character of a truly good act that it can be done "in the name of God."

A traveler on trains may easily find his mind filled with a genuine religious feeling with regard to the experience he is undergoing. Lying in his berth at night, while the train is rushing through space at great speed, he feels security in the thought of the experienced, dependable engineer at the throttle, the fireman on the lookout, and the crew at their posts of duty. But these are only surface aspects of the larger situation. The construction of the cars, of the track, of the signals along the way, belongs to the ground of his security, while the laws of nature, gravitation, light rays, temperature, atomic action, and tensile strength, play their part. The action of an indefinitely extensive set of factors is involved, all of which and more may be included in the passenger's sense of the agencies and forces which sustain and carry him safely on. Whether his attitude is scientific, æsthetic, practical, or religious depends upon the manner in which he reacts to the experience. All of these attitudes deal with the same phenomena but in different perspective and emphasis. The feeling of safety and comfort while being transported through space to a desired destination may easily fall into the imagery of personal terms and beget the attitude of being upheld by a great, encompassing Power for which the name God is used. From that stage it is but a step to the expression of gratitude, of reverence, of awe.

The empirical view of religion emphasizes the advantage of seeing the religious experience from such an approach, rather than from the side of inexplicable, unanalyzable aspects. Usually the idea of God, in religious literature, is more characteristically employed in experiences which baffle analysis, as in surprising coincidences where the individual narrowly escaped death in an accident, or where good fortune brings a chance meeting with a soul-mate equal to all possible emotional demands. So long as only the surprising and the incalculable phenomena awaken religious feeling, and the better understood, orderly occurrences are barren of religious sentiment, religion remains merely mysterious, non-rational, and ready to be dismissed.

The inclusion of the human experience in the order of nature, and the use of it as the key to a personal attitude toward life, gives justification to the religious feeling of being in a friendly universe. Through our intimate, congenial personal associations, we have the realization of friendliness, and we frankly make it the avenue to God. From infancy we live in a world of persons. They nurture us, enfold us, and stimulate us. This human world stretches about us in a wide area and in a vast past. We find at hand a rich record of this human experience and the more we make our way into it the more we see our indebtedness to it. Not only the names which are preserved, but the multitudes of unknown workers, thinkers, and artists who have contributed something to the process, are of kin to us. In them the divine is manifest, not wholly or always in clear terms, but recognizably and wistfully.

It is too much the habit of our time to allow ourselves to be blinded by the external, quantitative view of the world, and in consequence we cannot rid ourselves of a tendency to undervalue and negate the significance of the personal aspect of life. Around our little earth there runs out into fathomless space the great picture of physical nature, and over man we see the impending doom of material forces and swiftly moving, all-devouring time. Instead of taking our stand

within the human and the personal, we allow ourselves
to be decoyed out into a realm conceived as implacable
force and relentless law. But what reason is there for
not also insisting upon the reality of the inner point of
view, upon the constant experience in all human beings
of love, sympathy, and cherished values?

There is a sense, surely, in which the scientific conception of the world is abstract and partial. No doubt
it is legitimate for what it is, but to assume that it
is the whole or that it is the truer conception is to
surrender the only means of living a genuine human life.
For that life is one of personal values, of imagination,
purposes, and ends. To say that this is "merely," or
"just," or "only" our human point of view, assumes
that it is in some sense unreal and illusory, while from
the side of the living, vital sense of things, it is far more
"real" and important than anything else. In an empirical assessment of life as we live it, nothing is so
actual and so meaningful. Why should an empiricist
overlook or minimize these facts? They loom large
and beautiful to our human estimate and therefore are
for us actually large and beautiful.

It is important not to confuse transiency with insignificance. Human life need not be small because it
is short. Value is not measured by time. Finite things
in their little day may be the carriers of meanings and
experiences which transcend their forms and limits.
Even if the human race itself is destined to cease, are
not our human loves and aspirations profoundly significant? The scope of life, by the calculations of the
scientists, opens out toward a future of millions of years,
and by the estimates of moral values, it acquires spirit-

ual dimensions of more significant magnitudes. The individual knows that the end will come for him, yet he clings to life and enjoys it. May it not be the same for the whole of life? It is good while it endures, and its values are great and wonderful beyond all such calculation. Life is good in the feel of it, even when mixed with pain and evil. Otherwise it would be abandoned. Man holds his life in his hand, and could make his exit from the scene instantly any day, but he clings to it, usually with laughter in his heart. The paradoxes are indeed marvelous. This suffering, perplexed mite of being, still wishing to live! In reality his life is not to him so drab and pitiful as some of his reflections make it seem. Actually it goes on, under the shadow of smoking volcanoes, in the presence of danger and death, with an astonishing energy and joy. And when the brighter scenes are considered—domestic bliss, happy friendships, successful labor, achievements of discovery and creation—man appears as a happy, productive, and well-adjusted child of Nature. What disturbs him most are his own dreams of something better yet to be, in contrast to which his present attainments are partial and inadequate. His "divine discontent" is itself prophetic and inspiring.

If "nature" includes man and all his works and aspirations, then the idea of God based upon it becomes cosmic in its significance. Here is found the answer to those objections which derive from the difficulties of interpreting God from the side of personality. These have their force only in that sharp dualism which conceives the physical universe on one side, and the human world as a little realm outside it. When nature is itself

humanized by the inclusion of man, personality and the
social process become legitimate in defining the entire
picture.   The physical becomes the abstract, partial
aspect of the world, and the personal is the more adequate characterization.   It is when we allow ourselves
to be imposed upon by the natural-science point of view
as more real, more actual, that the human sphere appears as subjective, illusory, or unreal.   If we hold
consistently to the facts of experience, empirically
given, man has good ground for asserting the importance
and the centrality of his feeling for himself and his kind.
It is just one of the interesting and impressive phenomena of human thought that it is able to take an outside
look at the world, but that it is truer or more essential
than the inside apprehension of reality through genuinely human estimates is a wholly gratuitous assumption. This may be a very vital instance of "the will to
believe," but it is not merely arbitrary or fictitious. It is
in fact the only method of giving *meaning* to the world,
and at last it is *meaning* which constitutes any "world"
at all.   Starting with the richness and fullness of life as
experienced through social and personal relations, it is
possible to abstract certain aspects and treat them as
the physical sciences do.   But to assume that we can
begin with the external, and the purely objective material realm, is to desert the empirical procedure and to
lose grips upon the most immediate and worthful forms
of reality.   When this simple fact is realized, it may be
seen that the abstract, natural-science interpretation of
nature is indirect, round-about and exceedingly difficult of attainment; while the personal, social conception is more original, more real, and more appreciable.

An important feature of the interpretation of God through human experience is to recognize that man's life itself presents something more than a chaos of impulses and wishes. Just as consciousness always tends to be "figurate," so interests and values appear in hierarchies. Some things are worth more than others. There is a scale of values. Bodily welfare, possessions, social relations, spiritual ideals suggest a series of goods in an ascending curve experienced by every normal personality. The higher concerns are those for which others are held in abeyance at any given time, and for which those others may be sacrificed. Each person displays a pattern of interests, more or less definitely organized within his behavior, in reference to which he selects and acts with some degree of consistency. A man will let his hat go if it falls under a train rather than risk the loss of an arm in trying to recover it; he will give up an arm to save his body; he will forego profit in preference to committing a crime; he will forfeit his life to save his loved one. Moral goods are dearer than gold, and integrity is of greater value than life itself. The specific appraisement in different individuals may vary greatly, but there is always some structure and constancy in human conduct.

In different cultural groups, custom may establish widely varying systems, but throughout the race there are distinguishable marks of the human assessment of objects and deeds. Heroism in battle, fortitude in labor, shrewdness in emergencies, excite universal esteem. As Mill asserted, those who have experienced the pleasures of the beast and the pleasures of the intellect choose the latter as better. Among civilized men the refinements of art are cherished as superior to the gross and meaner things of merely sensual indulgence. There has come to be a virtuous way of living in contrast to vice and ignominy. Intelligent men seek the truth about practical things and ideal things with a conviction that some measure of truth may be found. These judgments of morals and truth constitute a frame of reference through which all reality is measured. By that frame the conception of God is assessed. Some things are not worthy to be attributed to God any more than to a noble man. And certain characteristics are inevitably identified with reality, conceived as God. At any stage of culture, what is good in man is good in his God, and while we have shown the progressive changes in the idea of God, corresponding to different levels of morality, it is apparent that the character of God reflects the best as men feel it for themselves. When men lived brutally, so did their gods. When they discovered sympathy and good will to be good for themselves, they saw these qualities in God. At the time when persons attained worth in their own right, and not by station or favor, then God was held to be the champion of every soul on the ground of its own worth. Slavery among men was matched by an arbitrary and tyrannical God. Righteousness on earth called for goodness in heaven. As personality became clearer in human nature it defined more clearly a personal God as the Father and Friend of man.

The idea of God may thus be seen to express more than the mere projection of human ideals, for that expression still carries within it the old dualism between an alien cosmos and man's little world of interests and values. No doubt the ideals arise in human experience, but they are not on that account to be discredited by saying that they are merely human. They are as real as the body or the rock on which the body rests, and they are as much a part of the cosmos. In these ideal aspects of experience God is immediately possessed through human insight and feeling. God is not supernatural, but wholly natural, just as ideals are natural. The word "natural" may be dismissed, for it came to have significance at the point where an order of nature was distinguished as the experienced opposite of the supernatural. Neither term can properly be used without the other, for each implies the other. Only if natural be made synonymous with the real, can it be adequate to express all that is experienced; but when the natural is given this meaning it includes the ideal, the mental and the spiritual, as well as the so-called physical and material.

Many advocates of modern "humanism" commit this fallacy of supposing that one term of a dualistic conception may be dropped while retaining the other. Convinced that the empirical values are the only values discoverable, they conclude that this justifies their naturalistic, humanistic interpretation of the world. They are therefore compelled to devote much of their strength to denying the existence of God and the supernatural. But as a result, they are left with a truncated world, and the lower half of the old dualistic order. They have unwittingly separated man from nature by the same stroke, and have left their humanistic realm suspended between the void of matter on the one side and the vacancy left on the other by the removal of the old supernaturalistic deity.

What the logic of the change to an empirical view involves is that there should be recognized one process of life from the lowest to the highest forms, ever emerging in new creations. That which is new is not sharply discontinuous with the old, but neither is it simply identical with the old. The process is illustrated in man's outreaching life through all the stages of his growth. Through conflicting interests, imagination develops plans and ideals which impel to their realization in definite, objective form. Thought and action are not discontinuous, but represent steps in the movement of the life man lives. Desires for more adequate living arise out of the conflicts occurring in the partial and imperfect adjustments of the organism; conceptions of means for attaining more satisfying conditions appear, and these are embodied in attempts to reconstruct the ways of life. It is these ideals, springing from blocked desire, which have been hypostatized into entities of another order. The misunderstanding of them gave rise to the contrast between the natural and the supernatural, and the error cannot be corrected by assuming a static realm of physical nature on one side, and man as a helpless dreamer in an alien world on the other.

CHAPTER XII

HOW GOD IS USED

Professor Leuba has said: "God is not so much known as used." He seems to regard this fact as weakening the significance of the concept, and to imply that it means that God does not have reality, but has only subjective existence. In another connection, he explicitly says: "I cannot persuade myself that divine personal beings, be they primitive gods or the Christian Father, have more than a subjective existence." [1] Evidently this conclusion is based upon the idea that God must be conceived as a metaphysical being of the anthropomorphic type. It does not apply to the conception of God as experienced reality, taken in a socialized way; nor does it suggest what Mill saw, that religion may be a social process not generated from metaphysical concepts, but itself the occasion and source of certain ways of viewing reality.

The position here maintained is that the reality to which the term God applies, like the reality to which the term Alma Mater applies, is not the word itself, nor the image it suggests, but the reality of a social process belonging to the actual world. The reality of Alma Mater is not to be found in any particular noble woman, much less in the picture printed in a college annual. The name designates an organization of actual things and living people, the college or university. So

[1] J. H. Leuba, *A Psychological Study of Religion*, p. 10.

the word God is not properly taken to mean a particular
person, or single factual existence, but the order of
nature including man and all the processes of an
aspiring social life.

In a sense, it is use which defines both concepts, as
it is use which determines other concepts. It might be
said of electricity that it is not so much known as used.
It is sometimes asserted that although we produce
electricity to light our homes, run street cars, and send
messages on wires and by wireless, still we do not know
what electricity is. But we do not cease to use it because we do not fully understand it. The same is true
of mind. Men go on with their thinking, studying problems, planning for the future, calculating consequences,
and enjoying their thoughts although the psychologists
and the metaphysicians have not satisfied themselves
entirely as to the nature of mind. Practical life constantly involves the use of objects, forces, and sub-
stances which are not wholly understood, and it is of
the very genius of the scientific procedure to formulate
conceptions of them in reference to their behavior and
function. Life goes on under the pressure of wants and
habits, with varying degrees of awareness of the factors
involved. It is doubtful whether any knowledge of
them is possible except in relation to that process
and their use. Attitudes are evolved, values are cherished, and controls are effected without clear insight into
all the events. Religious experience is no exception.
Its gods are not to be understood apart from that experience, as abstract, isolated entities. They have their
being in the action and outreaching of life itself.

God as Reality, inclusive and ideally evaluated, is

not to be thought of apart from that Reality. It is no more strange that religion should have this general term than that science should have the word "Nature," or that politics should speak of "World," or that philosophy should conceive the "Cosmos." If these are "concrete universals" may not God also be a concrete universal? Any universal is used to gather up facts and experiences into a system, to designate the system in which they are known to stand. It is therefore more than a class term, indicating a number of particulars. Such a universal means an organization of factors into a whole. Thus "city" signifies more than "men," for a city presents associations of men in certain relations, geographical, political, and economic. The term God expresses order and purpose and moral values in the great Reality which we call Life or the World. Reality conceived as friendly, as furnishing support for man's existence and for the realization of ideal ends, is God.

Accordingly God is used as the standard of reference for the adequacy of specific ideals. When a line of conduct is considered, the question arises for the religious man as to whether such conduct is consistent with loyalty to God. Is it God-like?

The scientist assumes the orderliness of nature; he studies the facts of given types of phenomena; he makes discoveries of their behavior; and regards his experiments and formulas as having general validity. Further investigation may require changes in his conception of the particulars and of the totality with which he is dealing, but his work has significance for him only as it is felt by him to be factual and real in reference to the nature of things. He does not discard his method

of scientific inquiry when he discovers errors or necessary corrections; he reinterprets them and thinks of his
new procedure as better because it is more consistent
with the entire order with which he deals. Man has
always had the problem of maintaining his life and
widening his control of the world. He is urged on to
this by the conflicts which he feels, by the pain and
hunger of his unsatisfied nature. The adjustments
which he makes are rough and loose, but they bring
some measure of satisfaction. It is satisfaction which
man seeks, and this is often obtained in some degree
without the solution of all the theoretical questions.
In practical life, which is the matrix and comprehending
sphere of all his life, he goes on by activities based upon
habit and partial experience, making such new adjustments as he must, and understanding the process as
much as the exigencies of his situation and his ability
allow. His securing and appropriating of food do not
wait upon his solving all the mysteries of chemistry;
his establishment of society antedates political science,
however much this may be used as the development of
society continues; and his religion flourishes and grows
prior to anthropologists and psychologists. If the
growth of the sciences gives aid to practical living in
improving the food supply, and in managing society, so
it may conceivably modify and enhance religious activities. Scientific knowledge undoubtedly tends to
destroy superstition and to chasten whatever it touches,
but it is not the source of human action nor the deter-
miner of all values. It is only on the assumption that
religion is all error or superstition that science becomes
its antagonist and destroyer. When religion is con-

ceived as the fullest and the richest way of living, science may be seen to be a method of solving problems and smoothing the way to that more effective living. God is used as the "frame of reference" in religious thinking. He it is who sees everything, who holds everything in his hand, who rules all the forces of the world. Such a frame of reference is in principle characteristic of all thought. All particular numbers are given their place in a series; all moments belong to time; all spaces fit into wider spaces and they into inclusive space; parts imply wholes; change is unthinkable except in relation to permanence; and qualities demand substance. This does not mean that thought is completed in these directions, but the mind does tend to project this larger frame and to endeavor to place things in some system and setting.

It is the same in any type of thinking and practical interest. In reasoning, men seek a procedure which validates their arguments. They appeal at last to the nature of reason, to the law of contradiction, or to the sufficient law of reason. They cling to the conviction that there is a measure for the true and the false, if they delve deep enough or carry the reasoning far enough. There is a body of principles or customs which is their ultimate appeal, a ground and basic condition of right and fruitful thinking. They make no apologies for this assumption but regard it as elementary and inescapable in any consequential reflection.

Moral concerns are treated in the same manner. Kant's dictum, "So act that the maxim of your deed may become a universal law," expresses this craving for the substantiation of individual conduct by a law or principle which includes and supports it. Only then does it become authoritative and commanding. Merely subjective impulses or chaotic actions have no moral significance. Only when they are made the subject of thoughtful, conscientious consideration, and put into adequate perspective, do they gain moral worth and justification. Duty is a social product and belongs to social order. It is the frame and structure of conduct to which, under some name, specific acts are referred. This is the way the religious man uses God. God is the judge, the umpire, the referee. Only by such an objective standard and guide is it possible to gain the sense of the relation of things. The formulation of custom into law provides a generalized expression of experience by which particular acts may be judged, and this law is conceived as the will or thought of the divine mind.

God has been used as one who gathers into himself the accumulated experience of life. To the Hebrew prophets he was the all-comprehending being in whom the wisdom of ages was contained. Like a great person seeing the whole panorama of life from the first, he possessed knowledge of the operation of the forces of nature and the motives of man's spirit. One could find in him the counsel and guidance necessary for the best course of action. He was from of old, had witnessed the cycles of life, and knew the ways which lead to satisfaction, and those which lead to defeat and destruction. His word was therefore a lamp to the feet and a guide to the steps of man. That man was truly wise who listened to this greater wisdom, and was willing to put his problems under its light. God was like a high tower from

which a wider survey could be made; he was like the sun
which illuminates all things; like the wide-spreading
heavens under which everything had its place and
where its meaning and outcome became clear.

God could not be deceived by appearances, by superficial show, or by passions and fleeting desires. Man's
life is but a day, while the life of God is the compass
of the years. A thousand years in his sight is but as
yesterday when it is past and as a watch in the night.
The life of God was made commensurate with the whole
of time, and his domain was the whole extent of space.
Man stood in relation to God as a little part in relation
to the comprehending whole. The thought of God was
the measure and rule for human conduct.

The natural tendency, in a society where the idea of
an anthropomorphic God has arisen, is to deal with him
as a great person without critical reflection upon the
precise form or logical validity of the idea. He is represented as the creator and controller of the world, as
the giver of life and of all things needful. Men feel
themselves in direct relation to him, able to converse
with him, and to deal with him quite as with a human
companion. He is used as the source of power and
comfort, as a refuge from evil, and as an ally for good
and the foe of harm. Men pray to him for individual
benefits, for health, for food, and for success in all
their enterprises. They seek his aid against untoward
forces of nature, against drouth and pestilence, against
depression and loneliness. Nothing is too small or too
great to be the occasion of appeal and petition. This
experience is variable. For some persons it is the habitual and continuous attitude, and there is the constant

consciousness of "the presence of God." With others it becomes defined in times of stress and pressure. Persons like Lincoln, carrying great burdens in the midst of conflicting advice, in the strain of many cross-currents, in perplexity and uncertainty of the best path to follow, may become habituated to dependence upon God as an ever present companion with whom there is the sense of vital and intimate communication. Many men, forced to decide issues of life and death for a cause, feel isolated and solitary, and gain strength for their duties in this alliance with God.

In such instances there may be little reflection upon the nature and existence of God, but there is the feeling of his immediate presence and help. There is comfort in this shared responsibility, in the sense that the agent does not assume to rely merely upon his own judgment. An element of resignation enters in and, if the issue of action is not apparently propitious, it is felt that God has some better thing in store and works in his own way. At a later time it will become clear that the conscious and seemingly wise course was not after all the one which would have brought the best results.

The history of religion shows that the conception of God has been subject to constant reinterpretation, but the tendency has been to attribute change to the mind and will of man alone. It is said that man achieves progressive insight into the nature and will of God, while God himself remains unchanged and changeless. It is not difficult to understand the ground of the appeal of that conception, for religion is so bound up with a sense of the absolute that it is felt that there could be no validity for the moral and spiritual ideals of life

unless they were guaranteed by a transcendent changeless order. Here the practical absolute required in all
crucially important conduct is carried over into metaphysical terms. But such a view has been beset by
practical consequences, often direful and deadening.
Not only is it apt to be assumed that God exists in an
untroubled realm of perfection, but that he may also be
trusted to exercise his power, in his own good time, to
fulfil his perfect will among men. August theologies
have been built upon that assumption, and their influence has sometimes eventuated in an attitude of complete dependence and patient waiting on the part of
religious people. They say, "His ways are not our
ways," and surrender to the conviction of the helplessness and impotence of man.

The "Crisis Theology" in Germany, since the war,
seems to be precisely of this character.[2] The works of
man are so insignificant, so lacking in wisdom, so constantly frustrated, that the function of religion becomes
that of teaching humility and patient acceptance of
events. Man's religious duty is to love God and trust
him unquestioningly. But it is possible that this theology is itself founded upon war psychology. At such
times the best of men's endeavors do indeed seem futile and empty. Measured by human estimates, everything human and earthly is thrown into confusion, and
the fairest dreams of social order and progress are
rudely destroyed. The lesson of these disasters seems
to be not to trust human intelligence, and not to hope
that man is able to make plans for a better society which

[2] S. V. McCasland, "The Crisis Movement in Present German Theology," *Crozer Quarterly*, January, 1928.

can be realized in such a world as this. The wisdom of man is foolishness with God.

Quite a different evaluation of human effort is possible upon an empirical basis. In specific lines of effort it may be held that man has reason to believe that his knowledge and labor have some honor and significance in this precarious world. If an interest like that of traveling from place to place is considered, it is possible to show that progress has been made. There is a vast difference between going on foot through trackless jungles and wastes and riding upon a horse, or by train, or by airplane. Improvements have been made in so many fields that it is not necessary to argue the point when stated in terms of specific ends. The world is sufficiently supporting and consistent to enable man to adapt himself to nature, and nature to his ends, enough to accomplish things which are marvelous in comparison with earlier stages of culture.

Corresponding claims may be defended with reference to moral attitudes, such as sympathy and good will. These have been extended from the limits of the little family or clan group to the immense areas of national and international relations. Enlightened men of all nations have more understanding. They assist each other by interchange of scientific knowledge, through trade and personal contacts more than ever before. International treaties have prevented some wars, even if they have not been equal yet to the entire abolition of war. For the fulfilment of the greatest hopes of man, there are elicited not only tireless energy, but also an appreciation of the vast length of time stretching before the race in which to gain such great ends.

The natural scientists, and now more than ever the social scientists, work at their tasks with increasing confidence that, though small in relation to the possibilities, their results are important, and their methods fruitful.

It is this sense of ability to discover truths about the processes of life, and in a measure to control them, which develops a new religious faith in life. When the great prophets of Israel gained new insight into the need of greater justice and righteousness among men, they attributed their insight to a revelation from heaven. Nor did they hesitate to identify their new social idealism with the will of God. They frankly declared that God had become weary of animal sacrifices and no longer required them. Jesus set aside many things which had been accepted for generations as the will of God and introduced what he felt to be simpler and nobler attitudes as the present will of God. Biblical writers conceived the character of God as more flexible and modifiable than some later theologians have done. The God of the prophets repented himself of evil and changed his mind and his methods in the light of experience. This appears in the story of the hardening of Pharaoh's heart and in the idea that "the prayer of a righteous man availeth much."

Religion is not always set in terms of surrender and dependence. Jacob "wrestled with God" and prevailed, and the Apostle Paul regarded himself and his followers as "co-workers together with God." The assumption was that much depended upon them. If they were faithful and in earnest, the kingdom of heaven could be realized faster and more adequately. God was thought

of as "the Lord of Hosts," a "Captain," a "Leader," a
"King" whose rule rested upon the fidelity and ability
of his subjects. So much was the life of God inwrought
with the lives of his people that they determined the
success or failure of his cause. This conception of a
"struggling God" is very old and very deep in the traditions of many religions. He is one who cannot win
his battles without armies of men, or without faith in
the hearts of his people.

It is not surprising that there is not entire consistency
in the conception of God. As Professor Fite asserts,
it is a vague idea, like the idea of human personality.[3]
Personality is a moving, changing form of reality, with
varying degrees of stability. Divine persons are not
exempt. In some relations they appear fixed and secure but in others they are incalculable, and uncertain
of attaining their ends. There is a tendency to put all
the permanence of the world on the side of God, and
all the change and variation on the side of man, but
this is quite gratuitous. If we secure our idea of God
by generalizing our observed and experienced living, we
see that it is everywhere marked by this double aspect.
It is at once both fixed and changing, like a river in
its course. We say the river is the same, that it is there
in its course from year to year, but we also say that the
river is running to the sea. The changes are not only
changes in the observer, but they are real changes in
the river itself, and they are changes in reality. The
world itself does not remain static, but moves throughout all observed parts of it in the flux and rhythm of
seasons and of sidereal cycles. Yet, like the revolv-

[3] Warner Fite, *Moral Philosophy*, p. 292.

ing earth, in relation to some things, it is stable and at rest.

Here again, the introduction of the concept of change is set in a context of emotional conditionings which seems to make it inapplicable to God. One reason for this is the assumption that change is in itself evil, and must lead to worse as well as to better conditions. It is at this point that a limit is reached in the reality idealized, for it is impossible to idealize that which is by definition bad. The very idea of evil is of that which is in conflict with itself and cannot be reconciled and harmonized. The quest for God as an intellectual possession is for a view of the world which can be to some extent rationalized and unified. When thus possessed, God may also be more effectively used in practical living and in æsthetic satisfaction.

CHAPTER XIII

MYSTICISM'S QUEST FOR GOD

Mysticism is one of the commonest and vaguest terms in religious nomenclature. It began to be used before exact definition was so much esteemed, and it was employed by those who did not attach importance to that careful thinking without which definition is impossible. The word has come to mean the doctrine that through feeling man experiences union with God. Mysticism claims that some individuals have reached a beatific state of rapport with God, the infinite, supreme Reality. This is an ineffable experience, beyond description. One who has experienced it can only give some hints of what it was by use of the poor analogies of human love and æsthetic ecstasy. According to this doctrine, it is an experience of the highest value affording intense satisfaction, but there is no known method by which it may be induced. One may seek for it most sincerely, through long years of self-discipline and effort, without being granted the coveted reward. Again, it may be reached by some humble soul quite unexpectedly, without such struggle. The mystics do recommend practices and exercises which have been employed by some who have reached the goal, and these are offered to aspiring souls without assurance that they will bring the result sought. It is part of the doctrine of mysticism that the reality with which one seems to be in union, during the ecstatic moments, is the divine Being, though it is also insisted that there is no means of proving to others that the being so found is really God. All of these features of mysticism show that it is, as it takes pride in being, a non-rational, emotional experience, which claims to be the highest form of religious experience.

Light is thrown upon the general nature of mysticism by noting the conditions under which it has been cultivated. Its earliest forms were in connection with cult ceremonials where, by drinking liquor, by exciting emotion through dancing, and ritualistic observances, the participants became stimulated into trances, visions, and various strange seizures and automatisms. These effects were attributed to the divinity in whose honor the rites were performed, and who was thought to be imparted to the participants as the ceremonies proceeded. To the primitive mind, such "possession" was evidence of the presence of the god, and the recipient of such favors was felt to be superior to his fellows. All religions have at times exalted such practices, and have attached unusual importance to the individuals who were most susceptible to their effects.

Modern psychological analysis of these phenomena makes possible a more careful description of them, and furnishes the means for some explanation of them. There can be no denial of the existence of such states, the evidence for them is abundant in all religions. But the more knowledge obtained concerning the nature of these states the more doubt is thrown upon the claims of mysticism. It is possible, therefore, for one to accept the fact of what may be called the mystical quality in experience, without accepting the doctrine of the *ism.* (We may acknowledge the factual nature of the mystic's states, without accepting his explanation of their origin or meaning.)

Description of the states has been given by the subjects of them. Professor James concluded that these states were passive, ineffable, transient, and noetic. Other terms may be used to describe them. The mystical state is involuntary in its onset and persistence. The subject of it may endeavor to put himself in a mood for it, but he can have no assurance that he will be successful. Many mystics report that they have prayed ardently, and through long vigils, without attaining the wished-for result. When the illumination or ecstasy does occur, it is felt as something given, something bestowed from an outside power. Throughout primitive society such phenomena—seizures, intoxications, manias, dreams, hallucinations, obsessions—were regarded as the work of spirits or divinities. In the light of modern psychology the causes of these states are sufficiently known to make it evident that they arise from secondary causes, from the state of the nerves or the blood, from fatigue or shock or prolonged fixation of attention.

The mystical state is intensely emotional, and is beyond the possibility of adequate description or communication by the subject of it. It is never possible to translate a vivid state of feeling into satisfactory scientific description. There is always something left over, unexpressed. The mystics are to a degree right in asserting that their ecstasies are indescribable. They have had unutterable transports and have seen and heard things they cannot tell. To this extent their

cherished experiences are individualistic, because they
are subjective, occurring for themselves alone. Such
moments are also transient and swiftly passing.

The vision or exaltation, whatever the imagery, is
pleasurable. It may be so intense as to be overwhelming and exhausting, and in a way pleasurably painful;
as the attainment of what has been anxiously sought, it
is satisfying and compensating. The mystic feels himself to be in union with reality, his striving is fulfilled,
his world is made harmonious and complete. The conflicts and complexities of ordinary life are swept away
and the Whole, the Unity of all things, seems realized.
It is the attainment of a height at which diversities and
discords are overcome, where all things flow together
in harmony and power. The tapestry of the vast world
is suddenly reversed, the seamy side is turned under
and a beautiful pattern is thrust up into view. Many
figures of speech are used by the mystics in their endeavor to convey their feeling. They have gained "illumination," they are enfolded in the "divine embrace,"
they have attained "spiritual marriage," they have
found "peace." At times they designate this as "cosmic consciousness" and believe themselves at one with
the universe. For the time being they have achieved
"adjustment to the total environment." They are "carried out of themselves." In all this there is abundant
mystery. That is, the whys and the wherefores of
such states are not clear. William James, great psychologist that he was, had to admit after a very fruitful discussion of the association of ideas, that when it
came to a complete and final answer, introspective psychology is compelled to "throw up the sponge." No

scientist of repute claims to know all there is to know about the phenomena with which he is most familiar. The physicist knows much about light but he still has unanswered questions about it. So has he about electricity, and gravitation, and the atom. The mystery of the mystic is partly a matter of the vividness of feeling, the sense of the freshness and vividness of a repeated, yet still strange, experience. There is a pleasing sense of the taste and of the general physical enjoyment in the repeated appropriation of food. This element of novelty in familiar and commonplace habits arises from the hungers of the organism. The saying that "hunger is the best cook" illustrates the dependence of novelty and freshness of feeling upon the state of the organism. Vividness of emotional response is often so acute that it seems strange and suffuses common things with glowing warmth and witchery. Thus old things may become new.

While admitting that the mystics have these involuntary, satisfying, illuminating moments, it is also true that all other persons of normal emotional experience have them in degree in some forms of action and thought. They are not distinctive of mystics. They belong to religious persons, artists, and plain people who know nothing of mysticism, and to those who do not classify themselves as mystics when they fully understand the term. In fact the characteristics named are familiar in common emotional states. (If the term mystical is to be retained at all, it must be allowed that there is a "mystical quality" in much normal experience.) The odor of a rose may awaken suddenly associations which suffuse the whole being with pleasure

and vibrant expectancy. Odors are peculiarly powerful in this way, the odor of new-mown hay, of lilacs,
of rain after a hot day, of salt sea air, of the timber
frame of an old house, of fire on the hearth.

When a person is not given to psychological analysis
he is likely to misjudge the nature of many experiences.
Hallucinations are often so intense that the subject cannot believe he did not have a real perception of an object actually present before him. It may be that there
has been but a single such hallucination in the whole
life-history, yet it may appear to have indubitable validity. The force of habitual attitudes makes a basis
for this mystical quality.

The recurrence of scenes, memories of places or people, may induce vivid emotional states, and make one
feel that something more than natural phenomena is involved. The emotional reaction seems to the subject
of it quite out of proportion to the recognized occasion
of it. It is due to this difference that the mystic is not
satisfied with dry scientific explanations of the phenomena. He feels that the analysis is woefully short of
the experience, and is inclined to posit some presence
or power beyond the matter-of-fact formulas.

It is from this that the alleged "noetic" character of
mystical states derives. A rare emotional state is so
impressive, so overwhelming, that it is regarded as carrying its own validation. It is not uncommon to confuse feeling intensely with knowing surely. Familiarity
with conditions may afford no intelligible causes for so
great an emotional experience, or at least none which
seem to the subject at all adequate. The doctrine of
mysticism has persistently insisted upon a theory of

such experiences which blinds mystics to the plain facts. This theory is that the sense world is itself unreal and cannot be the source of great moods. If a strain of music puts a person into a state of ecstasy, the assumption is that there is some greater and perhaps occult power at work. The ability of human beings to disregard what science shows to be the real causes of emotional states has a long history, and abundant contemporaneous illustration. Mysticism persists in its interpretation and denies the possibility of any explanation, but the psychology of emotion makes it possible to relate very great moods to seemingly small occasions.

The doctrine of mysticism deals with the phenomena of sensuous and rational experience in a way quite antithetic to that employed by modern psychology. It begins with the assumption that the physical aspects of life are inferior and spiritually indifferent or dangerous, whereas science seeks to take into account all factors whatever they may be, and to recognize any influence they are shown to exert. It is impossible to measure the hindrance to fruitful inquiry which has arisen from this presupposition and prejudice. Since it is assumed that the natural, describable phases of a situation have nothing to do with its meaning or outcome, it is held to be futile to take them into account. When, as the doctrine of mysticism teaches, the meaning of events has to be sought in the non-rational and unintelligible, all incentive to rational inquiry is foiled before it can begin. The mystics declare a taboo against such inquiry—not because it has been proved useless or harmful, but simply because it is contrary to the procedure enjoined by the tradition of mysticism.

It has been said that the knowledge of man is vain, and only a weariness of the flesh. The most devout souls have been represented as those who "hear and obey," and do not reason or inquire. The exercises of religion were early set in the form of ceremonials and practices which were commanded by custom. Thinking raises questions, and that is disturbing to the practical order and to the execution of the transmitted mores of the group. Socrates was regarded as impious and dangerous because he insisted upon asking questions, especially of the youth. He was thought to be a corrupter of the young and a disbeliever in the gods; he was a seditious fellow in the state, an enemy of the established order. So long as religion is thought of as something wholly supersensuous and irrational, it must be left in the realm of formal practices and of emotion. Whenever it begins to court understanding it appears to traditionalists to become confused, to lose its authority, and to succumb to the wavering and uncertain methods and conclusions of reflective thought.

The doctrine of mysticism has its stronghold in the view that knowledge, being partial and limited, only obscures and misrepresents what it deals with. This position is often shared by scientists themselves. They say that with all their knowledge of the phenomena of light they do not know what light is. They experience it, see its colors and the refractions which define objects; they measure its speed and analyze it through the spectrum, yet do not know light as it is in itself. What they mean by "light in itself" they can never explain except in the negative terms of denying that it is what they see and measure. This is a long-standing

fallacy in human thought and it is the main weakness
of the doctrine of mysticism.) If it is assumed that all
we know belongs to accidents and secondary aspects,
then the original and essential thing must ever elude
our minds. But why assume that what we know, and
can verify in use and control, is accidental and unreal?

Applying this view to God, the mystics refuse to
identify him in any way with the characteristics which
the world displays, except in terms of forces and laws
which may emanate from God but do not actually reveal him. If the experienced qualities of light do not
really show us anything of what light is, then how can
the various aspects of nature and human life be regarded as disclosing God? There seems to be no way
to avoid that conclusion, starting from that presupposition. It is not impossible to assume the opposite
point of view, namely, that what we experience is real
in its setting and context, and that experience discloses
in its own way the nature of the world and of God.
Everything is known to some extent and truly in the
functions which it sustains and the relations it main-
tains. An object is defined by its limitations as well
as by its uses. What it evidently is not is important
in determining what it is. The evils of life are judged
to be such in reference to the good. What is called
evil is a negative statement of what is good, and the
fact that evil is not directly included in God shows that
God is identified with the good. The difficulty in this
matter, especially in the field of religion, is complicated
by powerful emotional reactions. Religion has been
steeped in mystery so long, and identified with the unknown and the unknowable and the unnatural (often

called the supernatural) to such an extent that the
slightest suggestion of the possibility of dealing with
it by any rational and matter-of-fact method is revolting. Some religious groups train their adherents from
childhood against any inquiry into religion, and insist
that obedient acceptance of the attitudes and doctrines
of an authoritative system is the only allowable course.
So-called instruction with them is dogmatic affirmation
and repetition of the formulated beliefs. A kind of
fear-complex is developed against any investigation or
discussion of religious problems. Mystics have appeared within ecclesiastical systems of this kind.

It is possible to prevent intelligent and fruitful discussion by discounting the results of study. Without
prohibiting inquiry, it may be made to seem useless and
wasteful, as compared with the highly emotional experiences of reverie and action. Much prescribed
"meditation" is simply memorizing devotional literature and the unthinking repetition of sayings of the
authorities. Science would not be greatly advanced if
youth were taught only to commit to memory, and to
recite on occasion, the formulas and the results which
scientific leaders have authorized. The word science
is sometimes used for systems that are essentially of
that kind. In them there is no free, first-hand consideration of actual facts of experience, no experimentation,
no adventure of thought, no original problems. Everything is according to rule and in keeping with preconceived conclusions. While mystics have often been
rebels against the prevailing order of religion, and have
refreshed dull periods with pulsating life, yet they have
agreed in the position that knowledge is impotent to

find and report on supreme reality. It is this fact that makes them truly mystics in the historical and strict meaning of the word. This is the distinguishing doctrine of mysticism, the doctrine of the futility of knowledge to penetrate the real mysteries of life and afford access to the heart of reality; and the necessity of turning to feeling and direct action to reach its goal. This begets a patronizing attitude toward science and reason, and fortifies the assumption that those who busy themselves with these things are to be pitied like people who are handicapped with a kind of blindness in a world where there is so much to see.

Mysticism has separated the life of feeling from the life of reason, and chosen the former as superior to the latter. The effective criticism of mysticism is therefore to be found in the fundamental conception of modern psychology that there is no legitimate diremption between these aspects of mental life. Normal, productive experience is at once reflective and emotional. Reason gets its problems from the situations which produce practical and emotional conflicts, and the results of reflective thinking are significant only as they resolve those conflicts and free experience. The history of science shows how human wits have been quickened and sharpened in the search for solutions of difficulties which were distressing and disturbing. Hunting animals, sailing ships, building temples, elaborating language, have required attention to physical and social facts and to the invention of tools and devices for accomplishing desired ends. Likewise, man's craving for adjustment to the larger world of his hopes and dreams has given rise to knowledge of the history of his faith, of religious customs, and of the religious nature itself. Such knowledge has afforded deep satisfactions which have released the emotional life and given encouragement to further study. ⌈In scientific medicine, it is possible to see the union of knowledge and emotional satisfaction.⌉ The deliverance of a loved one from suffering and his recovery to happy living create appreciation of the value of scientific knowledge.

In religion the same relation is becoming apparent. Those who have become familiar with the Bible through literary criticism are as appreciative of its value for the religious life as are any who reject such study. The appreciation is doubtless of a different character but it is just as real and vital, and this is the point in question. The mystic claims a kind of exclusive experience of intense appreciation, but genuine appreciation is also found among those who take a very rational and scientific attitude. Similar evidence may be cited with reference to the conception of God, and the sense of union with him. There are many who find their critical ideas of God are more satisfying than were their earlier, naïve conceptions. They believe in God and "practice the presence of God." But they do not accept the doctrine of mysticism that one cannot find God through knowledge and thought. ⌈Their emotional life runs with their reasoning and not against it.⌋

If this emotional quality of all effective thinking and living is called the "mystical quality" in experience, then it is true that all adventurous and expanding living has this mystical quality, and there is justification for the view that all religion is mystical. Still it is doubtful whether even this use of the term is possible without misunderstanding. The devotees of mysticism are accustomed to insist that all religion is mysticism when it is only mystical. If the word mystical could be identified with the emotional quality, and released from its association with the doctrine of the futility of knowledge, it would be a serviceable term. At the present time all admissions of being mystical are likely to be interpreted as adherence to the doctrine of mysticism; and very often being religious is identified with the acceptance of a non-rational system of practice and belief. It is this fact which makes it so difficult to secure a fair hearing for the discussion of the question of the relation of science and religion. Those who regard religion as identical with mysticism cannot see any positive reconciliation between science and religion, whether they are themselves religious or not. Some who identify religion and mysticism regard this identification as indicative of the futility of religion, while others see in it the basis of reality in religion.

If the mystical quality of religious experience were considered apart from the specific doctrine of mysticism, many of the conflicting views would be resolved.[1] When once this position is adopted the way is open to recognize the mystical quality in a great variety of situations. Every event which has vital and pleasurable meaning becomes mystical in this sense. It brings a feeling of harmony, of union, of expansion, and of mystery. Different people will react in different ways, but many will find this quality in common occurrences, in

[1] See my article, "The Mystics: Their Experience and Their Doctrine," *Proceedings of the Sixth International Congress of Philosophy,* 1926, p. 115, where the mystical experience is distinguished from the doctrine of mysticism.

the sight of fresh, drifting snow; in crystals of sleet on trees and shrubs; in the odor of newly turned ground in spring; in the song of the robin, the cooing of doves, the feel of down, or the soft warm flesh of a child. These are sensuous experiences, but the quality may also be found in the performance or contemplation of effective and masterful action. A fleet runner in a race, a performer on a trapeze, a skilful wood-carver or sculptor, a ballet dancer—each moves with ease and power in the execution of his part, and the spectator participates in the feeling of mastery and grace. In the field of science this quality is often in evidence, in the delicacy and marvels of the phenomena of nature, in the swift motion of light and its long journey to earth from a distant star, in the wonderful velocity of electrons in an atom, in the growth of plants from the seed, in the working of the Mendelian law of heredity. The same type of experience arises in the more abstract fields of mathematics and the pure sciences. The number forms, the unfolding of elaborate equations, the uses of logarithms, have implications, order, and structure which are of endless interest, mystery, and fruitfulness. Philosophical thought has this quality when it finds the meanings and the implications of experience. The very attempt to deal with the whole of reality, with the nature of mind and material things, with space, time, and cause, sets the mind in an attitude of expectant inquiry which is often the preparation and condition of finding a mystical quality in the severest kind of logical and metaphysical thought. When one discovers a solving idea, a penetrating insight, or a productive working hypothesis, one gets a thrill which is of the essence of the mystical feeling.)

Nowhere is this phenomenon more frequent or intense than in social enterprises, in lodges, labor unions, corporations, learned societies, political conventions, patriotic celebrations, church assemblies. In each case those who know the situation most thoroughly and respond most sensitively to what is sought and intended are those to whom the experience is most genuinely mystical. When they feel the forces present in the committees and in the great representative gatherings, and see the movement of organized thought and energy toward a cherished ideal goal, the emotional release is apt to be of the most demonstrative character. When organizations like churches celebrate their anniversaries, dedicate a beautiful building, or promote some worthy and unselfish cause, they are permeated with stirring moods of power and mystical alliance with the deep forces of life.

All æsthetic experiences, all romance, all love motifs, all successful satisfaction of ideal ends, possess this mystical quality. It is a fundamental and natural aspect of zestful and sensitive living. Some individuals have more capacity for it than others, and it is manifested in different ways, but in some line of interest, in some field of achievement every normal person finds a degree of this wistful, releasing, elixir of life.

An interesting view of the whole problem of mysticism is that now designated as "the milder mysticism." [2] The effort is made to distinguish the defensible and

[2] J. B. Pratt, *The Religious Consciousness,* p. 339.

desirable forms of religious experience from the more extreme pathological forms. From this milder mysticism there is absent the kind of phenomena which were so much in evidence in the older type. Little importance is attached to visions, voices, trances, hallucinations, and the like. These mild mystics live quite normal lives, eating and drinking and guarding their health, instead of keeping vigils, emaciating themselves, and practicing all kinds of hair-shirt and spike-bed exercises. They live comfortably but earnestly in this present world. They appear so sane and so much like nonmystical persons that they would not be recognized as mystics if they did not insist that they are such.

Professor Pratt gives a number of instances of such experiences, and admits that they are not easily described in mystical terms to an extent which clearly differentiates them. One person says: "I have experienced God's presence so that I felt the lack of nothing and feared nothing. It is hard to describe the feeling, but everything seems bright and clear ahead, and I feel as if I had the support of some great unimpeachable authority behind me for everything I may do then. It feels as though I were not standing alone." Pratt adds: "It is extremely seldom that a mystic of this milder type gives or even attempts to give a detailed and exact description of his experience. There are several obvious reasons for this. One is that the mystic is not usually interested in exact description and never thinks of taking the psychological point of view. Poor introspection on the part of many is another reason. Most fundamental of all is the fact that exact psychological description of an emotional experience must necessarily

be in sensuous terms, while the mystic often feels that
sensuous terms are unworthy to be applied to his purely
'spiritual' experience."

Some, like St. Augustine, recognize the sensuous elements but call them by figurative names, speaking not
of light, sound, and fragrance, but of "a certain kind
of light and a certain kind of sound, and a certain kind
of fragrance and food and embracement." Only a little
psychology is needed to see that the sensuous experiences are still present and but thinly disguised. This is
true to a much greater extent with the typical mystics.
They describe with the utmost detail their intense sensuous experiences, but insist that their words are in
reality only "figurative."

Professor Pratt goes on to show that the mystical
experience is essentially an emotional experience, and
that what is said of the mystical quality is said also of
the emotional states. They are ineffable; they have an
expansive quality and suggest the "Beyond" that is a
wider possible range of experience, something more. It
would seem from this that the milder mysticism is just
an equivalent of pleasurable, welcome, and mysterious
qualities of tender emotions and their concomitants.
No one need doubt that the mystics are religious persons or that their emotional states are very real, but
that is quite a different matter from ascribing to them
peculiar powers of access to the divine nature of reality. In the meaning of Professor Pratt every religious
person might claim mystical experiences, but no one
need regard himself on that account especially favored
or peculiar. Well-rationalized forms of religion yield
this quality, and it is not necessary to deny the natu-

ralness or the intelligibility of the experience in order
to accept it as mystical in the sense indicated. An appreciation of this fact would allow religion to be a matter of normal experience and would make it clear that
in normal experience there is what may be called a mystical quality. The studies of Professor Leuba and others have identified this quality in æsthetic, scientific, and
practical life, and have thereby placed these phenomena within the normal life of man.

CHAPTER XIV

PRAYER

The common conception assumes that prayer implies on the part of one who prays an idea of a personal God to whom prayer is directed. Such an idea may be present, but to assume that it necessarily is present overlooks those types of religion which lack a clear idea of a personal God and yet employ prayer. Such, for example, are many early cults which have not risen to any definite conception of personality. Such is the case with the ancient and far-spread religion of Buddhism, in which the notion of personality is rejected as inapplicable to supreme reality, yet prayer abounds in this religion. There are forms of pantheism in the western world that deny personality to God, yet practice prayer. Many mystics have done this; they have thought of God as transcending any forms of personality that we know and yet they have been ardent in the use of prayer.

Modern psychology throws light upon these facts.[1] In connection with studies of language and the reflex, impulsive types of expression, a new point of view has become possible which resolves this seeming paradox. Human beings are naturally expressive, and they are from birth bound up with a social situation. They could not survive helpless infancy were it not for being carried and nourished in the embrace of an adult group.

[1] Cf. Ames, *Psychology of Religious Experience.* Ch. VIII, "Prayer."

These human beings are constantly using signs, gestures, and sounds, in their interaction with one another. "Significant symbols" come to be used habitually and without consciousness of them as symbols. Not only the child but the whole tribe comes to employ speech without realizing that it is language, just as birds and dogs develop signs and signals without definite conceptions of them as instruments. At this stage spoken words are used without addressing them to "persons." It is a psychological fallacy to conclude that because at higher levels speech may involve reference to minds or persons it is necessarily so at all levels. The most sophisticated use of language is far more of a reflex, habitual activity than it is a reflective, conscious process.

Acts which secure responses are not always performed in order to get those results. The cries and calls of children may be just organic reactions, though they may secure needed attention. Much prattle goes on within the field of auto-stimulation and circular response. Similar processes may occur within groups of people, as in ceremonial chanting and dancing. To the observer, these may seem to indicate deliberate interactions, but to the participants they may be merely concerted, habitual performances, lacking in any clear ideational content. Chants and prayers of primitive peoples often have this character. It probably would be astonishing to discover how much of this verbal repetition occurs in modern ceremonies. It is well known that trains of words, as in droning songs or memorized lines of poetry, run themselves off in this mechanical fashion. They may contain forms of address, petition,

and appeal without the substance of conscious thought.
When it is remembered that in primitive life prayer
does not appear except within the total action of the
ceremonials, it is easier to understand how far below
the threshold of clear cognition the uttered words may
lie. This approach to the phenomena of prayer does
not imply an effort to reduce it all to this level, but it
affords an opportunity to gain a more comprehensive
understanding of all later stages.

The use of language gained by all normal human
beings through the social process in early childhood
conditions all mental processes to essentially a social
pattern. When the organism is isolated from physical
proximity to other organisms, mental images tend to
flow in the accustomed social channels. The individual
continues to talk. Under such circumstances we say he
"talks to himself," but it is more accurately descriptive
of what happens to say that he talks with persons present in memory or imagination. Social psychologists
maintain that each individual is a community of selves,
owing to the activity of imagination, and is able to represent himself to himself in a variety of "rôles." These
rôles are reflections of the social environment in which
the individual lives. They are taken over from other
persons, and the mind represents the individual to himself in the parts played by others. It is impossible to
isolate a man so that he is psychologically alone. There
is no real solitude possible for one who has once become
a person in the processes of social interaction.

Prayer, in its basic character, is this kind of conversation with another, but the "other" may be one of
these idealized selves. Often it is another, such as a

common object, fused into the life of the group—a totem, a revered ancestor, or whatever gods there be for them. So constantly and deeply are these objects bound up with the daily life of the group that they are easily stimuli and carriers of conversation, which is prayer. Some of these objects become so symbolic of the group, and of the social selves of the members, that they live vividly in imagination, and prayer-conversation goes on with them as habitually and naturally as with physically present members of society. In the more highly developed religions, where the attention of the group is centered upon an historic person, accepted as the representative of God, prayer is quite obviously communion with that symbolic person, or with God represented by this symbol. The literature of Christian prayer testifies abundantly to this psychological fact. Otherwise, why all the figures of saints, and of Christ, in Christian churches? Why also, all the prayers in the devotional literature of the church addressed to the apostles, to Mary, and to Jesus Christ? Prayer thus appears to be a normal and general form of conversation, due to the source and nature of man's mind, generated as it is in social intercourse. It is the inevitable result of his habit of speech, of "talking to himself" in thought. The nature of the "other" with which, or with whom, he talks, is determined by the level of social experience and by the character of the social group in which he lives.

Such analysis carries the experience of prayer into the psychological realm where it belongs, and thus saves it from being confused with some particular ritual or liturgy.

A man is not through with prayer just because he has discarded some familiar form of words, or some particular conception of deity. In the depths of his mind's dramatic action there persists a form of converse in which his actual self wrestles with the ideal nature that he projects into some Other. He may call it his conscience, his better self, or God, but he cannot escape it or eliminate it from his inner world. The precise form which dialogue takes depends upon the training and temperament of the person. In the usual churchly individual, it becomes the prayer of more or less formal petition, adoration, and communion, but in others it may be just the experience of meditation, day-dreaming, or conscious planning for the realization of a better self, or surrender to an objective, personal supreme Being.

In discussions of the effects of prayer, there has been so much tendency to consider its influence upon physical nature that the really fruitful phases of the problem are scarcely treated. The first questions are often with reference to the value of prayer in bringing rain, or making the ground yield its fruits, or restraining storms or disasters. Curing and controlling disease and determining success for an individual in business or sport lie very much in the same category, though obviously more complicated with personal effort. These questions are sharpened and hardened by the underlying assumption of a complete cleavage between the physical world and the world of persons. To defend the efficacy of prayer in such a universe would require the interaction of two distinct orders of reality which by definition cannot influence each other. But that is not the only possible conception of the relation of the world of persons and the world of things. The dominance of the physical sciences has given prominence to the outward, material aspect of experience, and has left the human, social phase secondary and almost unreal. Prayer therefore, as a mental and social attitude, seems at once impotent and futile. It becomes "subjective," and merely a play of fancy. With this approach, and its back-lying assumptions, there is nothing to be said for the reasonableness or efficacy of prayer. Such is undoubtedly the conclusion of many scientific men.

But if the phenomena are regarded from the side of the social process within which they occur, a very different conclusion may be reached. It might be said that the social interactions of the members of a college housed in buildings set upon a hill, would have no appreciable effect upon the hill, but yet it could not be denied that those interactions might be of the utmost consequence to the members of the school. No social experience of the individuals is negligible to them. The first place in which to look for effects of prayer is in the experience of those who practice it, and in terms of the foregoing discussion, those effects are very real and important. Prayer as here stated is the direction of thought and affection toward those ideal selves and persons that engage the attention of all idealistically impelled people. And there are few, if any, who escape this impulsion in normal associations with their fellows in work and school and community co-operation. It is scarcely necessary to argue the subjective effects of prayer, but it is important to appreciate their significance. The sense of communion with an ideal personality may strengthen one's morale; it may suggest useful ways of looking upon one's self or the tasks of the day; it may yield the sense of companionship that is so essential to joyous living.

A person is obviously a better member of society when he can maintain these traits. He is more likable, radiates more health and happiness, and helps others to accomplish their part in life more adequately. If prayer aids a man to maintain better control, to achieve relaxation, to think more clearly, to sustain courage and initiative, it is certain to have social consequences. These are objective, relative to him. They are not merely subjective and within the field of the individual's feeling or fancy. It is not difficult to show by following this line of thought that prayer has objective results in the world of nature. When men are moved by common purposes and plans they may transform the physical world about them to a great degree. If by prayer a common task is held before a company of people, the tendency is for that task to be undertaken. It would not therefore be absurd for a community such as the college upon the hill to pray for protection against fire, if they followed the impulse thus stimulated and provided the means for such protection.

It is significant that prayer is seldom conceived as the sole factor in accomplishing the ends sought in it. "Work and pray" is the injunction of enlightened religion. Even where enterprises claim to depend upon prayer, other influences are at work. The case is often cited of Mueller, who maintained orphanages in England by prayer. With hundreds of children in his institutions he would sometimes find the provisions nearly exhausted and no calculable source of supplies available, but always, he claimed, his prayers were answered in due time and the orphans fed. It was undoubtedly an impressive experience, but in appraising his system it is important to recognize that when the provisions came they came through human channels, and they came from those who knew that the orphanages were maintained by prayer and not by any budget system of the usual business-like kind. It does not seem to be impertinent to point out that it was widely known that the orphanages were maintained by prayer. That hundreds of little children were dependent upon these institutions for their very lives would make many sympathetic, devout people responsive to their needs. The spectacle of seeing them assigned to the influence of prayer would alone stir the religious enthusiasms of believers in prayer. They could not let such faith and trust fail. Therefore they answered the prayers by their generous gifts, not taking credit to themselves for their charity. Probably no more effective advertising plan could be imagined among people of such a religious faith than to make them believe that the enterprise was entirely dependent upon prayer to God. But it is also obvious that the plan could hardly have succeeded if no human being had been informed that the sole resource of the management was prayer! It might even be suggested that the experiment could only prove what it assumed to be its real support, if all contributions from human patrons had been declined! In reality God "heard" the prayers only as they were heard by men and women, and he answered them through human agencies.

Is there, then, any significant theory of prayer which also recognizes this mediation of human beings? Any satisfactory reply to such a question goes back to the problem of the relation between man and God. If God is conceived as reality, characterized by idealistic tendencies, and by the emergence of personality, then it is possible to see prayer as a real, vital, and intelligible experience. Such reality includes at least human intelligence, and in the sphere of that intelligence, hears and responds. The most realistic expression of prayer is that which occurs within the social group, as in a worshipping assembly, or in an earnest congregation of like-minded religionists. The prayers are indeed addressed to the deity, but to a deity felt to be present in the hearts of his devotees. Prayer, thus conceived, has something in common with an address made directly to the thought and feeling of those present, but it also has additional meaning. It is directed to that deeper nature which all share and in which they realize their profounder kinship. It is not so much in the form of speech intended to enlighten and convince others, but in the quest for a right attitude, for a more adequate point of view, for a submergence of selfish interests, for a clarifying and quickening of spirit. There is thus renewed the sense of the wider life, and greater movement, within which the deliberations and aspirations of the group are set. Nowhere is the sense of God more real and potent than in a company of devout souls sincerely seeking insight and guidance. God is surely found there, if anywhere, in the Spirit of the World, flowering in that Presence; in the Oversoul, brooding through those hearts attuned to noble purposes and endeavors. So long as man has a genuine, organic place in the order of reality, that order is marked by at least so much personality as man attains. To reject this medium on the ground that it is "merely human," and therefore not integral with the divine, is to reject the only means of establishing intelligible relations with God as conscious and personal. To forfeit this inter-action of individuals with God through the medium of the social group is to leave prayer in the realm of blank mystery or of meaningless words. Because of their un-willingness to recognize this relation between human beings and ultimate reality many have surrendered any rational meaning for prayer.

But with this starting point it is possible to under-stand and to justify other phases of the experience. It lays a basis for the sense of a personal relation to the whole order of nature. Nature, being now inclusive of known and experienced intelligence, becomes an object with which the individual may communicate, and to-ward which it is possible to feel the attitudes of inti-mate and tender relationships that are so vital to reli-gious moods. Divorced from man, poetic moods may be set up in fancy, somewhat after the manner of Wordsworth, but they are always liable to disillusion-ment from recognizing the artifice. It is easier to take a social attitude toward a house which is warm with the presence and activity of a family who reside in it than toward a building that has not the association of living human beings. Or, taking an illustration still more per-tinent, nature viewed as the physical organism in which the life of thought and feeling exist inherently is more appealing than nature conceived as mere rocks and weather. Disspirited nature, as compared with inspirited nature, gives little scope for prayer. Nature, credited with the actual possession of the spirit of man, is far more consistent with the exercise of prayer than nature truncated below the human level.

Prayer is the expression of the sense of being at home in the universe, and the expression of this sense strengthens and enhances it. One of the deepest elements of religion is this at-homeness, what Schleiermacher called the feeling of dependence, of surrender, and of adjustment. It is through the warmth of association with one's fellows that this harmony is most readily achieved. When this is felt, the tides of outward fortune, of physical distress, have little power; but when this is lacking no outward comfort compensates for its loss. Colonel Younghusband recounts an experience in Tibet, where he had gone as the representative of the British government. He was desperately ill and in his suffering came to have a sense of the divine significance of the circle of nurses and doctors by whom he was sustained. God was present to him through their sympathy and care.

We have seen that prayer is a natural expression of the human spirit. It is not destroyed by atheistic views of the world. Man would still continue to talk to, and reason with, an impersonal world just as he now unbosoms himself to mountains and rocks and oceans in the poetic outpourings of his soul. But there is more than this impulse to express himself in the prayers of man. They are really in relation to a world that has intelligent, responsive persons in it. Summing up known reality in terms of its inclusive Being, as it is natural for man to endeavor to do, he is not misled by attributing to that reality personality such as he knows in himself and other persons. This indubitable fact adds meaning and conviction to his prayers, and enables him to derive help from them.

It is impossible to measure the force of prayer in the universe, precisely as it is not given to any man to know the force or influence of the words he speaks. What he says in secret may be heralded from the housetops. (Conversation with a friend may carry molding power that runs beyond any limits that men can see. (The words men utter in prayer have not only a reflex effect, but they have moving and directive power in other hearts and in widening circles of unknown range. No deed of a man is limited to the instant and to the sphere within which it originates. It may have an indefinitely great magnitude of power and force within the sphere of known and of unknown events.)

There is an elevating effect in sincere prayer that is proportionate to the moral dignity and worth of a man's conception of God. The more adequate and impressive the God men cherish, the more uplifting and purifying is their communion with him. Prayer is a genuine experience of communion, it involves a rapport between man and God, bringing man into the presence of the highest and best that he is able to conceive. This is an elevating and ennobling experience. Meeting an exceptionally great and fine human being has something of this value. It tones up a person's thought and feeling, and widens his perspective; it deepens his sense of the value and the meaning of life, and fills it with the glow of something vastly beautiful and satisfying. People affect us according to our estimates of their character and spirit. Some inhibit and antagonize us; others release and relax us. How a man feels at the thought of being alone with God is an index to his conception of God. If he attributes to the divine being sympathetic understanding, generous friendliness, interesting fullness and novelty of personality, he will be refreshed and find strength in the most intimate companionship with God.

Prayer is far more than any form of words or conscious thoughts, although it may employ these. It is an attitude, a habit, a disposition in which is sought the fullest possible participation in that larger reality into which all significant thought and action radiate. Professor Wieman uses the word "adjustment." He says: "To worship is to turn one's whole attention to this present, ultimate, sustaining condition of human life called God, with all the fullness of attainment which is to be achieved through right adjustment to him. The religious man is stirred with this vision, is given assurance and peace by it, is inspired by it to reconstruct our human way of living with respect to personal habits, social organization, and intellectual, artistic, æsthetic, and moral endeavors, to the end of making those adjustments which will enable God to fill our lives with the good which may be ours." [2]

[2] H. N. Wieman, *The Wrestle of Religion with Truth*, p. 131.

CHAPTER XV

DEATH AND THE FUTURE

One of the most striking changes in religious thought and feeling during recent times is a new attitude toward death. It is no longer thought of as the result of Adam's sin, nor as a special judgment of God, but as the consequence of natural causes such as the disintegrating effects of old age. The most virtuous and the viciously wicked finally reach the grave. Even where individuals escape the ravages of disease, violence, and accident, they eventually pass from this mortal life. Though some scientists may see possibilities of prolonging the normal span of physical existence to one hundred and twenty years, there is no reasonable hope of avoiding indefinitely the breaking down of the body. Nor is it believed that at any time, in any race, men ever did live for hundreds of years. The average longevity has been greatly extended in the last half century, largely through the reduction of infant mortality, and through the development of hygiene, medicine, and surgery, but the end comes to all at last. Insurance companies bring home to all classes knowledge of the life-expectancy and seek to instil practical attitudes concerning it. Religious ceremonials for the deceased have been attuned to more restrained and rational views, celebrating with greater dignity and appreciation the meaning of the individual's life and his experience of the common destiny. It is recognized that man

is subject to the natural cycle of all living things, and
the meaning of life is sought in the spirit and manner
of it rather than in length of days. The greatest possible longevity is sought, but it is the quality and character of personality which makes this effort significant.

Much of the terror of death for the individual has
been removed by realization of the fact that nature
often softens the final act of the human drama, bringing unconsciousness quickly, or gradually and gently
inducing the quiet of sleep. The agonies of death are
experienced more in anticipation than in the event, and
more by the watchers than by the subject himself. Not
infrequently the end comes like a welcome release from
suffering, and like deep peace after hard struggle. The
pathetic imagery which has centered about death has
given way to saner emotions, and even to the triumphant naturalism of the poetry of Walt Whitman.
What appals and overwhelms men most in leaving this
life is the forced withdrawal from their tasks and from
the intimate associations of their love and labor. Death
is most tragic when it falls upon youth opening out upon
the plans and hopes of a promising lifetime, or upon
vigorous manhood or womanhood, bearing the activities
of joyous and fruitful living. Then it reveals most
poignantly the instability and precariousness of life.

It is one of the most amazing traits of human nature that it lives in such a world with so much zest and
joy. Men are astonishingly absorbed in their immediate concerns and in the brighter pictures of the future
just ahead. Only with difficulty and under great pressure do they make real to themselves the risks and the
final event. As Robert Louis Stevenson says in *Aes*

Triplex, "although few things are spoken of with more fearful whisperings than this prospect of death, few have less influence on conduct under healthy circumstances." In days of vigorous health the end never seems imminent, and attention cannot be made to dwell upon it. The prophets of religion who remind us that our days are but a handbreadth, as fleeting as the passing shadow, sound plaintive and unreal; we revel in the joy of living and will not be dissuaded even temporarily from its zest and thrill. To reflective thought this unwillingness to face the facts and to take account of them betrays a superficial and naïve attitude. What is needed is an interpretation of life which recognizes the brevity of human life, yet affords appreciation of its dignity and value.

The Hebrew religion of the Old Testament had little or nothing to say of a life beyond death; it centered attention upon this world, and sought to instil those habits and practices which would bring a man to his grave full of years and in honor among his fellows. The proverbs and counsels of prudence in the wisdom literature magnify the virtues which fulfil the natural duties of kinship, of neighborliness, of national loyalty, and of true piety. The righteous are held in remembrance but are not conceived as having personal immortality.

Christianity cherished an ardent faith in a future state of bliss because of its great emphasis upon the value of the individual, and because of the circumstances of its historical development. Jesus taught the infinite worth of the individual and the security of the virtuous soul against all the forces which kill the body.

The society in which his religion was launched could afford little opportunity for the acceptance of such a faith. In all its ruling elements the world was alien to his ethical and spiritual conceptions. Militarism, aristocracy, hedonism, and moral despair permeated the reigning culture. Christianity became subject to contempt and persecution because of its teaching of the worth of the individual regardless of social status, its suspicion of worldly riches and learning, its rejection of the popular idolatry, and its cultivation of mysterious rites. Forced by terrible experience to feel that it could not be at home in such a world, the leaders of the new religion turned their gaze toward the heavenly abode, and comforted themselves with the assurance that the sufferings of this present life were but for the moment and would work out for them a glorious destiny in an immortal life hereafter. The Synoptic Gospels, which reflect more directly the teaching of Jesus, are not dominated by this despair of the present life; but in the letters of Paul, who had bitter experience of worldly enmity and persecution, the heavenly realm is the great goal of faith and hope. In the later writings of the New Testament the importance of the celestial as over against this evil, transient life is further magnified. Through succeeding centuries, persecutions and oppositions deepened the conviction of the impending doom of the existing social order, and heightened the Christian's assurance that though compelled to live for a time in the flesh his true abode was in the heavenly courts to which death would bring him home.

That this emphasis upon the greater excellence and importance of the heavenly world was not exclusively a Christian idea may be seen in the fact that when this religious faith required formulation in doctrinal conceptions it found already prepared for it the elaborate forms of Greek speculation regarding the celestial realm of the gods and of the purified souls of men. Christian theologians took over from Platonism, more than from their own traditions, ideas and arguments concerning the immortality of the soul and the state of the blest. Metaphysical conceptions of the unity and indestructibility of the soul were adopted into traditional theology from pagan literature, as were so many other doctrines which have long passed for orthodox beliefs. Such speculations were not characteristic of early Christianity although they were congenial enough to the faith in its practical exigencies when the pressure of circumstances forced it to find a refuge from the fire and sword of earthly hostility.

How much the doctrine of otherworldliness depended upon these two influences of an antagonistic society and the ready-to-hand Greek philosophy is further revealed by the diminishing appeal of this doctrine in the modern world. As Christianity gains recognition and prestige in this present life and becomes the religion of the state or is protected by the state, extreme concentration upon the future life as the only opportunity for the realization of its ideals is relaxed, and more attention is given to its applicability within the world that now is. Christian thinkers realize with growing conviction that extreme occupation with thought of the future life leads to neglect of conditions in the present which it is the duty of all good men to meet with practical wisdom and religious idealism. No severer criticism is passed upon orthodox religion today from within and from without, than this, that the churches stress a sentimental, metaphysical notion of salvation and fail to deal vigorously with glaring mundane evils.

Another ground of discontent with the old doctrine of immortality is that it was often stated in such a way as to foster an immoral theory of rewards and punishment. That doctrine advocated the good life, not for its own sake, but as a means of escaping the torments of hell and gaining the joys of paradise. This made the issue of conduct external and arbitrary, whereas genuine moral behavior generates its own good and its own intrinsic satisfaction. Unless the religious life is the best life possible for man on the earth, why should it be considered a fit preparation for a moral and desirable life hereafter? If the religious man lives according to the highest conceptions of a thoroughly virtuous life today, why should he be anxious about the morrow? On the other hand, if immortality is a gift of God without reference to rational and intelligible moral character, there is no means of knowing what one should do to achieve immortality. The idea that a divine being requires obedience to certain rules and ordinances which have no discernible moral quality, and makes man's destiny dependent upon their observance, is repellent to human reason and moral judgment. Popular religion has not yet shaken off all its inheritance of magical rites, and the survival of practices which are thought to assure immortality regardless of their bearing upon character signifies how much of that inheritance still persists. The opposite side of the case makes the matter still more impressive, for if eternal punish-

ment should follow upon the failure to comply with requirements which are themselves non-moral, there could
be no faith at all in the justice and goodness of God.

For scientific knowledge, the answer to this question
of the future life is as lacking as is the answer to the
question of the origin of life. The Society for Psychical
Research has for many years gathered material upon
the subject of life after death. It has patiently re-
corded the efforts of mediums to communicate with the
departed; it has toiled over dreams, visions, and
séances; it has sought the wisdom of psychological experts, but thus far no positive results of scientific worth
have been secured. There has been found an abundance
of strange coincidences, and not a few men eminent in
their special fields have given credence to the evidential
value of some experiences. But those psychologists
who have gone deepest into the matter have remained
skeptical and unconvinced. William James was one of
these. If any competent observer, with an open mind
on the subject, ever gave the case a fair hearing, it
was he. He reported that many of the alleged cases
of spirit communication were proved to be fraudulent;
in others, the mediums were sincere but mistaken in
their conclusions; and in some instances there were coincidences of a startling nature, yet not affording sufficient evidence for decisive judgment. He was impressed by the inconsequential character of the alleged
communications. They were the merest generalities,
vague and insignificant, and not on a par with the mental life of the persons during their lifetime. More than
most psychologists, James was convinced that the phenomena were of sufficient importance to justify contin-

ued investigation, but this was due partly to the value
he saw in them for the better understanding of many
other problems of psychology, such as the subconscious
and the phenomena of suggestion.

One factor which greatly complicates inquiry into
this subject is the intense emotional interest in it.
Where there is such eagerness to be convinced, the
way is already prepared for all manner of false judgments. The cheapest tricks, often exposed, are still
sufficient to lure and persuade those seeking comfort
and assurance by such means. Perhaps nowhere is it
more difficult to secure scientific impartiality and thor-
oughness. Certain discoveries of physical science have
furnished analogies which are eagerly seized upon to
confirm belief in the future life. The development of
communication by radio appears to the unscientific to
be much the same as thought transference without a
material medium, and suggests the possibility of tele-
pathic converse with disembodied spirits. The reduction of the material world itself to non-substantial terms
by physical science has opened the way to new hope
of confirming the primacy of spiritual existence apart
from material bodies, and of its survival after death.
But these are conjectures quite beyond any present
scientific justification.

The problem remains unsolved, and the powerful
wish to believe seizes upon the fact that nothing is
clearly proved against the hope of immortality. Imagination, supported by the long, intense faith of religion,
clings to its dreams and continues to cherish the bright
pictures of reunion and unending bliss. This projection
of life into a vast future is felt to give dignity and

worth to human life, and to provide for the realization of frustrated ideals. Such a faith gives courage and fortitude in the presence of the manifest ills and wrongs of earthly life, and although chastened by the disciplines of the cautious and tentative attitude of modern science, that faith is not likely soon to disappear completely. The conception of the hereafter, however, has undergone significant reconstruction. Instead of a place of infinite leisure and passive enjoyment, it is now conceived as a state of continued activity and growth, of enlarging knowledge and achievement. The old imagery of a deity receiving unending praise and adulation from choirs of the redeemed palls on the imagination and repels by its lack of adequate moral tone and strength. The stirring picture of a glorified, creative democratic society actively working out a higher order of intelligence and co-operative achievement is more appealing, and illustrates anew how men have always imaged the celestial life as an idealization of the values that they have treasured here below.

With this lightening of emphasis upon heavenly immortality has come a new appreciation of other ways in which man's earthly life runs on beyond his death. He lives on in his children, in the works he performs, in the ideas he evolves and in the influence he exerts. The nobler and more significant his life the more certainly it will continue and the farther it will reach. Even if his name is forgotten the impress of his personality and work may go on with increasing force and meaning. What is so conspicuously true of great men, is true of men in humble spheres and interests. A celebrated cartoonist has represented the stature of Abraham Lincoln rising in statelier grandeur through the unfolding cycles of American life. At his death he was indeed somewhat taller than his fellows, but as his spirit was better understood, he rose to loftier proportions, and now when he has become so much the symbol of rugged honesty and democratic idealism, his figure rises over the social aspirations of the whole world in towering spiritual strength and greatness. With each generation he becomes mightier and speaks to increasing numbers in all lands. Compared with the thought of his continued existence in some remote and silent world, this dynamic energy of his living presence is for our human estimates more precious and more enduringly fruitful. The contemplation of such a triumph over death and time awakens incentives which stir men to a new assessment of the spiritual values of devotion to the concrete ends of idealistic social endeavor.

It seems now a pathetic fact of history that the continuance of the life of Jesus after death should have been so long and so literally associated with the idea of his bodily resurrection. The importance of his alleged ascension through physical space into the heavens has been so magnified as to withdraw attention from his real ascendency in the moral realm. No one can doubt the fact that he came to life in this world after he died upon the cross. No argument is needed to prove that he rose from a grave of obscurity to a life of renown; from a grave of weakness and silence to a life of power; from a grave of ignominy to a place of love and honor. Already, in comparison with some thirty years of ordinary life, he has lived for nineteen hundred years beyond his death! And the secret of this conspicuous fact lies not in some miraculous magic but in the moral and spiritual quality of his character. It was the power of his living word and gracious spirit that carried him over the gulfs of death and gave him immortality. It may be said that such interpretations are beside the point since they do not relate to the continuance of the self-conscious existence of the individual after death. They do, however, have a decided bearing on the question of the effect of death upon what men hold most dear; for, after all, men are not so much concerned with their own personal preservation as they are for the work, or cause, or ideals for which they spend their lives. There easily comes to be something revolting about a man who consciously puts his own safety in the foreground of his plans and actions. Decent regard for his own health and well-being is doubtless his duty, but when it is a choice between his own comfort and a friend's need, or between his life and his honor, his concern for himself gives way. He would rather forfeit his existence than preserve it at the cost of self-respect. It does not seem likely that this is because he reasons that if his life is thus given up it will be recovered after death. Scarcely can it be contended that bravery in battle and willingness to die for the cause rest upon the hope of immortality. There is a decisive and final choice in favor of the action which may lead to self-destruction and the triumph of a great hope, as against the course which would save the self and lose the cause. Perhaps this means that men do not have so deep a longing for a life after death as has been thought, and that they are more concerned to help forward this present life than they are to share in another.

Man lives an associated life, and it is to the values of that shared life that he is most devoted. It is by the victory and fulfilment of those values that he realizes the greatest satisfaction. To live is to enter into appreciation of them and to further them in every possible way. They are precious through the functions that they represent in the life of society, not because of any transcendental permanence. And the same is true of man's own personal life. In reality it is a derived and dependent life, bound up with his fellows and set in the intimate yet wide bounds of the whole human world. In imagination, by means of which alone a truly human life is possible, he participates in the real past and the possible future. Constantly he transcends the moment of the present, and by the same power he oversteps the bounds of death. To some extent he anticipates what the future will be, and it is part of his privilege and duty to live in the light of that future as aiding in the determination of what is worth while in the present.

Throughout the whole of experience there runs the limitation of man's knowledge and power. He accepts life with the responsiveness of his innate disposition and finds zest and worth in it, in keeping with the endowments which nature has given him and those that it has enabled him to achieve. He may lament his lot, or he may utilize what it offers, with zest and wisdom. There is no other kind of life available except that which his imagination conceives in terms of experience and reflection. To its tides he must intrust himself with such adaptations as he may contrive, and with the measure of such satisfaction as it affords. Before him, over the course of years, he sees dimly the end of his earthly way. If he is wise, he takes his bearings in the stream of time which carries him on, and gives himself with thought and patient labor to the tasks he finds, not pondering too much nor contemplating too lightly that coming day of which from the first he has had fair warning. All the way he is intrusting himself to the encompassing life of God, and with God he may rest the final issues of both life and death.

CHAPTER XVI

CREATIVE RELIGIOUS BEHAVIOR

It is a commonplace that man greatly modifies the environment in which he lives. By the removal of forests to build houses and ships, to gain land for agriculture, to make paper, and to keep his fires burning, he has denuded great tracts in ancient and in modern times. This has resulted in the washing away of the soil of rich areas, and the turning of fertile places into desert wilderness. Civilizations have thus undermined the very economic foundations upon which they rested, and reduced the inhabitants of once powerful dominions to poverty or extinction. Modern men are effecting still greater and more rapid changes by the application of the inventions of science in industry, transportation and communication. Natural resources of mineral, oil, and animal life are developed and exploited on an unprecedented scale. New devices are continually created, like the radio and the airplane, which perform miracles of transformation in nature and in human life. Movements of population and the shifting of the physical scene were never so swift nor so vast. Control of the food supply, of disease, and of the conditions of existence for all living things is a fact shown by every landscape and by every hamlet on the globe.

These changes go on with increasing deliberation and conscious purpose. The blind struggle for existence, wars of conquest, and competition of peoples for territory and treasure wrought their results in the past; but today cities are built, industries set up, and nature harnessed with foresight and mastery made possible by scientific knowledge and conscious co-operation. Mankind is possessed by a growing sense of power as new and greater achievements are attained. Practical men in industry, commerce, and the useful arts have no doubts about the reality and the force of their ideas and their enterprises. They venture forth upon the quest for new inventions and new conquests with intrepid spirit.

In strange contrast with this attitude of engineers and executives stands much of the speculative, academic thought of the time. Philosophers and school men, in the presence of this creative, eventuating activity, often seem "sicklied o'er with the pale cast of thought." Professor Dewey would say it is because in so much of the prevailing philosophy there is an unwarranted separation of mental activity from the world of affairs. Owing to a long standing effort of theorists to estimate the nature of thought and its function, apart from the bodily organism and its relation to the environment, they have been unable to credit it with genuine efficacy in the actual world of visible and tangible events. But when mental life is judged by the concrete performance of the whole human being, the puzzle disappears. "Knowledge" is then shown in the skill and resourcefulness with which adaptation is effected, particularly in the use of tools. Mind is no longer shut up within the head or brain, but operates through sense organs and muscles in the manipulation of objects. In ordinary speech we observe that a person "knows" how to weave, to sew, to cut with a saw, or to play upon a musical instrument. This ability to handle tools and materials in accomplishing definite results is the display of mental life in the wider and more fundamental meaning of the term, but in the refined processes of deliberation and reflection the nature of ideas and judgments is also finally exhibited in their applicability to the adaptation of an organism to its environment. Testing the validity of ideas at last comes home to some practical situation, to the solution of some problem of action.

From a common-sense point of view the superiority of human beings in respect to mental life may be estimated easily in a comparison of their behavior with that of the lower animals. While ability to learn must be credited to the latter, for example, to the white rat in learning to run the maze or to solve simple box puzzles, yet man outdistances all his dumb kin by inventing and using tools, and particularly in and through the use of language. Men create literatures, sciences, works of art, voluntary societies, and a world of cultural agencies which exhibit a mental life shared by no other animals. Moreover, such productions are projected, planned, and carried through with awareness and critical reflection. They do not occur at random, nor elsewhere than in the realm of human experience.

It is especially in the sphere of the conscious life of deliberation that the significance and fruitfulness of the mental life appear. Here the practical man proceeds with assured reliance upon the powers of memory, reflection, and imagination. He thrusts his enterprises into the future for full realization, and measures the correctness and adequacy of his thinking by the actual outcome. When his plans fail of completion or satisfactory operation, he does not attribute that failure to the impotency of ideas in general to operate in the practical world, but only acknowledges that his particular ideas in this specific situation were false or partial. Characteristically he sets to work again by knowledge revised in the light of his experience to carry his work to completion in some modified forms.

Curiously enough the recently formulated behavioristic psychology, which rightly insists upon the functioning organism as the central fact in man's relation to his environment, has undertaken to dispense with the fact of consciousness and all its alleged significance in the foresight and direction of activity. Dr. John B. Watson has endeavored to explain language as merely habits of the speech organs, organic responses to physical stimuli, devoid of all conscious meaning. When a person meets an old acquaintance, words called out by their earlier contacts are reinstated and flow from his lips with a smile or a frown, quite as automatically as an organ pipe sounds when the key of the console is touched. But, as Bertrand Russell has pointed out, there is actually such a variation in language habits, without loss of effective intercourse, that the theory loses its applicability, or is compelled to resort to assumptions which are as full of mystery as any doctrine of consciousness. Mr. Russell suggests that one may say, "I met Mr. Jones in the train today," or, "Joseph was in the 9:35 this morning," and in both statements relate the same fact, yet the recollection is not identified with the same verbal habit in the two instances;

furthermore, the experience of meeting Mr. Jones may not have been put into words at all until the moment when it was reported.[1]

Psychologists now generally agree that thinking is bound up with the use of language, but this is far from saying that thought is nothing more than the movements of the vocal organs in the production of words. Otherwise, parrots and phonographs would have to be credited with essentially the same behavior as human beings. Speech is not merely the association of words with objects, but it is a social process in which vocalizations are subject to modification by the responses of other persons. The speaker finds the meaning of his words modified by the reactions of those addressed, and is thereby led to discover fuller and richer meanings. The whole context of discourse is essential to the understanding of terms, and this context is fluid and never twice quite the same. The behaviorist is involved in the dilemma of regarding speech as the mere repetition of identical verbal habits, or of resorting to the assumption of mysteriously subtle bodily changes that are beyond observation and become the equivalent of the psychic factors that he is anxious to dismiss. The awareness, or consciousness, recognized by most psychologists in common with ordinary experience, need not be regarded as any more of a mystery than living itself. The simplest habits, so freely admitted by the behaviorist, are mysterious enough, and the attempt to load them with the whole task of explaining human thought and language does not make them less so.

Another more familiar argument against the creative

[1] Bertrand Russell, *Philosophy*, p. 74.

influence of man in the world is based upon the conceptions of physics and the older doctrine of evolution of the last century. Modern science began to make real progress when it discarded the notion of special forces and causes from the world of nature. It then conceived the order of physical things as under one law of cause and effect, held in equilibrium through the conservation and correlation of energy. In this view there could be no gaps, no leaps, no breaks in nature. That was a metaphysical conception adopted by the natural sciences, not upon the ground of empirical observation but in reaction from the older idea of special agencies and supernatural invasions of the natural order. It was concluded that man himself must be under this same dominance of uniform law and that what might appear to be his creative activity was only an illusion owing to his misinterpretation of his feeling of effort, or to a wish to exempt him from the common fate of all natural phenomena. Therefore it was asserted that the conditions and causes of all his conduct were given in his past, and that if these were known his future acts would be entirely calculable. The fact that the situation was complex and of a high degree of refinement only made the conception more difficult but none the less theoretically sound. The effect of this materialistic philosophy was to deny reality to the mental life or at least to make insignificant its relation to the actual world.

Nothing has been more revolutionary than the course of the physical sciences themselves during the present century, and particularly in physics. Experimental work with electricity and light, and accompanying studies of space, time, and matter have given a radically different picture of the world. The once solid atom has disintegrated into electrons and protons, and has taken its place with the "ghosts" of other supposed realities. So-called matter has lost its independence, its substantiality, and its continuity. The objects which appear to the senses dissolve under inspection and become organizations of events to which cannot be attributed any such permanent substance as was once supposed to belong to them. Doctrines of relativity have introduced modifications into the ancient and long-accepted ideas of space and time, and have brought into question the foundations of Euclidean geometry. The old three-dimensional space has a rival in the addition of a fourth dimension, and the universality of the categories of substance, permanence, and causation has been denied. The consequence is that physicists now talk much in the language formerly characteristic of the idealistic philosophers and the whole realm of being is unshackled from its thraldom to the fixed and static laws that once ruled it.

It was in terms of the now discarded doctrine of physical determinism that the theories of moral determinism were formulated. Not only did the atomism of Democritus present a materialistic, mechanistic conception of man in the firm grasp of physical law, but the hedonistic ethics of modern thought took a similar position. Its chief contention was that since the object of desire is pleasure, the will is destined to be influenced in the direction of the strongest desire, or what the agent regards as the greatest pleasure. Bentham undertook to state a calculus of pleasure by suggesting that those pleasures are the most powerful that are most intense, durable, accessible, affecting the most people, and so forth. Since it is pleasure which a person seeks, it is the pleasure which has the greatest force, estimated in terms of quantity, that will determine his action. While it is not possible in all cases to specify what these pleasures will be, the principle is clear and the theory consistent. A man's acts are not within the province of his will or choice; he is always subject to the compulsions of relentless forces, and has no more option as to the course of his conduct than has a stone to determine its course when thrown through the air.

The refutation of such theories has come from a more comprehensive psychological analysis of human nature. The substance of the criticisms is that human activity is not moved merely from external forces, and that the conception of pleasure reveals its fallacies when subjected to analysis. Determinism in all its forms takes an external view, and regards the person as passive. The more scientific psychology recognizes the activity of the organism as original and ever operative; it concedes that the environment is not indifferent to the state of the organism, since what is agreeable at one time is disagreeable or indifferent at another, and the objects which are sought are first of all sought as a means of fulfilling the needs of life and action, not for the satisfaction of a love of pleasure. It is not pleasure in the abstract, but the concrete experience of a pleasure-yielding object or activity which is wanted.

The question of the creative power of man is of the utmost concern to religion, as to every other human interest. Religion continually demands the enlargement and enrichment of life, and exhorts the individual to renounce his evil ways and pursue the good. It can only do this with conviction where there is intelligent understanding of the possibility of men responding to its appeal. It is often cited as waste and weakness on the part of religious leaders that they urge men to change their lives and enlarge their conduct without making clear that this is really possible, or showing the means whereby it may be accomplished. Probably nothing would more vitalize religion than the presentation of the facts of modern psychology in reference to the methods by which conduct may be modified and developed. The old assumption that men are by nature bad, that they love the evil more than the good, is a vicious dogma of an outworn theology. Little is gained by the reiteration that we are all sinners unless some light is thrown upon practical methods of overcoming our sins.

Perhaps the first great step needed is to make it clear that sins are plural and concrete, that there is no such thing as Sin, an abstract and pervasive entity. This doctrine has led to the fallacy of supposing that it could be counteracted by some great emotional upheaval that would convert the individual at a stroke. When sins are seen to be specific and particular, they may be attacked in definite and effective ways. The problem is then that of finding ways of changing habits or uprooting them by directing interest to other ways of acting. The individual may thus have some chance of realizing his own responsibility for his deeds, and of achieving that enlightenment and self-discipline that will free him from his old self and enable him to achieve a better self. Religious conduct is all of a piece with moral conduct, so far as the attainment of the good life is concerned, and the great instrument for this purpose is enlightenment with reference to the formulation and the realization of desirable ideals. The cultivation of intellectualized emotion, and of emotionalized intellection, is a general statement of the need, and for this religion must employ both intelligent criticism and appealing forms of conduct.

Ethical theories defending freedom of the will have generally made the assumption of the independence of the will, a faculty belonging to the transcendental realm outside the domain of cause and effect. This was the doctrine of Kant, and he held that within the natural sphere man is bound by causation as are all things which have a physical existence. For him the moral law reigned in its own intelligible world from which it gave commands to the human will. He was thus in the difficulty of having human conduct guided by a principle which belonged to one part of man's being, while the other part, the physical, moved within a rigidly determined causal order. As the hedonist made a dualism between desire and pleasure, so the intuitionist divided the world of action between inner motives and outward deeds. In both the relation remained external and logically one of such separation that no consistent account could be given of moral conduct and of moral responsibility.

Modern moral theory has the advantage of a more adequate psychology, and has provided criticisms of both the extreme deterministic and the free-will positions. It insists upon the unity of the psychical life, and affords a basis for a more thorough account of moral behavior. It recognizes that man is at once a creature of impulse, habit, and reflection. From blind, impulsive acts, through memory and imagination he becomes aware of the course of his action, and by reflective selection follows routes of conduct that appeal to his disciplined judgment. While the patterns of his behavior are developed out of his impulsive needs in relation to his environment, they are modified by his insight. Through memory he becomes aware of the consequences of his acts, and is able to set up in imagination various options. By means of "dramatic rehearsal" he projects in imagination different possible procedures and chooses that which appeals to his character as good. The choice thus made is not arbitrary nor independent of his formed habits, but neither is it merely the repetition of previous experience. There is something novel in the situation in which he acts, and the consequence is an achievement of new developments in his experience. In all such acts there is a thrust into the future, an invention or creation which goes beyond the old habits, the full import of which the agent himself must await and witness in the attitude of expectancy.

The measure of a man's freedom may be said to lie in the range of his habits, and in the quality of his reflective insight. Formal freedom lies in the absence of barriers to action. A prisoner locked in his cell is not free to travel about; the paralyzed individual has the formal freedom that is denied the prisoner, but lacks real freedom, that is, ability to take advantage of his opportunity. A person skilled in playing the piano has the ability, the real freedom, but may not have an instrument at hand, or may be denied the privilege of its use. Freedom to converse in the Latin language requires the appropriate speech habits, and also the presence of another similarly versed. When a moral situation impends, both the formed character of the agent, that is, his body of habits, and opportunity for action through a favoring or manageable environment, are required, and also an imaginative survey of various lines of possible action. It is true that the decision, so far as it is deliberate, expresses the nature of the individual acting, but it is a mistake to suppose that his nature is necessarily so limited that he has no field of exploration and selection. It is just the quality of moral action that it involves alternatives presented to the mind of the agent for his consideration. Human beings are capable of "delayed responses." When a plan is proposed they may say, Let us think it over; or, Let us make a decision on a certain day when pertinent information has been secured. This ability to delay the answer, to weigh various factors, to investigate numerous suggestions, and to try them out in imagination, is the heart of the matter. So long as the proposal is in suspense, various courses of conduct may be projected in imagination and their consequences estimated to some extent. If a person has no opportunity for this deliberation, being forced to act through the exigencies of the situation, or if he lacks knowledge and experience for such forecasts, he has little or no freedom. Thus children and uneducated people do not have as much power to direct their behavior as do those of greater maturity and intellectual development. Freedom may therefore be said to be a matter of degree, as well as of kind, and all education to be in a true sense an extension of freedom.

Much has been made, especially in old controversies, of free choice. In its extreme statement it means the power arbitrarily to enter upon a line of action, but few would now undertake to defend such a conception. It is the counterpart of the position which holds to the complete determination of behavior by antecedent influences or by the mechanics of desire, or other forces operating from without. A man's choice of ends is the outcome of his character, but that character is not a fixed, unchangeable entity. The very fact that he is called upon to make decisions indicates that he has a moving, changing self that confronts a changing social and material environment. If the world about him did not change there is little reason to believe that he would be subjected to so many demands for choosing his way. It is the requirement to maintain himself in a changing world, changing within and without, that precipitates moral problems. Man is a creature of many impulses, of many interests, of waxing and waning moods, of shifting social relations and varying obligations. To have habits rigidly fixed is to lack the ability to make needed adaptations, but to have no organized habits would be to exercise no power whatsoever in the face of life's demands. Often habits become so stereotyped, so grooved, that they limit freedom. It is the process of reflective thought, of wary, watchful criticism which alone is able to cope with the situations that normal experience presents. Thus is developed the most important of habits, namely, the habit of modifying habits, of discarding baneful or useless ones, and forming new ones. Such modification is required in response to the needs of life. There is no virtue in making changes for their own sake, any more than there is value in constant, extreme self-criticism. The occasions for the exercise of freedom are the natural problematic situations incident to all growing, vital living. Family, school, and social life continually offer moral questions to be settled. Reading books, travel, business and social contacts stimulate to varied activities which have to be related to the customary rounds of the individual's vocation and to his tastes and interests. The wider and richer the social and cultural environment, the more resourceful a person's intellectual and imaginative experience may become.

It is of the nature of all living things to have appetite, impulse, and craving, impelling the organism to search for food and for whatever is congenial to it. Plants seek light and moisture, animals hunt for prey, and man, whose wants expand in more directions and on a greater scale, is ceaselessly in pursuit of many kinds of goods. Even the blind, explosive manifestations of impulse make differences in the organism and in the environment, but those forms of intelligently guided activity disclosed in civilization work far greater changes. Organization of states, conduct of relations among them, both peaceful and warlike, the development of literature, science, religion, and art, constitute creative forms of behavior that vastly modify human nature itself, and the world of which it is a part. The institutions thus built up constitute patterns and molds to which children are shaped and through which they obtain the skill and knowledge that give them freedom in wider ranges of activity than belong to primitive peoples. Customs are transmitted by many forms of suggestion and stimulation, as well as by direct education. They are channels of release, currents of free movement as well as defining and limiting modes of behavior, and they provide manifold occasions for the individual to select ends for his labor and means for its direction. As human life becomes more conscious of its processes through acquaintance with its past and awareness of its possibilities, the free impulses of childhood are regarded as the opportunities for new forms of behavior and the enrichment of the general social life.

The freedom realized in such a society is that of specific ability to meet in some measure the exigencies of concrete situations as they arise. It is not freedom in the abstract, nor a theoretical determinism of sheer conformity to external conditions. The older metaphysical views of both free will and causal compulsion were abstract doctrines based upon transcendental conceptions of the soul or upon generalizations of the laws of physical science. They were not embodiments of the actual concrete behavior of reflective activity. Physical science presents averages and summaries of numerous events, but it is not able to tell what will be the issue of the individual case. The characteristic of moral conduct is the demand upon a specific individual to act in a particular situation. Because it is not merely routine, and not the demand for re-enactment of a previously given procedure, it requires of the agent a venture into the unknown, an experimental deed for which there is no exact precedent. No two persons are just the same, nor is their social or physical world ever twice the same, and therefore each confronts the necessity of adjusting his conduct as best he may in the light of his judgment and capacity.

Hence the individual is responsible for his deed. While his responsibility is partial, being shared by the group to which he belongs, he is the medium through which conduct is realized and society rightly holds him to account for what he does. He is the bearer of the conscience of the shared life of which he is a part, and the burden of the consequences of his reflection and his choice is put upon him. He is told that he should foresee the nature of his acts, and the penalty placed upon him for evil results is the discipline by which he is developed into appreciation of the character of his behavior. Just as no one else can perform a moral act in his stead, so no one is able to take moral blame or reward for him. It is only by accepting the proper measure of responsibility for his acts that the individual can increase his realization of his own nature and that of the world in which he moves. If he were completely determined, no blame could be attributed to him, and if he were entirely free he would be equally irresponsible. It is only because he is able, as a conscious, reflective person, to exercise some estimate of his performance that he is a moral agent and the bearer of moral worth or guilt. Every man is supposed to know the laws of his society and to be responsible for his ignorance. In actual practice the second offense is more severely condemned because the first experience is a lesson by which he should have profited. Without this assumption of the capacity of the individual to learn from the consequences of his conduct there could be no ground for moral judgment, but the assumption is the evidence of the responsibility, that is, the freedom of the person.

All members of society are subject to these conditions. It is a fallacy to suppose that any one is in possession of absolute standards of right and wrong. The law itself is constantly undergoing interpretations and consequent modification. Legislators and courts are in the same process of change as the individual, and the right and wrong of conduct are differently estimated in different stages of social history. Nowhere is this more dramatically displayed than in the great innovating personalities who venture to deny the claims of established customs and conceive new standards of the good. Often such men are misunderstood by their time and condemned by the conventions as criminals, while the generations which come after them are able to see in a wider perspective the justification for their ideas and deeds. Socrates and Jesus were put to death as criminals but were afterward acclaimed as righteous men. They displayed that courage of adventurous faith which is an essential of all moral conduct. Their tragic deaths were the outcome of the assumption on the part of their contemporaries of a static, social code of morals; and their recognition as moral leaders by later times is proof that there was no such final, absolute moral standard. They themselves believed in freedom through insight—that truth makes free. But truth is not once for all given; it is developed out of a growing experience and is learned by taking account of the outcome of experimental living.

CHAPTER XVII

GOOD AND EVIL

An account of religion in terms of experience cannot state the nature of the good in conceptions of absolute standards derived from revelation or from transcendental metaphysics. This has been attempted in various systems of religion, but the result has been external and superimposed. All transcendental interpretations are formal and dogmatic, subject to varying interpretations and to ultimate skepticism. They set over against their claims of ideal perfection the actual stream of human experience, condemning its partial and shifting character, regarding it as impotent and unavailing, so that only miracles of supernatural transformation are able to invest human beings with valid moral and spiritual worth. To this end magical rites and mysterious powers of faith are invoked, while the unresolved dualism of evil human nature and divine perfection remains to discredit natural good, and to leave man's noblest endeavors futile and confused. Practically all traditional theology assumes this *impasse* and suspends the natural man in clouds of doubt and impotence, leaving only mystical, emotional ecstasy and unintelligible symbols to religion. Doctrines of vicarious atonement and of abject surrender to arbitrary authority continue to be the strongholds of popular religion.

The intellectual revolution of this scientific age is rebellious against this assumption that the best of life should be consigned to irrational attitudes, while in other spheres the fruits of reflection and experimental living are being gathered in rich abundance. More ardently than ever the human spirit, achieving emancipation and mastery in every other field of endeavor— in politics, industry, and art—seeks an understanding of the good life which is within the comprehension and control of intelligible conceptions and practical methods of realization. Modern psychology and the development of a science of morals give encouragement in the quest for an interpretation of religion which shall bring to flower a vital and appealing insight into the natural spiritual life. It is from these sources, from psychology and morals, that the nature of the highest forms of the good in religion may be sought.

Psychology shows that man is a creature of impulses and desires, of wishes and cravings, aware of needs and wants, and able to discriminate among different forms of satisfaction in their fulfilment. Those courses of conduct are found to be best which most fully satisfy these needs, leading on to enlarging desires and satisfactions. The measure of the good life may be said to consist in the expansiveness, harmony, and happiness experienced. Fullness of life, variety of interest, depth of insight, scope of social participation, are the insignia of the good. Growth in sympathy, in understanding, in skill and power are characteristics by which life is made worthful. These are relative terms, but they are meaningful and appreciable, are applicable to all stages of development and afford means of estimating the concrete experience of the child and the adult, of the plain man and the genius. Such standards lie within the field of natural effort, they are derived from concrete experience in the normal relations of men with one another and with their environment. They do not depend upon special revelation, nor upon the example of superhuman beings. Daily vocations utilize such judgments of excellence and the finest of the arts have no other criteria.

The athlete does not aspire to reach some mark of perfection; he takes note of what has been accomplished by others like himself in his specialty and undertakes to "break the record." Athletic standards have been built up through a long history of experimenting, and success is measured in reference to these empirically determined capacities of men. To insist that the ideal time for running every race is not a certain number of minutes or seconds determined by what has previously been done, but is zero, would be to erect an abstract and meaningless standard, reducing the problem to absurdity. Yet it is some such theoretical and impossible conception of perfection that has often been set forth as the goal of the spiritual life.

A business man does not try to gather to himself all the wealth of the world, to become perfectly rich, but he pushes ahead to exceed what he has accomplished before. The quality of his conduct is determined by what is done, by the customs of people with whom he deals. Honesty and justice are partial and imperfect because they have to be practiced in concrete relations, as is conspicuously illustrated in matters of taxation, and in the actual administration of the law. Human justice is "rough," but it is valuable and good. Telling the truth may seem a very clear and obvious requirement, easy of fulfilment if the heart is right, but the old questions as to whether the truth should always be told to sick patients, to insane persons, and to men bent on murder and theft are extreme illustrations of the complexities of right conduct. It is a sound maxim that a man should have the intention to do his very best on all occasions, but he can only intend to do what appears to him to be the best and his knowledge and judgment of what is the best are never perfectly complete. Hence tact, sympathy, and regard for all concerned are important qualities in the appraisal of the good.

The attempt to define the good by formal rules encounters the same difficulty. The Golden Rule does not afford direction for the exact path of duty, but has value in stating the desirable attitude. Its spirit is of the utmost importance though it leaves something to be supplied by the agent in dealing with the complex situations in which moral action eventuates. It is not always evident what a person would wish to have done to himself by others, and it is more difficult to put one's self in the exact position of another to determine how he should be treated. People of the finest intentions notoriously make mistakes in their effort to render charity to others. It is one of the amazing discoveries concerning benevolently intentioned persons that their philanthropies have unexpected results in weakening the character and complicating the moral behavior of those whom they seek to benefit. Organized charity has for this reason become exceedingly wary of direct help to individuals. Increasing attention is given to the underlying conditions of economic social backgrounds, to family histories, and to community environment. Philanthropy turns more and more to medicine, education, housing, and means of recreation.

Individualistic conceptions of the good have not only shown their limitations on the side of the recipients of charity, but also with reference to all members of society. The person who strives for his own development is seen to fail of success unless he reckons with demands for his participation in the manifold, complex relations of an associated life. While the incentives to personal effort in a profession or some field of art tempt a man to concentration upon his particular problems, the good life involves him in demands to share responsibility for the common interests. One of the greater evils of the present time is the narrow, specialized activity of business and professional men in devotion to their chosen occupations, withdrawing them from any significant part in the public affairs of their communities. Politics is allowed to fall into the hands of specialists who often come to regard their offices as their own possession and the spoils of office as their natural rewards. But in a democratic society there cannot be properly any really private citizens. Unless the burdens of the general welfare are made subjects of intelligent concern by business and professional men, by artists and devotees of saintliness, these persons lose in breadth of character, and the community is exploited by other selfish men who do not feel the support or the restraint of a vigorous social conscience and group spirit. This demand for living a shared life does not arise from any external authority of the state over its citizens but is an inherent condition of their own fullest development. Nor is it merely because each requires protection and order about him in pursuing his particular ends. It is because every man is thereby enriched and enlarged in his own character, and makes his own contribution to the enhancement of life for his fellows.) That religious teaching which has pictured this life as alien to genuine spiritual values, as a temporary habitation of pilgrim souls destined for other worlds, might justify to itself withdrawal from secular affairs; but a view which regards the development of personality in terms of enlightened and socialized character as the supreme good must reckon with the conditions and the relations within which alone such character is possible. In contrast to a salvation obtained by a miracle of grace and concerned chiefly with a future life, a religion of experience offers a salvation which is worked out with fear and trembling to be sure, but also with intelligent participation in concrete, aspiring, human tasks fused in an organic social whole.

An unsocial individualism is not cherished merely by a religious tradition, but is found as a common trait of many modern intellectually emancipated idealists who seek to escape conventions, to realize independence, to fulfil themselves. Our age prizes novelty, initiative, adventure, and mere strangeness. New modes in dress, in poetry, painting, and literature are symptomatic of an attitude often superficial and jejune, but significant. It is an expression of desire for the tang and thrill of first-hand experience, of "reality." Reaction from the restraints of puritanism, from fear of naturalness, and from the claims of sheer conventions, has brought a great quest for pleasure and the joy of life. Nothing is more pronounced in this tendency than the attitude toward problems of sex. Here, where suppression and ignorance had reigned, frank inquiry and full knowledge have sprung up, while freedom of discussion and license of conversation obtain seemingly in disdain of all older standards. Perhaps the change is particularly marked in its effect upon women, who have within a generation attained freedom of many kinds, political, economic, professional, and domestic. Their dress, their hair, and their cigarettes symbolize emancipation and their entrance into the customs of the masculine world. But with the superficial and negative aspects there are signs of an awakening to larger social responsibilities. Civic movements, political campaigns, culture clubs, and welfare enterprises have enlisted unprecedented interest and support. The development of individuals and of institutions through such experiences reveals the impossibility of escaping the social bonds within which we are set, and it exhibits the possibility of constructive changes.

The dependence of individuals upon association for realization of the good life has been emphasized by the students of social psychology. They point out that it is in face-to-face groups like the family and neighborhood that the human world comes to be and continues to grow. Thought and language arise simultaneously, and the interaction of persons in kinship circles, in labor, and in sport provide the occasions and the means for mutual stimulation and response. Their lives are interwoven with the phenomena about them, with the animals and objects of their daily concern, with industry, warfare, and ceremonial. In the most advanced societies the same influences operate on a larger and more complex scale. The use of machines and literature makes wider intellectual contacts and gives play to the imagination through the refinements of science and art. All the natural associations are educative in some sense, and the schools are now including in their methods the practical disciplines of actual living, by establishing closer relations with the ready-to-hand laboratories of the household, the market, and the street. This permeation of common life by the habitual use of machinery and scientifically determined attitudes has given new thought-forms to men of this age, extending far beyond the conscious, technical terms of scientific method. This means the elimination of magic and superstition wherever machinery and science dominate, and it is inevitable that the moral and spiritual life should also be conceived more and more in practical and reasonable ways. It is scarcely thinkable that religion should remain under the control of primitive ideas and practices when the rest of life is dominated by the self-vouching and fruitful experience of the more reflective and critical procedures. No wonder the conviction grows that religion is either destined to disappear or to be reconstructed in harmony with the modern spirit.

The conception of the good man brings into definition the nature of the good itself. He is one who responds to personal relations with sensitive regard for the values of personality in himself and in others. He is neither an egoist nor an altruist, for if he were either he would set up a one-sided standard leaving out of account half of the relations which require fulfilment. A person who selfishly centers his attention upon himself, disregarding the claims of those about him, cuts off the possibility of meeting his own needs; while one who neglects his own interests to serve others soon loses the resources of possessions and power to be of help to others. There is something just as repugnant to normal, wholesome people in having too much done for them as in being ignored. Persons who spend too much time in preening their own virtues or acquiring self-culture become sentimental and self-righteous; and those who are over-officious about other persons' welfare or morals lose sympathetic insight, the real basis of social influence. The really good man has concern and respect for his own affairs, for the duties of his vocation, for his own integrity, for time and opportunity to live a healthy and happy life; but he recognizes that in doing these things he is sharing with others with whom he is associated in work, in the family, in friendships, and in the larger spheres into which he is naturally led. The social relations which he is morally obligated to sustain are not remote or separate from his personal activities: they require of him thoughtful and imaginative attention, for otherwise the very children and companions of his household could not hold a vital place in his plans and affections. When members of the same family are strangers to one another in their deeper intellectual and emotional life they break the inner bonds and mar the ideal social unit that tends naturally to spring up in such association. Every person, child and man, is a member of many groups and in all of them the same sharing of life is offered; when there is mutual interaction in thought, sympathy, and action, individual characters are developed through their own unique relations and functions in the whole.

The good life may be viewed as conditioned by the social order, though it is inept to regard the environment as wholly decisive in the development of persons. Society has its complexion from its constituents and they have theirs from it. In simple, homogeneous groups the patterns of behavior are cast in fairly uniform molds, there is little suggestion of conduct which is novel or digressive, the range of imagination is limited, and the natural impulses are quickly set in the casts of approved habits. In societies of less solidarity, as in modern cities, contacts are numerous and conflicting; where education has introduced persons to still wider perspectives, the standards of conduct are more diverse and suggestions toward innovation are multiplied. Then what guides can there be for the good life? Obviously they cannot be found in family and racial customs, for these are the very things in conflict, especially to the minds of the young. Nor can they be found in abstract rules, which are the condensed formulas of old customs. They can be found in general principles of action and in the taste and wisdom of the participants in the living drama. Principles are more flexible than rules, and imply the need for intelligent adaptation to varying conditions; they are the funded experience of mankind; they invite critical and experimental use; they are the criteria of the good, of fullness, harmony, and growth in satisfying experience. The virtues of courage, wisdom, temperance, industry, sympathy, honesty, and justice are good because they are conducive to satisfying experience when they are fused together in the active conduct of a thoughtful and expanding character. The good is inherent in the quality and functions of living; it encourages consideration for the examples of the past and of the present, yet puts a real measure of responsibility upon the acting agent for the deeds he performs and the character he achieves.

The nature of the evil may be understood in the light of this conception of the good. The good represents the outreaching, constructive movement of life and therefore is positive; the evil is the aspect of obstruction, disintegration, and therefore the negative phase. Strictly speaking, both goods and evils should be stated in plural terms in order to avoid the fallacy of regarding Good and Evil as metaphysical, transcendental realities. They are concrete, particular conditions of experiences incident to an active, moving, evaluating interest. It would be less confusing if these terms were always used as adjectives rather than as substantives, for they describe the qualities of experience and have no independent subsistence in their own right. We speak of a good man or a good state of existence, an evil deed or a bad character, and the most general use of the words still holds this adjectival quality. Evil things and acts are those which thwart or defeat the issues of plans and efforts. The fundamental movements of living organisms are those of reaching out and accepting, of withdrawal and aversion; the consequences of action are those of fulfilment and preservation, of impoverishment and destruction. Material, moral, and spiritual goods have the positive, upbuilding quality in common, and the bads have the quality of weakening and undermining. Bad habits are those which hinder and mar the larger life-process. Lying, stealing, drunkenness, licentiousness, and murder violate, corrupt, and annul; but truth-telling, honesty, sobriety, clean-living, and kindliness reinforce, strengthen, and enhance conduct. The latter neither have nor need any other justification or sanction.

So-called physical evils—earthquakes, tornadoes, and diseases—are evils because of their destructive, disintegrating effects with reference to some ends or values. In a merely physical order there could be no good or evil. Evils appear only where there are plans projected and endeavors made toward some fulfilment. Only where there are beings which work for the attainment of desired objectives can there be good or bad events or things. Neither a static deity nor an immobile rock contains the conditions essential to evaluating anything as good or bad, right or wrong. Where sentiency, appetite, purpose, and desire appear, there values emerge in relation to the characters and activities manifested. Wholesale pessimism would involve constant and overwhelming defeat, and perfect optimism could obtain only where every impulse was successfully consummated. The world of actual experience justifies no such wholesale judgment, for life is plainly mixed, partial, and precarious. Every living thing pursues its way at some hazard, with risk and uncertainty. It is useless to argue whether there might be worlds of other kinds; it is equally futile to deny that the world in which we live has adverse, pathetic, and tragic aspects. How there could be good in a world that was not also the scene of evil is beyond the comprehension of beings con-

stituted and environed as are human beings. The very
nature of a moral act lies in its problematic character,
in its being a venture into the future, a voyage of discovery. If the end were known from the beginning, and
the issue of every deed guaranteed in advance, there
would be no consciousness of right or wrong, nor any
need for it. The essence of the moral and religious
conduct of life lies in the fact that there is in it something novel, creative, and unpredictable. The moral
quality of actions cannot be entirely known until after
they have been performed and their nature displayed in
the objective field of their practical and social consequences. Yet these consequences cannot be fairly estimated in complete disregard of the motives of the agent
who occasioned them, for the deeds of a man are colored
and qualified by his personality and intentions.

It has been the bane of moral theories that they have
so often separated the deed from the doer, or the doer
from the deed, picturing on the one side only physical
results, or on the other only subjective impulses.
Physical things as such have no good or evil in them;
mere intentions are no more than passing fancies or idle
dreams. Only ideas burgeoning into overt acts, and
deeds warm with the life-blood of pulsing thought are
properly good or bad. The assumption that the original
impulses of human nature are bad in themselves is a
vicious inheritance from an old mythology. Psychology
has at last brought freedom from that ancient curse,
as it also affords protection from the opposite error that
all natural impulses are good. In themselves they have
no moral quality. Only as impulses are transformed
through reflection and developed into conscious habits

do the real objects of moral judgment emerge, and even then it is not these in isolation, but the whole person active in them through the medium of a concrete social process who is rightly judged good or bad. Men are not endowed with impulses of cruelty, or pugnacity, any more than they are endowed with impulses of kindliness or pacificism. These are traits which are learned, acquired through conditioning, by means of the varying experiences to which they are subjected.

The good and the evil are more than matters of individual conduct; they are social facts as well, since the development of the native capacities of the child are fashioned and directed through the common life that he shares. As the race itself becomes educated to the complexity of the process through which its individual members grow up, there is deeper and more widespread recognition of the necessity of affording more adequate means for children to acquire those habits of behavior and of moral judgment that will enable them to intelligently pursue the good and avoid the evil ways of conduct. To this end they are made acquainted with the lives of the good and the bad in the record of history, are led to appreciate in their moral significance various actors in the great human drama; they are helped to sense the moral situations in which they themselves daily live and act; they are encouraged to reflect upon the events of current history whose tides flow through the living world-wide movements of politics, trade, art, and religion.

It is interesting that the old view of evil as proceeding from the machinations of an Evil Spirit, Satan, or the Devil has nearly disappeared. That monstrous demon lives now almost wholly in profanity. His realms of eternal fire and endless suffering have receded into unbelievable myth and dogma until it is almost forgotten that he once served the function of dramatizing the reality and the horror of the actual evils of life. In his abode of darkness and pain the long consequences of momentary deeds were shown as warning reminders of the seriousness and the magnitude of the results of careless and vicious living. That picture is not without its meaning as an illustration of the nature of evil, for the lost souls experience all those negative and self-defeating conflicts that constitute the second death. They are cast into outer darkness where there is wailing and gnashing of teeth; they seethe in the fires of their own lusts and cruelty; they are forever tantalized by hopes that turn to ashes, and by infinite labors which bring forth only new pangs and penalties. The lord of that region broods in gloom and wrath, rebellious against the greater King he cannot dethrone. He is the incarnation of evil itself, always divided, disappointed, striving with plans that will not eventuate, hated of his subjects, betrayed by his minions, and forever unable to escape from the bonds of his own perverse mind and will. It is not possible for modern men to believe in the literal hell of Dante and Milton, but it is equally impossible for them to deny that in those vivid pictures were portrayed the real and poignant evils that shadow the human world.

CHAPTER XVIII

CHURCHES

Churches, like other social institutions, have a curious double function. They are at once the effect and the support of the interest which they represent. Schools are the outgrowth of the love of knowledge and they are for many people the occasion of intellectual life. The religious zeal of individuals creates churches, and the activity of churches awakens interest in religion for other persons. When the former fact is emphasized it leads some to conclude that churches are not necessary to the religious life, and when the latter fact is stressed it invites the conviction that these organizations are the sources of religion. Each is a one-sided and partial view. All institutions are at once the product and the origin of the attitudes which they embody. Love of learning draws scholars together; organized scholarship stimulates the search for knowledge and aids in its extension.

Institutions have a longer life than individuals, and the persons born into a developed society find families, schools, the state, and churches present as given and seemingly fixed realities. To these new and naïve members of the rising generation there is at first little understanding of the origin and growth of the various forms of associated life. Only gradually, if at all, does it appear that the institutions of the community and the interests which they represent have a mutual and reciprocal relation. Nowhere is this truer than in religion, which tends to magnify its antiquity and authority. Churches appear to stand over against the changing individuals with an objective and enduring persistence, prescribing the forms of faith and the ceremonials of worship. They come down from the past and impose their standards of thought and action. Only in times of crisis and reconstruction does it become clear that their life is amenable to the needs and aspirations of their constituent members. Only then does it occur to discriminating, creative minds that the sabbath was made for man and not man for the sabbath.

Perhaps there never has been an age in which this relation has been so well perceived as in the present time. The study of social origins has been pursued in every direction, and all phases of institutional life are now viewed genetically. All moral, practical, and religious customs are seen to have a history, and to undergo changes in relation to the general cultural processes. The worth of institutions tends to be estimated not so much in terms of age, prestige, and numbers as in terms of the service which they render in the enrichment and fulfilment of human life. What is its value for the fullest life of mankind? is the question asked of every association and organization.

Churches, once developed, tend to persist according to their form and habit. They gather to themselves like-minded people, and discipline them to their ideas and forms of behavior. So much is this the case that familiarity with the sects of Protestantism makes it possible for a shrewd observer to judge what kind of a person an individual is likely to be who belongs to a given group. One sect attracts those who love forms and elaborate services; another appeals to those who crave doctrinal clarity; others make their converts from the more emotional types. Some denominations are mystical, some practical, some æsthetic, some authoritarian, some conventional, some insurgent. Many religious bodies in America follow racial lines. The affiliation of Germans, Swedes, Italians, and English is apt to follow the systems which have arisen within the tradition of those peoples. It does not require extraordinary intelligence to predict what types of faith have the best likelihood of success in frontier communities, or in the new industrial centers of modern cities. There are decided limitations to the power of any ecclesiasticism to impose its forms and doctrines upon the citizens of a particular community, but each continues to make its claims upon the attention of all and to speak as if it had a universal message to which in time all men must respond. Seldom does a religious movement recognize that it has inherent limitations. It tends rather to attribute lack of response to the perversity or weakness of those whom it addresses.

The extent to which churches are subject to the limitations of habit and custom may be seen in striking exemplification in the great cities of America. Here changes in the character and population of neighborhoods often bring out in pathetic clearness the inability of churches to meet changing conditions. The growth of the business district encroaches upon old residential sections where churches have had a long and successful existence. With the approach of business houses well-to-do citizens seek other locations. They may continue to make the long journey to the old home church, but their participation in its activities is lessened and the children drift into church schools of their immediate neighborhood. If the loyalty of the congregation has been highly developed the church may continue for a considerable time through the support of its long-range membership. But in the course of time, particularly with a change of pastors, the older families drop out entirely and the congregation declines.

There may be an influx of new people, but if they are of a different social class, or of different nationality, or of different race, there is little success in reaching them. The old church has its type of service and its established forms of appeal. It seldom is able to blend the newcomers with the older members or to adjust its methods to suit the mixed community. Not infrequently the remaining members are disturbed by efforts of a zealous new pastor to bring in persons of a different social class. They cannot fraternize with these poor or foreign persons. At last the burden upon the diminishing faithful becomes too great, and in spite of special contributions from former parishioners, or from a missionary society, the old building is closed or turned over to other uses. This is the story of hundreds of churches in the great cities that have been compelled to move out into newer localities, or to merge with other better-situated groups. What is needed to make churches more flexible and more serviceable to changing populations is recognition of the fact that authority for their procedure lies not merely in the past, but also in the spiritual needs and aspirations of the people whom they seek to serve.

A similar problem arises with references to churches

and the scriptures. With an accepted canon of sacred books there is a tendency to regard the writings as prior to the churches. In modern times churches appeal to the books as guides for the pattern and direction of the organization. Protestantism especially has exalted the authority of the Bible and turned to it for the settlement of questions of doctrine and Christian living. This usage through a long history has made the literature appear to be the permanent, unchanging source of religious faith and practice, while the churches have passed through many modifications and transformations. In its quest for a reliable standard, Protestantism has set up the Bible as the final court of appeal and has overlooked the historical processes in which the documents were created. The theory of inspiration commonly accepted has proclaimed the divine origin of the scriptures and identified them with the infallible and unchangeable word of God. Since they contained a divine revelation, their contents were felt to be independent of the accidents of time and the events of the social process. All Protestant reformers took their stand on this foundation of a Book, inscribed by the Deity, and held it to be the means, when rightly interpreted, of determining the substance of the true faith and the character of the proper ordinances to be administered.

One of the results of the application of the historical method in the study of early Christianity has been to show clearly, and to stress the importance of the fact, that churches were organized and the faith propagated for two or three generations before the New Testament writings were produced. The earliest of them, the letters of the apostle Paul, were written probably thirty

years after the death of Jesus, and it is evident that
Paul had no thought that his epistles were to form the
major part of the permanent literature of the churches.
Even the sayings of Jesus, which may well be regarded
as the most basic and essential expressions of the spirit
of Christianity, floated about among his followers in
the free and changing form of oral tradition for several
decades. It thus becomes obvious that organized
churches were established before written records took
definite form. It is equally clear that the sayings of
Jesus were prior to the development of the local groups
of his disciples. The records and the organizations grew
up together, both attaining settled form and elaboration
in the course of centuries. Indeed, the rewriting of the
scriptures through more accurate scholarship, new interpretations, and the needs of new cultural developments still continues; and at the same time, under these
and other influences, churches are still modifying their
beliefs and modes of procedure. In principle the social
process is not now radically different from that of the
beginnings of Christianity. The growth of institutions
and the expressions of their life in various types of
literature go on together in mutual and reciprocal interdependence. History does not disclose one true, supreme, and continuous church pattern, any more than it
affords one fixed, unchanging, and infallible body of
scripture. Both are empirically fashioned by the numerous and subtle influences which permeate all human
relations and achievements.

The significance of these facts in the understanding
of the nature of religion is profound, and the implications are far-reaching. Religion is seen to move with

the whole life of society and not to be a thing apart. It is subject to the limitations, and is carried forward by the powerful idealisms, of human nature. There is nothing infallible about it. Neither churches nor scriptures, councils nor individuals, show proofs of perfection, and yet all of these have their value, and make valid claims for recognition and appreciation. The efforts of churchmen to lift their cherished institution above the qualified and finite sphere of human judgment and experience are pathetic expressions of human nature to find or invent something which is safely above the changing, concrete world. They appeal to the decisions of councils and popes, or to the texts of ancient scripture, or to mystical visions, but never do they transcend the sphere of practical reality. From all their authorities they bring back what has been gathered out of experience and reflection, and from the aspirations of fallible men.

Institutions, like individuals, have the defects of their virtues. They multiply the strength of people by organizing them into united and orderly action; they encourage specialization through which each is able to contribute his best; they give form, objectivity, and vastness to the will and purpose of the many. Continuity and power lie in association, and by participation in the group the single life feels itself enlarged and enduring. But institutions may also overwhelm the individual, inhibit his initiative, and discipline him into the acceptance of traditional customs and ways of thought. The institution, its success, maintenance, and defense, may come to enlist all the energies of its members until it is regarded as an end in itself, rather than as a means of furthering the growth and welfare of its constituents. Many a minister or layman has been subdued into silence by fear of disturbing the peace or conventional efficiency of his church, though convinced that new ideas and methods would accomplish better results.

The assumption that churches have an infallible standard of faith, and an equally dependable authority for conduct, tends to make them intolerant of dissent or criticism. They have so commonly required attitudes of submission and acquiescence that they do not readily provide for free discussions of ways and means of possible improvement. Their officials and leaders regard themselves as charged with the responsibility of maintaining a system which they in turn have received from others. The experimental spirit has not been encouraged and because it suggests change and novelty it is looked upon with suspicion. Yet it is only by a wise and reasonable use of criticism and experiment that improvement is possible. It is when churches become more concerned with being serviceable to human beings than with defending the faith of the fathers that they consistently and fruitfully encourage conscious and deliberate experimentation. Inquisitive and adventurous minds are not likely at present to feel at home in the churches, but these are just the minds which are needed in religion, as in other fields, in order to accomplish the best results.

It would be of assistance toward a better practice if the plural term churches were used instead of the expression *the* Church. Analogy with other social organizations makes this evident. When the home is mentioned it is understood that reference is made to a class of entities within which there are great variations. In reality there is no one home which includes all; neither is there one church which designates all religious societies. The general term, school, likewise signifies a kind of group within which instruction goes on, but it does not suggest any one school including all, nor any one particular school superior to the rest. "The church" is employed not only as "the home" or "the school" may be used, but in two other senses which are misleading. One of these is intended to designate the church universal, as if the church had continued from apostolic times with a continuing identity and consequent sanctity and authority. Sometimes this is thought of as the mystical church, or as the spiritual church, as if it had an ideal life apart from the actual churches existing concretely in specific places, and constituted of actual people. The other misleading use is that which designates some denomination, or organized group of congregations, as *the* Church, meaning that it alone is the true church among all the existing sects of various names and creeds. It is surprising to what an extent this meaning is intended by the representatives of the many denominations, though fortunately this is less the case than formerly. In the beginning each movement probably had leaders who thought of it as a more perfect embodiment of religion. Sometimes they were convinced that they had received a new and more authentic revelation, and it is certainly quite essential to the driving power of a movement that it be persuaded of its own importance. But a knowledge of history and of the inner life of churches makes it clear that no claim of age, doctrine, power, or prestige can justify any organization in using the exclusive title, *the* Church.

This is a fact as important for the critics of churches as for their defenders. It is a common error to generalize the particular evils of certain churches into charges against all churches by using the expression, *the* Church. Thus *the* Church is often arraigned for the crimes of the Inquisition, or for warfare against science, or for bigotry and conservatism. There have been local churches of that kind, and in certain periods and places such may have been the prevailing temper, but it has not always been so, and it is not true of all churches today. Not only do denominations differ widely in their attitudes of tolerance and open-mindedness, but local congregations within the same brotherhood are marked by varying degrees of comprehensiveness and enlightenment. Nor is it always the newest sect which is the most modern, or the oldest which is the most tolerant.

The sources of these sentiments of the universality and infallibility of churches are not difficult to find and understand. In early society all institutions were so regarded, and in the biblical tradition such convictions were continued and consciously formulated. The church was a divinely founded order, and it was natural to suppose that but one could be the true and perfect embodiment of the divine will. Through human error and perversity many pseudo-churches would arise and impose themselves upon the credulity of mankind, but since there could be but one authorized type it must be sought out and exalted above all others. The scriptures gave accounts of numerous departures from the one true faith and warned against their mistakes and corruptions. The course of religious history has been marked by the tragic conflict of these many claimants to one perfect pattern. It is only through a developed historical sense, and a deeper insight into the nature of religion itself, that emancipation from the fallacy of the conception of a single perfect institution has been achieved. It is now seen that from the first religion has been borne in earthen vessels, and all forms of its expression have been marked by the traits and genius of the people who have constituted the organizations.

The attempt to make a metaphysical separation between religion and its manifestations is equally futile. An illustration of such a view appears in a recent scholarly work of Horace Kallen, *Why Religion?* He shows by abundant illustrations that religion has been objectified in manifold types of churches, reflecting the cultural and social genius of different societies, but he discounts all of them just because they are thus involved with the concrete life of their times. Religion therefore remains for him a kind of mystical, transcendent reality, ever seeking outward expression but always limited and corrupted by the forms which it assumes. He is therefore completely baffled in his effort to define or justify religion in actual experience. Religion remains an ideal, unattainable thing, while the churches and societies which it generates are weak and changeable human products. But an empirical, realistic interpretation of religion takes these historic forms for what they are, and estimates their worth in terms of the values which they cherish and the ends they serve.

Mr. Kallen rightly holds that churches reflect the economic features of the societies in which they appear.[1] He shows that in the religion of Hebrew and Christian

[1] Horace M. Kallen, *Why Religion?* p. 241.

white

cultures agricultural interests have dominated. Christianity still continues to be largely a farmer's religion, and there are accordingly many incongruities arising from the industrial revolution that has created a machine age, and a new type of urban life. Biblical figures of speech and ceremonials are remote from the habits of great areas of the population, making it difficult for the modern city man to appreciate and appropriate the religion of his ancestors. Such undoubtedly is the case, but there are also signs that new symbols and fresh adaptations of old symbols are being fashioned under the influence of these new social demands. It is as unlikely that religion will fail to find means for its expression in these new conditions as that justice will not make for itself laws and forms of administration in keeping with the needs of a society which develops corporations and labor unions, and uses automobiles, airplanes, and radios.

In the view here presented churches are voluntary associations of individuals for the cultivation of the highest forms of life that they can conceive. In them persons band together to instruct themselves, their children, and the community, in finding and following the most ideal manner of living. For this purpose they may select leaders—ministers, teachers, artists—who will give their time to studying the experience of the past and the resources of the present, in order to transmit to the group such materials and methods as promise for them the fullest and finest development. Such churches tend to propagate themselves throughout the community and the world by the same natural, dynamic impulsion with which schools, clubs, fraternal orders, and commercial enterprises project themselves into wider and wider areas of influence. All of these have the missionary spirit just as religious institutions have. Groups of similar spirit and cultural outlook fuse together and become movements, brotherhoods, or denominations.

The community church enterprise is a contemporaneous illustration. In many centers people have recognized the waste and weakness of supporting numerous feeble organizations which have largely lost zest for their traditional names and creeds, and have seen the desirability of making the terms of church membership broad enough to include all persons who desire church affiliation. The result is that community churches, formed either by uniting struggling organizations or by broadening established ones, have sprung up in great numbers in response to the religious needs of their localities. Such churches already have begun to affiliate together through national officers and official publications. This illustrates the manner in which churches have always originated and functioned, except that in this case the movement has been unusually rapid and widespread. It may be that this movement is symptomatic of a decadent Protestantism, and may prove to be a temporary makeshift in a struggle against overwhelming tides, but the process is illuminating and impressive. The fact that this movement is promoted by representative leaders who travel from place to place, or distribute literature to encourage the formation of such churches, is only another indication of the manner in which all causes have been extended. Such was the work of the early Christian apostles, and such is the method of modern missionaries at home and abroad, but their success presupposes genuine interest and responsiveness among the people reached by them.

Community churches mark a new stage in historic Christianity, a stage in which for the first time the traditional doctrinal standards have been so modified as to be in effect abrogated. The basis of association is practical and empirical. Doubtless the things held in common by the evangelical churches are emphasized and the differences largely ignored, but this of itself discloses significant changes, for it is only a few years since these differences were insisted upon with divisive tenacity. Even more revealing is the fact that the accepted beliefs are held far more lightly than formerly. The old ideas of inspiration, revelation, incarnation, atonement, salvation, and future rewards have become secondary, and stress is put upon practical living—neighborliness, sobriety, honesty, intelligence, and devotion to social ideals. Sanctions for the duties taught by such religion are not sought so much in the authority of the Bible, or in any ecclesiasticism, as in their value for human life itself. More and more this gradual transformation of the old creedal religion is coming to consciousness, and the justification for further experimentation is being recognized. Whereas proposed changes were once tested by the possibility of finding texts of scripture to warrant them, or worthy precedents to justify them, it is now common to adopt methods that "interest the young people," or that increase attendance and interest in the church school or the regular services.

A definite attitude is arising in all churches which may be the forerunner of new doctrines and philosophies of religion. This attitude is the practical one of measuring religion by its contribution to the character and wellbeing of those who cherish it. When this conception is made explicit it puts the standards of truth and value within experience, and makes them subject to the judgment and conscience of the churches themselves. By this means a complete release is won from the conventional forms of religious authority, and the way is opened for free experiment. It is perhaps the vague sense of these profound implications that makes the constituted officials and sponsors of the older denominations suspicious and cautious of present tendencies, for they do not believe that the faith can be conserved without the customary acceptance of the authority of the Bible and the recognized precedents of ecclesiastical practice. The laymen and the young people, however, have fewer inhibitions, and are ready to support intelligent efforts to bring religion into more effective procedure.

It is in this direction that the real solution of the problem of Christian union seems to lie. For centuries some of the wisest and devoutest leaders have sought scriptural and creedal grounds upon which Christians could unite, but with little practical effect. No clear biblical instructions could be agreed upon for the correct organization of churches, and no satisfactory body of beliefs could be formulated. With the finest of spirit and the best of scholarship such endeavors have come to small results. But in recent decades many practical movements have grown up which virtually have ignored the more official conceptions of the proper means to union, and these movements have been surprisingly pro-

ductive. Young Men's and Young Women's Christian
Associations, Societies of Christian Endeavor, Religious
Education enterprises, and many other agencies have
circumvented doctrinal issues to a large extent, and have
demonstrated their effectiveness in uniting church members in great numbers and in beneficial ways.

But the officials of denominational organizations have
not been able to ignore the question of the union of
churches. There have been notable conferences, as at
Stockholm and Lausanne, in which the ecclesiastical
representatives of Christian bodies have come together
to consider frankly their differences and their common
faith. The very fact of such gatherings exerts a salutary
effect, and quickens thought concerning the desirability
of better understanding and closer fellowship. But they
labor under two great disadvantages. One is that the
participants, both clerical and lay, are those who are
most deeply attached to the forms and the doctrines of
their respective groups, and are therefore inclined unconsciously to give undue weight to historic convictions
and practices. The other is that they are disposed to
view the problem of union in terms of the closer co-
operation of denominations. They tend to take the
attitude of diplomatic statesmen, representing their various organized constituencies. They do not sufficiently
reflect the needs of local communities, and the cravings
of non-theologically minded people who constitute the
membership of the churches.

Probably the most significant and fruitful tendencies
toward union are to be found in local congregations of
the free churches, where doctrinal issues are likely to be
weakest, and where the natural social impulsions to

neighborly co-operation are strongest. The progress of the community church movement has been cited, and there are other important evidences of these more basic influences. Especially in the cities all congregations are fast becoming union churches. Letters are passed back and forth with an unprecedented freedom. It is not uncommon for a Protestant church of any denominational affiliation to have within its fold people who represent in their past connections fifteen or twenty denominations. Even immersionist bodies, so tenacious of their forms of admission to membership, are rapidly adopting the practice of "open-membership," that is, the reception of unimmersed persons on the same terms as those who have been immersed.

In practice, the creedal churches have relaxed insistence upon acceptance of the ancient articles of faith. The clergy are more concerned to draw people into fellowship for practical ends than they are to preserve purity of doctrine. Not only do they allow all degrees of mental reservations, but they forgive outright dissent from the orthodox beliefs. Matters of residential convenience, family bonds through marriage, social congeniality, and æsthetic interests are becoming more influential. Underneath these practical considerations new intellectual processes are at work that signify growing emphasis upon the human, social values of religion. Motivation in seeking membership in churches is less that of finding salvation of some transcendental kind, and more that of establishing satisfying and fruitful aids to right living here and now.

There is an increasing awareness that Christianity is not primarily a doctrine or a theory, but a system of attitudes and aspirations. Churches are moving away from their Pauline theological inheritance toward the deeper and more practical spirit of Jesus. With him, love and radiating good will were the master motives. Men were invited into his fellowship to learn and cultivate love of God and love of their fellow men. With him, faith in such a way of life was the supreme thing, for from it flow naturally that sympathy and insight which are the best guides to happy and useful living. That faith constantly begets repentance and readjustment toward a nobler and fuller life. It was with him superior to all external authority, and to all formal doctrines and codes of conduct. It pointed beyond all worship of himself and beyond all slavish devotion to his example and teaching. It gave room for the discovery of new and greater forms of association, and impelled to the conception and invention of more adequate means for the realization of a society of justice and mercy. He was willing to rest the justification of his religion upon experience, to let it be tested by its fruits, and to encourage it to expand beyond anything which he had seen or done.

Churches are free associations of individuals, endeavoring by every means to cultivate the highest forms of life that experience and imagination may devise. They are not bound by any historic model or by an established set of doctrines. They have evolved many types and many formulas and, like all other institutions of society, they are impelled to continue their quest for still more satisfying beliefs and practices. Every local congregation has the right and the duty to examine its methods and teaching in the light of man's growing knowledge of himself and his world. It is obliged by the very urgency of the religion that it cultivates to search and experiment for better forms of public services, for more effective methods of training its members, young and old, for more compelling and illuminating symbols in all the arts, and for more appealing and sustaining sources of comfort and courage in the great adventure of reasonable and idealistic living. Organization and institutional structure are necessary to practical operation in society but these are always provisional and temporary. They are not ends in themselves and there are no given and universal forms by which they may be constructed. In the nature of the social process there will always be needed many types of churches according to the occupations, cultures, and stages of development of the people who constitute them. But when this fact is recognized, the old exclusiveness which has characterized the churches of the past will disappear, and they will accord to one another the right to be what the circumstances and needs of their members require. The mutual understanding and good will which spring from this comprehension will express the only measure of union that is possible or desirable. Congregations which cultivate such attitudes are already one in spirit and may co-operate in many practical ways for the common good.

CHAPTER XIX

RELIGIOUS EDUCATION

Can religion be taught? This proves to be a more searching question and much less easily answered than at first appears. It has all the implications that Socrates suggested when he asked whether virtue can be taught. The answer depends both upon the nature of religion and the methods of education. If religion comes by way of inner illumination, independent of instruction, as some have held, then obviously it cannot be taught. If it is a response of the individual to the social values of his group, then it is a question as to how far any formal training can make certain of eliciting such response. If there are tone-deaf persons who cannot learn music, may there not be emotionally stolid people who cannot sense the meaning and value of religion?

If education is identified with the intellectual process of learning facts and cultivating analytic processes it may be possible to achieve much knowledge without appreciation of idealistic values. There are men who know the literature of the Bible and the history of religion but who do not enter sympathetically into the aspirations and ideals which these records signify to religious minds. There is much factual instruction that does not eventuate in idealistic motivation and appreciation. If there were any guarantee that knowledge about religion could secure religious feeling the case would be altogether simple, but experience does not justify this assumption. All religious educators have sufficient occasion to realize that something more is needed beyond familiarity with biblical stories and theological doctrines.

This fact is impressively illustrated in the futility of much of the current stress upon so-called character education. Setting forth the traits of courage, honesty, temperance, love, and patience does not necessarily result in evincing these qualities in pupils. Knowledge of them may remain formal, isolated, and barren. The very process of calling attention to them may result in fruitless sentimentality or even in aversion. If the end of education is to elicit these virtues as active and spontaneous forms of behavior the mere intellectual apprehension of them is insufficient. Not even a kind of competitive effort to excel in virtues pertaining to games and set projects of action assures their attainment. Bringing desirable traits to consciousness in this way is in danger of defeating the end sought by creating conceit and priggishness. The desired naturalness may be frustrated by the very effort to instil these elements of character.

Religion is so much a matter of attitudes and working habits that it is susceptible of cultivation only by those vital and delicate processes in which knowledge is operative within a living experience moving toward the fulfilment of interesting activities. Unless the will and emotions are enlisted, the ideas, however correct and important, are pale and inert. All classroom instruction involves this risk, and nowhere more than in the fields of morals and religion. It is an old saying that we learn by doing, and for this reason education in the sciences goes on in laboratories and in concrete tasks. Similarly in the kindergarten, which has pioneered in so many new methods for the schools, the development of the child springs from his activity in doing things within the range of his power and interest. It is in the area of his spontaneous motivation that he experiences the joy of creative and progressive achievement. This principle remains fundamental for education at all stages and in all subjects. Knowledge is in a real sense a by-product and when it is obtained it becomes a tool, an instrument, in the system of activity through which it arose. When separated and abstracted from this concrete stream of interests it becomes dry and cold.

Religious knowledge is no exception. The conceptions which have arisen through religious experience refer back to that experience and have no content or meaning apart from it. When abstracted from their historic and social setting they become mere counters and empty words, capable of endless manipulation without power of proof or refutation. In this lies the futility of much casual conversation about religion and the disheartening discussions of many pretentious theologies. Here is to be found the cause of the failure of much well-intentioned religious education. Religion is a life-experience, and without sympathetic participation in that experience its dogmas and formulas are lifeless and unappealing. Its richest adventures become as idle tales and its profoundest sayings appear as meaningless chatter. Much religious literature has permanently lost its vitality for the present age because the modes of life which it reflects have disappeared from the world. Old civilizations have passed into oblivion with their sacred scriptures and their theologies. They can be recovered only by the archæologist or the historian, and only by them in so far as they are able to enter into what were once living experiences for men of the ancient world. To a surprising extent the same fate has overtaken many sects and cults within the ages of Christian history. It is exceedingly difficult for the modern mind to enter fully into the consciousness of men of the Middle Ages, such as Anselm or Thomas Aquinas, owing to radical changes in modes of life and more intimate acquaintance with the world of nature. Consequently their proofs for the being of God and their doctrine of salvation seem remote and unconvincing. In the last century developments occurred that make it almost impossible for the college youth to understand the religious vocabulary of their orthodox grandfathers. The latter lived in a world of revelation and miracle, of supernatural authority and otherworldliness, that is unreal and unintelligible to the new generation, trained in physical and biological science, in modern psychology and philosophy. Under these circumstances effective religious education demands more than cleverness and proficiency in the technique of transmitting conventional literature and doctrine. Scholars in this field are keenly aware of this but the task before them is radical and testing in the last degree.

Religion is an evaluating attitude in which individuals of a group share. To this attitude some things are of highest importance and other things are of lesser value, or of no value at all. In every religious system, from the crudest to the most civilized, interests range themselves on a scale which is disclosed by noting the attention and care given to the various factors in it. This scale differs widely among different peoples. With some the supreme object is head-hunting, with others it is the sacrifice of a humble and a contrite heart. In one age it is the quest for salvation in a future life, and in another it is the attainment of welfare here and now. At the present time the development of individual and social life, free and rich, is the evolving ideal. The specific features of this ideal are stated variously, and are yet vague and inarticulate, but it is in this direction that aspiration is moving. Criticisms of our time as materialistic and lacking in spiritual insight indicate the craving that marks all finer minds. Perhaps just this outreaching quest is to be the chief characteristic of the religion that is forming, rather than insistence upon settled codes of rules and standards. The task of religious education then becomes one of influencing people of all ages to share intelligently in this view, and in the effort to make it the chief end of thought and experimentation.

How may such attitudes be instilled? Something more than analysis and mental exercise is required. A pervasive and earnest co-operation of the leaders of society is essential now, as in the past, to create an atmosphere and pervading spirit on behalf of religious living. If churches and church schools are regarded as institutions specializing in ancient lore and in impractical ideals, they are thereby cut off from the possibility of inculcating vital faith. There is evidence of pathetic confusion at this point in the most enlightened communities of American life. Parents who themselves were reared in religious homes, but have lost the sense of the reality of the old religion, are sending their children to the churches for an hour on Sunday mornings to have religion "taught" to them. But what significant effect can be gained from such instruction, however competent and conscientious, when the children return to homes where such subjects are treated evasively or lightly? Very early children feel the breach between the church and the home, or between the church and the school. Even a dignified silence, or an assumed interest will not long deceive them. They become restless and bored in being subjected to ideas and forms that do not appeal to their elders.

Illuminating contrasts appear on other sides of family activities. In the world of sport, for example, there is no such perplexing indifference. These matters have much space in the daily papers, and are easy topics of conversations on all occasions. The heroes of the track, of the diamond, and of the ring are familiarly known and admired. Aviators are so much the center of attention that thousands of boys are dreaming of future exploits in the air, without any formal encouragement or instruction in the history of aviation. This kind of stimulation is the only kind that can make any interest dominant and commanding in society. It is achieved without conscious effort and it radiates through every type of home and stratum of society. Any interest which has this kind of approval and support rises toward the degree of intensity and universality which makes it a religious value. This is why industrial and commercial pursuits so generally captivate the imagination and the ambition of American youth. Financial success is respected on every hand, and the captains of industry are for most people the great men of the time. Such impressions do not have to be institutionally cultivated. They are generated by the popular run of attention. Other societies have by this sort of public opinion made reverence for scholars supreme, as was the case in old China; or they have given prestige to soldiers as France and Germany formerly did; or they have given superiority to artists as Italy has done in certain periods of her history.

The pursuits to which adolescence turns reveal the commanding sentiments of any society, and the state of religion is shown by the number and quality of the young men who seek its offices as a profession. Dr. Robert L. Kelly, in his careful survey of theological education in America,[1] found that recruits for the ministry come from rural and village communities, that they are from poor families, and that they are largely second-rate men. Furthermore, the churches, in order to gain an adequate supply of ministers, subsidize theological training beyond that provided for any other profession, and means of self-help is given more than to any other class of student. If superior men pursue longer and harder courses to fit themselves for law or medicine with a prospect of a longer apprenticeship to gain lucrative positions, this fact can only be accounted for by the greater esteem in which these callings are held by society. Evidence of the place which religion has in the public mind is also found in the attitude of well-to-do parents with reference to the ministry as a vocation for their sons. Often the idealistic appeal of religion has invited a young man to give himself to its

[1] *Theological Education in America.*

tasks only to be checked by parental opposition. Or the youth has found, after some years of study for the ministry, that he is regarded as forfeiting better chances of success and social recognition. The young woman with whom he has fallen in love is not enthusiastic over the prospect of being a minister's wife! Numbers of men now thirty or forty years of age once fully intended to enter the ministry, but later discovered (?) that they were better fitted for business or other occupations. The opinion which people have of ministers is an index to their feeling about religion itself. Education of children and youth in a field whose leaders are at a discount can never reach maximum efficiency. It is lacking in the deeper sources of motivation and support.

The meaning of this is that successful religious education involves the development of an aspiring and ascending religious life. No elaboration of professional technique through teacher training, or intensification of devotion on the part of teachers, or urgency of parents in merely sending their children to church schools, or devices to foster and force engaging interest, can compensate for lack of widespread religious conviction among the intelligent and idealistic people of the community. When these leaders—teachers, lawyers, doctors, social reformers, writers, and merchants—are patronizing toward churches and ministers and church schools, religion is shorn of the first requisite to power. Only where there is a living social interest in a subject is it possible for that subject to be widely taught, and then there is less difficulty in reference to methods and curricula. That the foremost of religious educators are aware of these things may be seen in the studies they are making. They are investigating the nature of religion itself as it has grown up in the course of human history; they are asking the psychologists to determine what foundations there are in human nature for the religious experience; they are attentive to experiments in general education to discover materials and methods for their own work; and they are deeply sensitive to the fact that in such a profound transition as religion is now undergoing, the teaching of religion is involved with the task of generating a religion that is worthy to be taught. When religion is seen to be not so much a theory as a way of living, a body of attitudes rather than a set of ideas, a system of values more than a deposit of symbols and ordinances, a different conception of its inculcation becomes possible.

Modern psychology has discovered many things about the learning process. It began to get light upon numerous mysteries when it undertook to understand how the lower animals learn. This learning came to be conceived in terms of the attainment of efficient behavior in the satisfaction of wants. The use of the maze revealed the fact that animals like the rat will make definite progress in mastering certain "problems." When a hungry rat is placed at the entrance of the complicated runways which lead to the food box, he is already provided with the stimulus to exploration. Running in and out of blind alleys, he succeeds after a measurable time in finding the food. On successive trials he shortens the time used in reaching the goal, and this facilitation registers the fact and the rate of his education in that performance. By this process he is "conditioned" to the most direct route. While such achievements show mental aptitudes, the mind of the animal is operative only through the whole complex reaction of the organism. It is never a thing apart. All education is now regarded as such conditioning, and in human beings as well as in lower forms it is bound up with a great number of factors, neural, organic, and environmental. Higher up in the biological scale the motivating interests may be more numerous and subtle than the simple hunger of the rat, but they operate in the same general way as stimuli to action. With human beings the pervasive social interests of the group are among the most compelling incentives. Unless religious ideals have this kind of conditioning force they do not awaken appropriate and effective responses. It is well known that the approval or disapproval of the group is the most controlling influence in human behavior, and therefore it is impossible to develop religious individuals in a non-religious society.

It is often pointed out that in the fairly simple, homogeneous life of primitive men there is little difficulty in conditioning children and youth to the ways of society. In later stages, where there are so many conflicting customs and cross-currents, the process is vastly complicated. Where the home, the school, the play-ground, and the newspapers work at cross-purposes with the churches, religion is obviously handicapped in educating persons in its attitudes and values. Such is the plight of religious institutions in much of the modern world. Only when their objectives are felt to be important and integral with the whole of life can the churches attain that commanding interest that is essential to the accomplishment of their educational endeavors. That this fact is more or less clearly understood may be seen in the methods of various cults. They insist upon withdrawing pupils into their own undisturbed sphere of life in order to give opportunity for their views and practices to exert the desired effect. Many sects isolate their charges as far as possible from outside influences in order to gain that intensive training which molds the novices to their doctrines and practices. Some guard their protégés from opposing influences by warning them against conversations and discussions upon religious subjects. They thus build up psychological barriers against "the world" and "mortal mind." All education seeks to some extent freedom from the distractions of conflicting circles. The public school tends to take possession of the child, to enlist his home, and to supervise his play and his leisure in such a way as to avoid interference with its task. Advanced experiments in education, which seek to make the most enlightened types of civilization operative upon the child, seclude him from ordinary contacts. A striking illustration is the newly founded private school of Bertrand Russell in England, who has taken a group of eighteen or twenty children of three or four years of age, domiciled them in his own home, and set about a program to continue through their adolescence. There is truth in the assertion of Dr. Watson, the behaviorist, that if children are taken young enough and kept under a controlled environment they may be conditioned to any type of life desired. The use of sheltered and isolated religious instruction may thus foster its own peculiar ends, and the history of religion witnesses to the perpetuation by this method in many diverse faiths. But if religion is to be integral with normal social life it must cultivate the religious values that are inherent in common experience, and its educational processes must have the intelligent and sympathetic support of the general public. Society cannot long endure systems of religious institutions that are out of harmony with its fundamental convictions and spirit. Education, for such alien and exclusive institutions, works against the stream. It is only such religion as is open to the light of day, and in unison with the basic ideals of the common life that can yield permanently satisfying religious education.

Leaders in present-day religious education realize that they not only face the task of devising methods for religious training, but that they are also concerned with the development of a religion that can be successfully taught. They accordingly seek to enlist parents and ministers, and all available agencies, in reinterpreting religion in keeping with the demands of a scientific and socially motivated age. All progressive churches are increasingly responsive to this need. In the spirit of the public schools and of advancing knowledge in colleges and universities, they discard from religion the superstition and magic that have entered into it in the past. They reject the assumption of external authority and of magical rites, of sacred mysteries and saving ordinances, of preternatural persons and exceptional miracles. None of these is capable of such rationalization as modern education involves. Stress is rather placed upon moral and practical values, upon regard for human personality, and the development of rounded and wholesome character. Intelligent religious preceptors are endeavoring to cultivate appreciation of the possibility of utilizing the marvelous achievements of modern science for the amelioration of human suffering and the elimination of the conditions that hinder the development of the natural powers of all members of society. To this end they are introducing the story of the discoveries and inventions that fill our present world with miracles of mastery and healing. The patient, heroic studies and experiments of such geniuses as Charles Darwin yield materials of the most fascinating character to illustrate the growing knowledge and control of nature on behalf of health and happiness. The service of scientific chemistry in producing and distributing pure food reveals values that have full religious meaning and appeal. The single-minded devotion of thousands of scientists to the discovery and spread of useful knowledge shows a concerted and widespread movement that invites the muses of all the arts in celebration of victories and triumphs certainly as worthy as those of any battlefield or patriotic exploit. And these are achieved for no selfish or national aggrandizement but for mankind.

The developments of science have been so recent and so rapid that they have not as yet been assimilated into the general culture to a sufficient extent to make its methods and results familiar and appreciated for their deeper human values. They remain largely the possession of specialists, and are couched in technical vocabularies that withhold them from popular appeal. The identification of science with critical, reflective thinking also seems to the traditional religious temper to be antagonistic to the attitude of faith and subjection to authority. Religion has so long exalted commands of super-rational powers that it cannot readily accept reasoned modes of life as adequate to its needs. Science also has added to this conception of the radical difference between its claims and that of religion. It has often had to make its way without the sanctions of religion and in opposition to them. In many quarters the view has prevailed that each has its own realm, and that no conflict can arise between them because of this fundamental independence, but that this is due to the relative novelty of the scientific method and to the materials in which it works is becoming apparent. As the results of science prove their value in the service of a larger and richer life for humanity, their practical religious value cannot be denied. Gradually science is understood to be primarily a method of liberating and furthering the very processes and ends that religion cherishes. As this fact becomes clear, science stands forth as the means of realizing the goals of an enlightened faith. It docs not furnish these goals, but it may assist in defining and fulfilling them. It is the process of reinterpreting both the ideals and the methods of reaching them that is now determining the enterprises of religious education. It can only be successful in popular esteem when it is judged in the light of these two phases. Men today crave adequate and moving religious philosophies of life, and intelligent means of cultivating them for themselves and for their children. They are not content to take either of them on the authority of the past, but are ready to respond to what proves fruitful and satisfying in their experience.

An experimental curriculum in which the writer has had some part may serve to make clearer the problems under consideration. This curriculum was formulated with the conviction that religion is significant in the degree in which it is integral with the whole of life, and to the extent to which it emphasizes the values implicit in daily, common living. The method is that of utilizing the current experiences of the individual, and of emphasizing in various ways those attitudes that are seen to be essential in promoting intelligent, harmonious, and joyous activity in the members of society. The church school in which this plan is followed is in a city neighborhood of rather high cultural standards, with a fair mixture of children from homes of the professional and business classes. There are few from either extreme of poverty or wealth. The general atmosphere of the church is that of progressive, liberal religion, and the teachers are largely persons of college training with experience as parents or professional educators. The summer vacation takes most of the families away for all or part of the season and leaves the school nine or ten remaining months for its work.

All classes study the vital, recurrent social relations, with material and problems graded to the advancing experience and powers of the children. A wide range of subject matter is suggested to the teachers, according to the interests and capacities of the pupils. So far as possible the particular subjects of study are those that are suggested by the members of the classes from their contacts and work. In a large sense the plan followed might be called the "project method," but the projects are those activities in which all are naturally and constantly engaged, rather than artificially created or imposed activities.

The home and its affairs is a natural subject at the opening of the autumn. The family is just returning from travel or summer camp, and the city home is the center of attention. Toys and books, daily routine, neighbors and surroundings, have the charm of familiar things rediscovered. Free conversations bring out objects of interest and points of strain. Opportunity is afforded in the exchange of comments to discover and emphasize appreciation of parental love and care, of generosity or selfishness in the children's treatment of each other, of the value of pets and their care, of the pleasure in pictures and works of art, of the concern for cleanliness and order, of the necessity for labor and mutual aid. Matters of health, thrift, hospitality; the joy of co-operation, singing, reading, working together; and an indefinite number of actual situations and experiences give occasion for the children themselves to point out what is wholesome and desirable. Then from stories, examples, and illustrations, the teacher may find confirmations of the good and condemnations of the bad. From the first it is possible to show some reasons in the experiences themselves why they are good or bad. Regard for the reasonableness of moral judgments is of the greatest importance, to prevent them from seeming merely arbitrary, and to cultivate the habit of estimating right and wrong in appreciable terms.

The week-day school is a welcome second topic. It is common to all, and it suggests a wealth of occupations, companionships, difficulties, and enthusiasms that carry their own problems and values. Appreciation of the

task of the teacher, her helpfulness, patience, austerity
at times; regard for the school property; rules of the
play-ground and of games; the studies themselves and
the importance of doing work regularly, neatly, and
promptly; the desirability of truthfulness, courtesy, and
kindliness in dealing with others; acceptance of the will
of the group in choosing leaders or administering discipline, these are some of the questions always impressing
children, containing in miniature the world of social relations and its most vital obligations.   Enhancement of
the school itself as an institution that grows out of the
needs of the home and that is required to enable people
to get on in the world is worthy of note.   There are
special days of festivals, of celebration, of public exercises that fill the child's imagination with the larger,
mystical moods of his associated life.   These are re-
called, and allowed their emotional reverberation.

The third topic is the city.   With the youngest children, the policeman, the street lights, the parks, the fire
engines, suggest the aspects of the co-operative arrange-
ments which are everywhere in evidence.   Gradually
more complicated features are grasped, such as taxes,
elections, building regulations, zoning, and public char-
ities.   Beyond these are the censor boards, police galleries, clubs, associations of commerce, courts of justice,
civic enterprises of idealistic kinds, public welfare movements, temples and churches.

The fourth subject is the larger community, the state
and the nation.   The uniformed postman, calling every
day at the door of the home, is a kindly and important
representative of Uncle Sam.   Railroads, airplanes, national highways, pure food regulations, soldiers, ships,

public lands, politics, foreign trade, customs, patents, copyrights, penal institutions, education, marriage, health laws, are some of the abundant subjects that touch the life of every child and offer invitations to his imagination and his moral idealism.

These social experiences, discussed in each grade in ways suited to the knowledge and interest of the children, bring the program to the Christmas season, where the spirit of all these social situations may be related to the world-perspective of the Christian religion. The Christmas festival is so universal in our society, so brilliant and so laden with gifts of good will for all, that the celebration of the birthday of Jesus marks at once the culmination of the best impulses in all institutions. In terms of his personality and teaching, and the unfolding of his cause, it sets a natural course of study for the whole winter season. His life and that of his followers, expressed in the churches which have sprung from his religion, yield rich material for varied and vital instruction through the "church year" which comes to its climax at Easter.

Springtime naturally calls attention to the great life of nature, with miracles of the awakening earth, sprouting of seeds, springing forth of flowers, return of birds, and the release of the energy and joy of a marvelous creative life. The abundance of scientific information wrought into story and song, into parable and pictures, affords treasures of knowledge and religious imagery sufficient for endless reflection and inspiration.

It is not claimed that there is any special importance in the order of these topics, except that they are suggested by the environing experience of all persons. The general theme of religion as here conceived is that of intelligent, rich, and vital living. The religious life has no peculiar content of its own, for it is just a way of meeting and entering into all the basic relations of common life. It is differentiated by its approach and spirit, by its idealization and its evaluations. There is no other subject matter for it than that found in the public school, in the neighborhood activities, and in the fields of art. Failure to recognize this has made religion seem something separate, mysterious, and negligible. The church school has much in common with the week-day school, yet is as different as a special art school or music school. Like them it intensifies instruction through emphasis upon certain attitudes and materials drawn from the common store.

Such a curriculum offers continuous interaction between the church school and the home. The questions raised are just those which intelligent and right-minded parents constantly have occasion to talk over with their children, and they are matters which emerge in all thoughtful and fruitful conversation. Moreover they invite such candor and frankness as characterize all matter-of-fact discussions. It is no longer expected that religious instruction should be always cocksure and pretentious of absolute answer to all inquiries. Free companionship with the child is the only valuable relation for teacher or parent, and in such companionship there is frequent opportunity on both sides to confess ignorance or uncertainty and to suggest that the search for information be made a joint enterprise. One of the most educative and stimulating situations any person can encounter is that in which he faces the responsibility

RELIGIOUS EDUCATION 303

and opportunity of bearing a real part in discovering knowledge, or formulating a judgment, or deciding on a course of action.

In one sense the church school should be less a "school" in respect to primarily imparting information. Instruction might possibly be secondary, since the chief concern is to develop desirable attitudes and forms of behavior. On this account there should be other means employed in addition to class work. The general exercises are worthy of more time and care than they usually receive. In connection with the curriculum outlined above, there is a specially arranged program of songs, readings, and prayers, one for each month, built upon the central theme and interest of that period. Dramatization has been used for many years and the music has been conducted by professional musicians. Parties, picnics, excursions, and clubs have been used. All such aids assist in making the church an attractive and appealing place to children and youth.

A genuine, intelligent, and spontaneous loyalty to the institution and its work is essential to the desired results. But this cannot be secured by the teachers and children in isolation from the church itself, or from the home and social circles that directly or otherwise affect the child. Unless religion has the respect and understanding support of the environing agencies with which it is thus related, it can only accomplish its ends partially and haltingly. The great religious concepts, such as righteousness, love, and God, have no content aside from socially conditioned emotions. They become meaningful and persuasive only where the lives of individuals are set in some group, be it large or small, where there is the sense of commanding values, the realization of which determines the success or failure of life itself. Mankind is now undergoing the profoundest intellectual revolution that it has ever experienced. No wonder there is confusion and uncertainty. No quick or easy solution is likely to appear, but there are signs of a gradual reconstruction which may eventuate in a clarified and unified faith, built upon the values that are found to be necessary to wholesome, idealistic living. Religious education may aid in this reconstruction, and it will itself be facilitated by every step taken in this direction.

CHAPTER XX

RELIGIOUS KNOWLEDGE AND PRACTICE

Any searching inquiry into the nature of religion is likely to be met in some quarters by doubt as to the value or profit of such study. Inquiry of this kind raises ultimate questions, confuses minds untrained in such reflections, and seems to distract and paralyze old, familiar practices. People whose ideas and habits are fixed in inherited religious customs find their deepest emotional experience bound up with traditional forms and phrases, and if other conceptions appear more reasonable they may not elicit such deep and vital feeling. Those who are at home in the old-time religion prefer not to examine it critically for fear of losing the comfort and help it has given. They are annoyed by inquiries whose positive results are not at once apparent to them. What they have taken on faith they cannot risk subjecting to the uncertain outcome of reflective criticism. Their experience is somewhat comparable to persons riding comfortably in an automobile through pleasant roads to a desired destination when something goes wrong with the engine. For the time they are frustrated, and the mechanics who are summoned seem only to augment the delay by taking the car apart and studying its condition. Not understanding the mechanism themselves, the passengers do not see how all the discussion and tinkering of the workmen make for anything but the thwarting of their movement and arrival.

Religion is in some such position today; it does not function with the old smoothness and momentum. It is not only obstructed in its career by the failure of a particular conveyance here or there; it is needing the discovery and equipment of entirely new methods and means of going forward. The age has built new roads and motors to meet its demands for improved transportation, and it seeks better highways and instruments for the satisfaction of its spiritual aspirations. The scholars who are discussing and experimenting with the problems may only appear needlessly to be criticizing and analyzing the old equipment, but their justification lies in their hope, already gaining some substantiation, that they will provide greater stimulus and power for the religious life. This alone can give value to their great labor, and secure appreciation of it.

Not every individual is concerned, or able, to carry on first-hand inquiry in the field of religion, any more than he can do so in the art of farming or of producing chemically pure and wholesome food, but he is called upon to become intelligent about religion as he is about food and drink and every other fundamental interest. No one is competent to master the whole domain of knowledge; every one is under the necessity of depending upon specialists in every sphere of life except in that which he has made his own, if indeed he has mastered any one. The great majority of human beings live by means of the associated life through which the wisdom of experts and the habits of wont and use mediate to the average man the goods which he enjoys. Few could invent, or even understand scientifically, the numerous devices used daily in the humblest households for heating, lighting, sweeping, locking, polishing, cleansing, curing, and communicating. Everywhere we depend upon the expert and recognize his authority and usefulness. In religion there is no exemption from these limitations of human nature, but there is the same kind of assistance. It is therefore important to consider when we acknowledge a man to be an expert, and what kind of authority he exercises.

The true expert does not claim esoteric knowledge, private and peculiar to himself. He has no secrets, no magic, nothing which any other normal person might not possess by the same training and experience. There is no special mystery about his information and skill, for he has acquired them by methods open to his fellows. Experts in religion, so far as there are any, became such by similar processes, by study, observation, experiment, and long application. They no longer depend upon or claim special revelations, visions, auditions, psychic powers, or divine endowments. If they should make such claims, there are certain means of testing them. Where was he trained, in what school, by what teachers? What recognition does he have from those best able to judge? What has he accomplished in his chosen field? Such questions imply further inquiries concerning his teachers and the results of his work, and they are all questions susceptible of natural and satisfactory answers.

Enlightened communities have become very exacting in the case of medical experts. They are required to take extensive courses in accredited institutions in the sciences basic to the profession as well as in the subjects and techniques immediately involved in practice, and the state insists upon its own direct examinations before issuing licenses. Alert supervision of those admitted to the profession is maintained, and the most competent experts are still held accountable to the public will and welfare. The same is true of lawyers who are charged with safeguarding property and personal rights within the forms and the spirit of the laws of the land and the demands of justice. Bankers, bakers, butchers, builders; salesmen, shippers, seamen, sportsmen; artists, architects, authors, and aviators are allowed no secret procedures but live and work in the public eye, open to observation and under the judgment of their peers. In effect the spokesmen of religion are held to the same tribunal of public intelligence, and as society advances people estimate the leaders of religious cults more and more by the character of their training and the quality of their achievements. Perhaps the day will come when all priests, ministers, and teachers of religion will be required to possess as definite and significant credentials of expertness as are now demanded of physicians and teachers in the public schools. It would seem as reasonable to safeguard society as thoroughly in its spiritual interests as in its health and commerce.

The kind of authority which naturally belongs to the expert is indicated by the qualifications which constitute expertness. It is the authority of exact knowledge and proficiency in a chosen field. There is no occult source of wisdom in sacred things any more than in secular pursuits, and there is no means of compulsion in affairs of love and faith. The very claim of authority through apostolic succession, or supernatural gifts or endowments is an evidence of the absence of that kind of genuine and significant authority to which alone intelligent people respond. In so far as religion still depends upon such secret and esoteric sources of power it remains primitive and archaic in an age of science and democracy. The rites and ceremonies of religious services have their potency in their observable and demonstrable effects, and not in their age, prestige, or biblical source. Words and phrases may indeed have emotional appeal through their evocative force more than in their literal significance, but their value at last depends upon their whole context and upon their verifiable meaning in experience. The emotional tension or explosion obtained by the use of terms heavily charged with suggestive force through their associations may be deleterious and corrupting to the higher forms of religious feeling, and their use is often the sign of the most pernicious kind of religious malpractice. Lines from old hymns, passages of scripture, sayings of devout souls may illustrate this fact.

Unfortunately, legitimate and worthy authorities are often employed as external and spurious authorities. This may happen in two ways: in one, the words and deeds of a great man are accepted not because of their meaning but because they are his; and in the other case, one who is really an authority in some line is credited with significance in other lines. Both fallacies may be illustrated by the fate which has overtaken the great religious teacher, Jesus. When sayings are received as true because he uttered them the effect is very different from that which flows from thinking that he said them because they were true. In the former attitude there resides a blind faith; in the latter, an intelligent faith. The difference lies in the verifiability of the latter in experience, while the former neither asks nor allows such verification. In some degree, there is always temptation to extend the authority of a genius beyond its proper sphere and make it absolute in its own right. We frequently hear authorities quoted, not so much for the reasonableness of what they have said, as for the simple fact that they made the statements. That Jesus sought to guard his followers from the misunderstanding and misuse of his authority is shown in his insistence that the true prophet could be known by his fruits, and that "wisdom is justified of her children." He constantly cited objective and well-known experience in support of his teaching.

Perhaps the other abuse of authority is the cause of greater evils, for in this, one who is truly wise in some important matters is accepted as qualified to speak upon subjects quite outside his ken. The reporters are fond of interviewing a rich man on questions of morals, or a champion pugilist on letters and art. A great story writer is listened to concerning spirit-communication, and a specialist in the science of physics or mathematics is invited to illuminate technical problems in social psychology. Doubtless the opinions of men of distinction are of interest upon all matters, but that they are authoritative in proportion to this interest is a vicious fallacy. The consequences are far-reaching in the conduct of social enterprises, and in the affairs of religion. Organizations created for education or for social welfare are often dominated by strong personalities whose real strength lies in other domains, and churches are frequently shaped in their teaching and policies by men who have succeeded in business or in non-clerical professions. Politicians are not always guided by political scientists nor school boards by educators.

It is one of the occasions of confusion in religion that the biblical writers are accepted as authorities on geology and history when their importance really pertains to moral and religious matters. Much less than formerly, however, is Moses referred to as the reporter of the exact manner and sequence of creation or the writer of the book of Revelation as the foreteller of the course of human history. Paul was a mighty force in founding churches of a noble faith, but his directions for women's dress, and his statements about other social customs have little claim to observance. Similarly it is hopeless to extract from the sayings of Jesus regulations for all phases of conduct. It is not likely that he thought of himself as setting a pattern for the whole life of man which could be copied in a literal way. He did teach and exemplify the fundamental attitudes of a thoughtful, socially minded, heroic, and devout life, but he also illustrated the fact that such a life moves freely, interpreting and facing situations as they arise by means of clear insight and helpful sympathy.

How slowly and with what difficulty men achieve rational estimates of systems of thought and practice may be seen in the survival of cults and techniques which have their roots in a long past and in association with questions of intense personal curiosity and concern. That there should be so much concern with occult, secret, and magical devices in our age of general education and scientific method is as astonishing as it is pathetic. Palmistry, crystal-gazing, astrology, phrenology, the magic of numbers, superstition associated with certain days, with animals, with dreams, with faith-healing, spiritism, transmigration and the rest still do a surprising business next door to scientists and philosophers. In all these fields there is abundant lore, and laboriously attained technique, which simulate significant learning and skill. They also have their "experts" and "authorities" whose following make them appear significant, and although repeatedly exposed and discredited they still find sufficient credulity to perpetuate them. Under the emotional stress of illness, bereavement, and the uncertainties of life human beings seem unable to maintain critical, practical judgment. Discriminating religious beliefs seem hesitant and weak to those seeking immediate and unqualified answers to their questions, cures for their ills, and anchors for their faith, just as scientific medicine often appears indecisive and baffled in the presence of some diseases and abnormalities.

The question of authority is therefore one which pertains to the subject matter and method of the expert as well as to his own personality and training. A man may be sincere and experienced in a practice which is itself unsound and futile. The age of a belief and the mere number of its adherents afford no sure proof of its present truth or value. The kind of people who make up its following is a better index to its importance, and the methods of its operation and promotion are still better indications of its claims to recognition. No insistence upon length of history or upon divine support can finally take the place of proved knowledge and of practical fruits in wholesome and happy living. Religion is therefore of necessity experimental, lives forward, and is to be judged as much by the direction it is taking as by the way it has come.

One great obstacle in the development of a working religious faith consonant with the best attainments in knowledge arises from the state of learning itself. Under the very laudable impulse of freeing intellectual inquiry from preconceptions and prejudices which long hindered its progress there has arisen an undue emphasis upon knowledge for its own sake. The cultivation of the disinterested scientific spirit requires detachment from practical concerns, and the consideration of facts and processes free from sentimental bias and ulterior aims. It is not strange that much modern scholarship has become so absorbed in its own technique and in its particular theories that it has lost touch with the wider social life and the demands of the final, legitimate uses of practice. The sciences have rapidly grown their own vocabularies, apparatus, and ideas, and have utilized them in the pursuit of intricate problems until it is impossible for the man untrained in them to appreciate what they are doing. The scientists are impatient of the task of making explanations to the uninitiated if they do not look with suspicion upon any of their number who condescend to instruct the popular mind. Philosophical and metaphysical specialists are in much the same mood, not only aloof and isolated by their vocation, but pleased with themselves for it.

The same spirit, generated by minute, technical scholarship, may be seen in studies which lie closest to religion, in biblical exegesis, history, and interpretation;

in comparative religion; and in the social sciences. Their work has been critical and analytical, meticulous and often highly speculative. This work has been so vast, so novel, and so revolutionary to traditional views that it could not be easily brought into practical relation to existing religious practice. Many scholars, and scholarly ministers, have not thought it desirable or safe to precipitate the issues which must flow from such an impact. It is not strange that to a great extent the scholars have been taken at their own word, and have been regarded as too remote and detached to be taken seriously by common people. Churchmen have contented themselves with being "practical" and have minimized the importance of technical studies and of the doctrinal controversies implicit in them. It is not uncommon to hear even the official representatives of religion say that it matters little what a man believes, if his everyday life is right. What they presumably mean is that it matters little about believing things which matter little, but when the statement is generalized into the idea that nothing a man believes, or fails to believe, is of importance in conduct, then a most serious and consequential dictum is pronounced. That position is a complete divorce between knowledge and practice, between doctrine and life, and it consigns religion to the limbo of authoritarianism and mysticism. It also separates religion from every other aspect of a man's experience, for in all other affairs, in politics, industry, engineering, and health, men have learned that real knowledge is of the utmost practical value. Furthermore it may be shown in the churches themselves that the effects of scholarship, which have in one way or another filtered into the public mind, have had widespread effects. A deep restlessness has been created, a groping and confused sense that the old structures are shaken, that the youth from high schools and colleges are indifferent to the old faith and its forms, that it is unadvisable to preach doctrinal sermons, and that it is more pleasing and popular to devote thought and ingenuity to the enhancement of "worship." Many ministers are unconsciously demonstrating that what men do not believe makes a great difference, for they succeed in holding and building up congregations of people whom they have induced to join by telling them that it is not essential to believe the creed or any of the traditional dogmas. Often those ecclesiastical systems most careful of the orthodoxy of their clergy have been compelled to be most lax with their laity. Therefore services in which the doctrines of the creeds recited and the hymns sung are no longer believed are continued for their "æsthetic" quality! Fortunately the deeper realities of religion may sometimes shine through the heaviest veils!

That the new knowledge in various lines has had other than negative and compromising effects upon religion will be appreciated by all who share what might be called the spiritual values of modern secular culture. Scientific knowledge has penetrated practical sides of the life of people identified with the most sequestered faiths, as is illustrated by a camp meeting of a strict sect in the days of the advent of the automobile. They discussed whether it is allowable for true Christians to use this product of worldly invention, but when it was found out that so many had come to the meeting in motor cars it was decided to permit them to return home in them and to continue to utilize them! The value of this machine for assembling the saints and the consequent effects upon their religious fellowship could not be denied. Scientific knowledge has displaced the biblical accounts of the origin of man, of language, and of religion itself, and has thereby helped to center attention upon the important and vital aspects of a continuing evolution of culture. Men have begun to be accustomed to look for natural causes of natural events, and to appreciate the marvels and significance of common occurrences.

New attitudes have arisen concerning present experience and the greater possibilities of the future. Men have faced about in their search for guidance and comfort; the golden age is no longer in the past; there is a fresh sense of youth in the race, and a larger expectancy for the deliberate realization of a happier existence in the world. There is a better-founded self-respect in the heart of man with the passing of the old dogma of the utter sinfulness and depravity of human nature and the dawn of the conviction that it is possible to remake mankind by reconditioning and training inherent, natural impulses. Life has taken on greater depth and breadth with the realization that work, art, and play have sources of strength and joy which the ascetic tendencies of traditional religion could not tap or develop. Naturalness and freedom have been substituted for repression and fear; inquiry and inventiveness have gained significance among the virtues in place of blind faith and abject obedience to authority.

There is indeed a legitimate authority of experts in

religion as in other concerns, but it is an authority responsible to reasonableness and open to investigation. Physicians no longer cultivate an air of mystery and speak to their patients in Latin or in high-sounding technical terms. They welcome intelligence on the part of those they serve and are ready to go as far as possible in sharing their insight and even their ignorance. It is a mark of the new time that authorities lose no prestige by admitting the limits of attained wisdom in their domains, and this is a lesson which spiritual leaders do well to learn. The claim of infallibility and the pretense of knowledge where no knowledge is only beget doubt and skepticism as well as suspicion of insincerity. The spokesmen for religion create confidence in their hearers and inspire a sense of reality in the things most surely known when they manifest that modesty and restraint which belong to the very essence of scientific wisdom and to genuine humility. The ignorance of the most enlightened is vast and obvious, and as Socrates asserted, it is the part of all true wisdom to know and to admit this ignorance.

The bane of religion has been the assumption on the part of its priests and prophets of some kind of inspiration not given to natural men and to ordinary mortals. By rites of initiations and ceremonials of investiture of office they have set themselves apart from the common people to whom they have denied the power and the right to acquaint themselves with the mysteries and the ways of the spiritual life. Such attitudes are not confined to the oldest faiths, but in recent times there are movements in this new world of science yet not of it, which expressly advise their novitiates against discus-

sions of religious problems and against the reading of
books which involve other conceptions of life and religion. By this means they bind the minds of their prose-
lytes with the old shackles of a spurious authority and
withdraw them into the darkness and bigotry of blind
faith and unthinking obedience. However pious the
intentions of such practices may be, their fruits are
dwarfed minds and destruction of the conditions of intelligent faith.

This is not to say that every one, in order to be
truly religious, must attain all the knowledge and understanding which professional leaders should have, but
it does imply that such knowledge should be open to all
who seek it, in the measure of their ability and endeavor. No fixed line can be drawn between the clergy
and the laity in respect to the right and privilege of inquiring into religious truth and observance, and the
common man should be encouraged to recognize and
improve the opportunity to make his faith vital and intelligent. Protestantism is to be commended for its
proclamation that the individual has direct access to
the whole field of religious truth through reading the
Scriptures and through reflective interpretation. This
principle has not always been fully operative in the
various sects, but it states the only conceivable basis
of genuine religious liberty and progress. Even for the
man who does not cultivate an intellectual interest in
religion there is a great difference between belonging
to a group which favors his right to do so, and belonging to one which denies or minimizes that right. In the
former he lives in a freer and more vitalizing atmos-

phere and is quickened by a sense of a more varied and stimulating association.

With the best of conditions, it must, however, be admitted that the great majority of persons will largely take their religion at second hand, as they are compelled by the exigencies of life to depend upon others for their ideas of politics, science, and art. But for this there is a great compensatory fact of human experience, and that is the fact that the power of receiving and appreciating the best things of life is far beyond the capacity to originate and interpret them. So much attention has been given in these pages to the highly important intellectual aspect of a satisfying religious experience that the value of religion in immediate use and practice has not received its proportionate emphasis. This has been due to the conviction that in the present revolutionary crisis the intellectual problems lie in the foreground and that their solution in terms of the dominant modes of thought is now the urgent task.

The ultimate justification of such reflection, as has been previously asserted, is the release and enhancement of practical religious living. All scientific and philosophical criticism, aside from the very genuine pleasure which such activities afford in their own right, is expected to eventuate in fuller and finer living. Men characteristically occupy themselves with the use and enjoyment of their religion rather than with its analysis and discussion, but it is a condition of this final and consummatory experience that its ideas and practices shall be harmonious with the general life. It is the heavy obligation of religious scholars and leaders in our day to reinterpret religion in concepts, and illumine it through forms of art and ritual, which shall make it real and moving. This is a more difficult undertaking than is yet realized, but the principle upon which it may be accomplished is clear, and this is to discern the moral and spiritual values in the daily life and social relations of normal human beings, and to enhance and beautify them with the weight and resource of public recognition and celebration. There are new perspectives of history in which the great spiritual drama of the race may be displayed; there are depths of heroism and heights of unselfish achievement in the annals of science and the pursuits of peace; there are forms of associated life generating dreams of more utopian conditions. All these unite with the best things of the older faith, for they fulfil the spirit of every religion of Christ-like sympathy and love. The method of Jesus in mediating the new values of his day, rightly appraised and applied, would perform the same service for the values of the present time. That method was to make vivid by parable and terse wisdom the ideal life implicit in homely occupations and in the direct relations of all men in their contact and influence with one another. He pictured the infinite value of the individual in the sight of God, and stirred into flame the flickering hope of discouraged souls by calling them into participation in a world-wide brotherhood of divine power and measureless riches.

INDEX

321

"Read + Reread"